The Federal Legality of EU Economic Governance

Martinho Lucas Pires

The Federal Legality of EU Economic Governance

On Law and Power in the Economic and Monetary Union

ASSER PRESS

Springer

Martinho Lucas Pires
Faculty of Law
Catholic University of Portugal
Lisbon, Portugal

ISBN 978-94-6265-746-5 ISBN 978-94-6265-747-2 (eBook)
https://doi.org/10.1007/978-94-6265-747-2

This work was supported by Fundação para a Ciência e Tecnologia.

Published by T.M.C. ASSER PRESS, The Hague, The Netherlands www.asserpress.nl
Produced and distributed for T.M.C. ASSER PRESS by Springer-Verlag Berlin Heidelberg

This T.M.C. ASSER PRESS imprint is published by the registered company Springer-Verlag GmbH, DE, part of Springer Nature.
The registered company address is: Heidelberger Platz 3, 14197 Berlin, Germany

I dedicate this book to my wife, Carolina, who is my staunchest supporter, my closest friend and my biggest companion. Without her, this work would not have been possible. I further dedicate this book to my mother, Maria Teresa, for her love and support. She always encouraged me (sometimes even without knowing) to do this project. This book, with all its imperfections, is my possible homage to two of the most important people in my life, gone since my youth: my grandfather, João, a former professor and researcher of economic law and public finances; and my father, Francisco, a constitutional and EU law scholar. I hope that this book, concerning public law problems of economic governance, makes them both smile, wherever they are. Finally, I dedicate this book to António, my son, who I hope will live in a better, more solidary Europe.

Acknowledgements

This book is based on parts of my PhD thesis, successfully discussed in March 2024 at Nova School of Law Lisbon. I would like to thank Nova School of Law, its professors, staff and students, and particularly Teresa Pizarro Beleza, Margarida Lima Rego, Nuno Piçarra and Francisco Pereira Coutinho for their support and help in researching this book.

I would like to express my utmost gratitude to Professor Rui Moura Ramos, who was my thesis supervisor. His wisdom, guidance and support was fundamental for the thesis to be concluded and, later on, for this book to take shape.

I would like to thank Diane Fromage and Joana Mendes for their discussion of the thesis and for the comments provided that helped me to produce this book. I would also like to thank Cristina Queiroz, António Goucha Soares, Miguel Poiares Maduro and Mariana Frnaça Gouveia for their comments. Further thanks must be given to Filipe Brito Bastos and João Francisco Diogo, who read and commented this work. I would also like to thank Faculdade de Direito da Universidade Católica Portuguesa and DLA Piper ABBC Advogados in Lisbon for the time they allowed me to work on this monograph.

I discussed this book and its ideas and conclusions with several people during its development. I would like to express my gratitude to them, in no particular order: Armando Rocha, Patrícia Fragoso Martins, Inês Quadros, João Brogueira de Sousa, Jorge Pereira da Silva, Maria Oliveira Martins, António Abrantes, Miguel Carmo Mota, Raúl Relvas Moreira, António Ulisses Cortês, Daniel Halberstam, Donald and Catherine Reagan, Mathis Batoul, Cristina Fasone, Samo Bardutzky, Nicola Lupo, Paul Dermine, Fabian Amtenbrink, Dagmar Schiek, João Capella Ramos, Sérgio Coimbra Henriques, Jeremy Sarkin, Emellin de Oliveira, Tiago Cartaxo, Leonor Queiró and João Freire de Andrade.

This work was made possible thanks to a scholarship granted by Fundação para a Ciência e Tecnologia. The scholarship allowed me, amongst other things, to do a research period in the spring term of 2018 at the Law School of the University of Michigan in Ann Arbor, duly guided by Daniel Halberstam. Furthermore, the scholarship allowed me to participate in a summer school on "Parliamentary Democracy in Europe: Parliaments, democratic accountability and budgetary powers", which took place in the summer of 2017 at LUISS Guido Carlo University in Rome and was organized by Nicola Lupo and Cristina Fasone. To the Fundação, my sincere thanks.

Finally, but not the least, I would like to thank my friends and family for all their presence and support while drafting this work, especially to Carolina, António, my mother Teresa, my brothers and sisters Jacinto, Sara, Rafael, Margarida, Simão, Nini, and to my in-laws, Paulo, Madalena and Paulinho.

Contents

Abbreviations

ABF	Annual Budgetary Framework
BEPG	Broad Economic Policy Guidelines
BICC	Budgetary Instrument for Convergence and Competitiveness
ECB	European Central Bank
EDP	Excessive Deficit Procedure
EEC	European Economic Community
EFSF	European Financial Stability Facility
EFSM	European Financial Stability Mechanism
EIB	European Investment Bank
EIP	Excessive Imbalance Procedure
ESCB	European System of Central Banks
ESM	European Stability Mechanism
ESP	Enhanced Surveillance Procedure
EU	European Union
GDP	Gross Domestic Product
IMF	International Monetary Fund
MSP	Multilateral Surveillance Procedure
NCP	Non-compliance Procedure
SGP	Stability and Growth Pact
SURE	European instrument for temporary Support to mitigate Unemployment Risks in an Emergency
TEEC	Treaty of the European Economic Community
TESM	Treaty of the European Stability Mechanism
TEU	Treaty of the European Union
TFEU	Treaty on the Functioning of the European Union
TSCG	Treaty on Stability, Coordination and Governance

Chapter 1
Does Brussels Vote in the Portuguese Parliament? An Introduction to the Work

Contents

Abstract This chapter introduces the book and its themes, by discussing the political and legal tensions surrounding EU economic governance in the aftermath of the Eurozone crisis, through the prism of Mário Centeno's provocative assertion that "Brussels does not vote in the Portuguese Parliament." It situates Portugal's 2016 budget within the broader framework of post-crisis reforms, highlighting the apparent contradiction between national democratic autonomy and supranational fiscal oversight. The chapter questions the effectiveness, legitimacy, and constitutional validity of EU mechanisms that influence national budgetary processes, suggesting a possible disconnect between legal form and political substance. It then introduces the book's central research questions and methodological framework, grounded in federal theory, to assess the balance of political authority between the EU and its Member States in the legal framework of economic governance.

Keywords EU economic governance · National budgetary autonomy · Mário Centeno · Federalism · Constitutional limits

1.1 The Budget and Mário Centeno

Tuesday, 17 October 2016. The Portuguese newspaper *Jornal de Negócios* (a daily newspaper covering economic and financial news) dedicates its edition to the Portuguese draft budget law for the year 2017, presented three days earlier by the Portuguese Ministry of Finance. Like all special editions, this one has in-depth analysis of the draft law's main measures, as well as comments from journalists and guest

M. Lucas Pires, *The Federal Legality of EU Economic Governance*,
https://doi.org/10.1007/978-94-6265-747-2_1

contributors from different technical and political backgrounds. But for all the analysis and comments, arguably the most significant element of this special edition is an interview with the main responsible for the draft budget proposal: the Portuguese Minister of Finance, Professor Mário Centeno.[1]

There was much anticipation surrounding this budget law, for it was the first budget proposed by the government of António Costa, Prime-Minister and member of the Socialist Party (*Partido Socialista* or "PS"), in power since November 2015. The socialists had succeeded the coalition government composed of the Social Democratic Party (*Partido Social Democrata* or "PSD") and the Centre Democratic Party (*Centro Democrático Social—Partido Popular* or "CDS-PP") headed by Pedro Passos Coelho, leader of the PSD. This centre-right coalition was in office from June 2011 until October 2015. Its tenure coincided with the crisis that hit financial markets from 2008 onwards, causing economic and social tensions around the world.

In Europe, the crisis particularly affected three EU Member States (Greece, Ireland, and Portugal) that had to seek external financial assistance to fend off escalating pressure from financial markets and make fiscal ends meet, therefore avoiding default on their external creditors. Assistance was requested from the IMF, the EU, and its Member States, and provided by a triad of assistance mechanisms established for that effect, based on international and EU law (the IMF facility fund, the EFSM, and the EFSF). Such assistance was conditional on the beneficiary countries' agreement to enact significant policy measures to correct public deficits. Measures consisted broadly of an acute reduction of expenditure, with the freezing of public wages, social provisions, and pension incomes, as well as measures for increasing public revenue through tax hikes, as well as liberalization measures concerning national labour markets.[2]

The implementation of austerity measures was met with social contestation in all beneficiary countries. Portugal was not an exception: the economic and social situations were very serious, and the measures put forward by the coalition government of Mr. Passos Coelho were very unpopular. The Socialist Party had initially showed their commitment to the conditions put forward by creditor institutions to provide financial assistance, but changed their approach for the parliamentary elections of 2015, making its governmental priority to "turn the page of austerity" and end budget cuts, restoring wages and pensions.[3]

Mr. Costa came second in the 2015 election, behind Mr. Passos Coelho's centre-right coalition; however, PSD and CDS-PP failed to win an absolute majority of seats in Parliament. Although Mr. Passos Coelho still took office as prime minister for a second term, his government was dismissed after its program was voted down by a grand (and unprecedent) coalition of left-wing parties, composed of the socialists,

[1] Miranda (2016) https://www.jornaldenegocios.pt/economia/detalhe/centeno_vamos_ter_de_viver_numa_restricao_orcamental_muito_bem_definida accessed 15 August 2025.

[2] A complete analysis can be seen in Moury et al. 2021; Ramalho 2025.

[3] Partido Socialista, 2025 https://phplist.ps.pt:8080/GabinetedeEstudos/SITE_GEPS/Programas_Eleitorais_PS/2015.4.out_Programa.Eleitoral.do.Partido.Socialista_Eleicoes.Legislativas.2015_Alternativa.de.Confianca.pdf accessed 15 August 2025.

the communists (*Partido Comunista Português* or "PCP"), the Greens (*Verdes*) and the Left Bloc (*Bloco de Esquerda* or "BE"). Mr. Costa then formed a government with the parliamentary support of these three parties.

Mr. Costa came to power a year after the conclusion of the financial assistance program to Portugal, and the country was now in post-program surveillance.[4] Given the fragile situation of its public finances, Portugal was also under EU monitoring within the Excessive Deficit Procedure ("EDP"), meaning that it had to continue adopting reformist policies and structural reforms to meet EU targets.[5] Therefore, it did not seem that Portugal could follow through with the intentions of the socialists and their parliamentary partners (who were all against the financial assistance programs and the imposition of austerity measures) and deviate from the previously established policy path, which made the possibility of a complete reversal of austerity not only intriguing, to say the least, but also problematic.[6] Mr. Costa's government seemed to have put itself in a very difficult position. How would they be able to present an economic policy program that satisfied both its parliamentary partners and still comply with EU rules regarding budgetary and debt maximums?

The interviewers asked Professor Centeno about the government's seemingly unsustainable position and its relationship with its political partners and the European Commission. Professor Centeno said that negotiations with Brussels were different from negotiations with its parliamentary partners. However, he said that there was "a significant understanding" of the Government's scope of action from Brussels.[7] According to Professor Centeno, the budget proposed by the government had a very well-defined restriction, and it was with that restriction that the country would have to live.[8] He acknowledged that his cabinet and the European Commission did not see eye to eye on the structural dimension of the country's situation, but he was confident that the proposed budget was the most adequate for the country.[9]

The interviewers continued to question the Minister on the challenges of negotiating with Brussels a draft budget that was accepted by the left-wing parties in Parliament only because of its commitment to reverse austerity, which led Professor Centeno to provide the following answer:

---

[4] According to the European Commission, the country was "making progress" but needed to do more to "consolidate its recovery". See European Commission, 'Post-Programme Surveillance Report - Portugal, Summer 2016 (Institutional Paper) COM 036 (2016), p. 7.

[5] The country had just been subject to a Council Decision in August giving notice to take measures to reduce the excessive deficit. Council Decision (EU) 2017/985 of 8 August 2016 giving notice to Portugal to take measures for the deficit reduction judged necessary in order to remedy the situation of excessive deficit [2016] OJ L148/42.

[6] Bugge (2016) https://www.reuters.com/article/us-portugal-budget-analysis-idUSKCN0UX1Z6 accessed 15 August 2025 and Barber (2016) https://www.ft.com/content/d03c408e-743b-11e6-bf48-b372cdb1043a accessed 15 August 2025.

[7] Miranda (2016) available at https://www.jornaldenegocios.pt/economia/detalhe/centeno_vamos_ter_de_viver_numa_restricao_orcamental_muito_bem_definida accessed 15 August 2025.

[8] Ibid.

[9] Ibid.

> Let us get this straight: Brussels does not vote in the Portuguese Parliament. It does not vote neither in the Spanish, nor in the Italian [parliaments]. What we are talking about with Brussels is an algorithmic procedure. Brussels has a code that applies with a certain flexibility, and I do not have to discuss with Brussels if my policy is more directed to A, B or C pensioners, or if I will increase or decrease taxes for the middle class, the upper class or the lower class. I do not discuss any of this with Brussels.[10]

The cover of the newspaper edition showed a picture of Mário Centeno descending the stairs of the Ministry of Finance. Above the picture stood, in white capital letters, the sounding catchphrase uttered in the interview—*Brussels does not vote in the Portuguese Parliament*.[11]

1.2 Does Brussels Vote in the Portuguese Parliament?

I remember being on the streets of Lisbon in 2016 and seeing the edition of Jornal de Negócios. The memories of financial intervention are still vivid, particularly the sense (or was it just a *mediatic* mantra?) that there was no alternative but to comply with the rules on balanced budgets and the wills of the creditors. And now I had in my hands a declaration from the new minister of finance basically indicating that the creditors did not have any say in Portuguese budgetary discussions.

I was both amazed and shocked at Professor Centeno's very clear dismissal of *the value* and *significance* of the EU's rules concerning the definition and execution of national economic policy, also known as the rules of EU economic governance. According to him, such rules were just *technocratic precepts* ("algorithmic procedures") applied by *technocratic public officers* ("Brussels") and therefore did not have (could not have) the same (*political and legal*) value as national budgetary law. The latter was a *significant political decision* (arguably the most important political decision of government) made by a *significant political body*: the Portuguese Parliament, directly elected (and therefore *legitimated*) by the Portuguese people. Being the most powerful political body in the country, the Parliament is supreme and autonomous in deciding the budget, and the consequence was clear: the EU cannot impose upon a national parliament its policy preferences, only request that specific economic targets be pursued, as an obligation of best efforts, but nothing more than that.

This view contrasted heavily with the official view of Portuguese authorities prior to Professor Centeno taking office at Terreiro do Paço.[12] From 2011 to 2014, Portugal did not have much autonomy in economic matters since it had to meet the conditions for receiving financial assistance from the IMF, the EFSF, and the EFSM. Furthermore, compliance with such conditions was subject to regular monitoring by the IMF,

---

[10] Ibid.

[11] The cover is available here: https://www.jornaldenegocios.pt/mais/primeira-pagina/detalhe/17_de_outubro_de_2016 accessed 15 August 2025.

[12] One of Lisbon's historical squares, where the ministry of Finance is located.

the European Commission, and the ECB. Although the conditions were previously agreed by the Portuguese government and legitimated by a substantial parliamentary majority (including the Socialist Party), it was evident that conditionality measures for the disbursement of funds reflected more the preferences of Portugal's creditors than of the Portuguese State. As per a common Portuguese saying, the creditors had both the knife and the cheese in their hands; given its delicate financial situation, Portugal was not in a good negotiating position to resist their pressure. The example of Greece's left-wing government (failed) resistance to austerity measures proposed by the EU and the IMF showed how powerless beneficiary States were in the face of creditor institutions and financial markets.[13]

But Professor Centeno's relativization of both EU rules and powers regarding national economic policies seemed to indicate that Portugal, now free from the procedure of financial intervention, had regained its full autonomy from external interference and could, once again, act freely with regards to its economic policy. The country's fate was in its hands (meaning *in the hands of the government*) and was not to be decided by external authorities. The conditions of assistance had been met, the money was paid, and the assistance program concluded. Life could go on as it was before the period of financial assistance.

However, how could that be possible? The political and legal landscape of 2016 was completely different from the political and legal landscape of 2010 concerning the EU framework of economic governance. Between 2011 and 2013, the EU went through one of the most important constitutional reforms in the history of European integration[14] with the objective of reinforcing, from a legal perspective, the prohibition of national fiscal profligacy and enhance compliance with common goals of EU economic governance. The consequence was a wave of normative production rarely seen, with two international treaties signed, together with a Euro Plus Pact; a revision to the TFEU to legally accommodate the signing of the ESM Treaty; and the enactment, by EU institutions, of eight binding legal instruments (six regulations, one directive, and one decision).

The enactment and implementation of these rules symbolized a renewal of the commitment of EU Member States to running balanced budgets. Such commitment was assumed in national constitutions with the transposition of "golden rules" for budgetary balance. Additionally, national duties of reporting budget plans and economic data for the short and medium term in regular intervals to the EU were instituted within an annual dedicated timeframe for economic coordination, called the European Semester. New supervisory procedures appeared, such as the Economic Imbalance Procedure ("EIP"), with EU institutions having more powers for requesting and monitoring national economic developments. Sanctioning powers were also added. Finally, a new institutional entity was dedicated to financial assistance, called the European Stability Mechanism ("ESM").

The events were not limited to the legislative field: a once technocratic institution reinvented itself as an essential economic and political actor (the ECB), seemingly

[13] Fatsis 2015; Mudde 2017, pp. 22–25.

[14] See, for example, Teixeira 2022, pp. 134–139.

going beyond what its primary constitutional mandate was. On the judicial side, there were three decisions of the CJEU on the EMU's constitutional framework and the powers of EU institutions in this realm, with significant effects for the character of the EU legal order in general. The last decision, *Weiss*,[15] led to a judicial conflict between the CJEU and the German Constitutional Court that raised fears of constitutional disobedience in the EU that could have had severe implications for the unity of the EU's legal order.[16] All in all, the EU of 2016 was not the EU of 2010: it seemed that a "constitutional mutation" had taken place.[17]

Hence, the EU legal framework of economic governance post-2014 was far from looking like a mere "algorithmic procedure – at least on paper." Professor Centeno seemed to be significantly downplaying the character of these rules and their significance, as if it were just a technical obligation with little political value, and few to no legal consequences. Considering his position as the Minister of Finance of a country that had recently successfully exited a process of financial assistance, and with the rough times of austerity measures still fresh in everyone's mind, Professor Centeno's statement sounded defiant while at the same time bordering on irresponsible.

But what if Professor Centeno was onto something? What if he was right about the relative value of such rules and procedures? What if, for all the new rules, treaties, and institutional structures in place, the obligations of economic governance that EU Member States had to comply with were not as binding and stringent as they seemed to be?

After all, *the EU continues after 2014 to have in the field of economic governance only the competence to coordinate national policies.* This means that the Member States continue to be the sole actors responsible for enacting and implementing their respective budgets. Unless a Member State is at risk of running an excessive deficit, economic governance continues to be just a preventive procedure of disclosure, consisting in the submission of reports, plans and estimations without any serious consequence for non-compliance attached. On top of it all, sanctions for non-compliance continue to be non-existent. Rules do not seem to "bite". Maybe the "emperor's new clothes" of 2014's framework of economic governance, for all its colours, fabrics, and designs, are in essence nothing more than a refurbished version of the clothes of 2010, more comfortable and sophisticated, but still largely uncapable of covering all the problems arising from the complex setting that is macroeconomic interdependence in the EU.

(This, of course, if economic governance *ever had* any kind of clothes: the king might, and may still, be running naked).

Or maybe not. Maybe it is the opposite: the rules and obligations in place nowadays, in the (apparently) sophisticated legal framework of economic governance, are sufficient and efficient, *effectively limiting* Member States' economic autonomy by establishing *strict obligations* for the Member States to follow. With the rules, EU institutions are not only capable of helping Member States coordinate their economic

[15] CJEU, Heinrich Weiss and Others, 2018, Case-493/17.

[16] Mayer 2020, pp. 1123–1126.

[17] Menéndez 2012, pp. 41–98 and 2014, p. 127.

policies but can also intervene more stringently in national economic autonomy and, ultimately, *orientate and influence* (sometimes decisively) *the definition* of national budget policy. A situation which is in line with the (traumatic) experience of the sovereign debt crisis, where these problems came to the fore.

The consensus after the crisis was that Member States' economies would have to start converging—even by force, if necessary. Discussions regarding the limits of economic autonomy of Member States led to a revamped concern of EU institutions on matters of macroeconomic and financial stability, with the conclusion being that, if EMU were to succeed, then the EU system of supervision of national budgets would have to be tougher and more interventionist. This would mean that rules and principles of economic governance would have to be capable of binding Member States's economic behaviour. In other words, such rules would bite.

However, if the rules are to bite, then there is a problem. To have legal control (or to have, by *legal* means, the capacity to exert a decisive influence or intervene) over a national budget is to have *de facto* control over a State's governmental apparatus, for a budget is not just a technical accounting exercise of incomes and expenditures but a democratically legitimate representation of a country's plan of self-government. Exercising control over a national budget is to control a State's political autonomy and its capacity for political *self-determination.*

The EU is a project created by its Member States to advance and manage political interdependence while achieving progress and welfare for local populations. It is founded on an agreement that was freely entered by its members, and such an agreement is premised on principles of respect for Member States' status as independent political units. This means that the EU is a space of political authority, capable of exercising government powers over its Member States and their respective populations, but such action can only go to a certain extent, so that it respects the political authority (and the consequent *right* to *political autonomy*) of the Member States.

There is, therefore, a form of governmental equilibrium established in the EU legal order that serves as a necessary structural basis for its existence and success. The EU should not be a "dominium", nor an empire, where a few rule over the rest; instead, the EU should be a political project for developing free and independent States under common goals, values, and objectives.

The Member States conferred many competences on the EU in the policy field of economic governance, such as the competence to issue money and supervise fiscal and financial developments in the Member States. However, the Member States did not (at least not explicitly) confer any competence on the EU to exert control over the specific definitions of national economic policy. Nevertheless, the powers granted to the EU in the reform of economic governance made during 2011–2014 enable the Commission and the Council to exercise stronger and deeper monitoring of national economic policy developments. Furthermore, sanctions can follow supervisory procedures if States do not comply with the rules or deviate from targets set by EU institutions. Finally, the setting up of a permanent instrument for financial assistance allows EU institutions and the EU Member States, in particular circumstances, to request specific economic policies for beneficiary States and to impose their enactment.

In summary, Professor Centeno's declaration leads to a reflection on two problems. The first problem concerns the current system of economic governance and the degree of EU intervention in national procedures for economic definition that is allowed under EU law. The second is, depending on this degree of intervention, whether a line of respect between spheres of authority has been crossed, and to what extent. Do such powers of the EU comply with EU law and legal safeguards against EU intromission in the protected spheres of national autonomy? Do these powers pose any problem in terms of their constitutional validity?

1.3 The Book: A Constitutional Analysis of EU Economic Governance

The purpose of this book is to comprehensively analyse the type, character, form, and scope of EU's powers in the field of economic governance to understand to what extent this legal framework (i.e., the combination of rules, powers, institutions, and procedures allowing the EU to act vis-à-vis national budget policy definition) respects the principle of organization of political authority as set in the Treaties.

With this in mind, the book wishes to answer the following questions:

- Does the legal setting of economic framework enables EU institutions to intervene, affect and control, in a decisive manner, the definition of national economic policy?
- If so, to what extent?
- Finally, depending on that outcome, what are the constitutional implications of the EU powers of economic governance, considering the fundamental principles of political authority set in the EU Treaties?

The first two questions require an understanding of, first, what the EU can do regarding national economic policy—in other words, *what are the EU's rules and powers of economic governance*—and second, to understand what is the *legal and factual* strength of such rules and powers, that is: *to what extent the Member States are obliged to follow them*? The research method must consider both the formal setting of EU economic governance (i.e., the norms and legal sources applicable, the competent institutions, and the different types of procedures at play) and its practical implementation by the institutional actors involved. By following such a method, it is possible to understand the effective "weight" of "Brussels'" leverage over national governments in the definition of national economic policy.

The last question, on the constitutional implications of the EU's powers of economic governance, requires a different methodological approach.

The complex character of the EU's framework of economic governance reveals several constitutional contradictions. After all, this is an intergovernmental area where the political power of the Member States holds a significant status, since national governments—acting through the Council—are responsible for enacting general economic guidelines, applying sanctions in supervisory procedures, and approving financial assistance programs. On the one hand, this would seem to protect Member States from the undue intervention of EU institutions. However, a paradox emerges, whereby relations of force that exist between different Member States come to the fore, given the weak institutional apparatus, henceforth making economic coordination either completely ineffective (and ruining the EU's goals and objectives of macroeconomic integration) or just effective for some, but not for all.

In this sense, the problem is not just a question of considering the division of competences set in the EU treaties and looking at how the EU framework of economic governance complies with it or not. It is necessary to go beyond the competence question and consider the picture from another point of view to see how EU rules respect or risk an important area of reserved national political authority.

For that purpose, it is necessary to adopt a methodological framework that is adequate to discuss the many ways in which constitutional balances between two levels of political authority in the EU are maintained. The framework chosen is federalism since the nucleus of federal (normative) theory concerns precisely this issue, that is, *the respect and balance of powers in a compound polity, between two levels of legitimate political authority*: the national (*the federal*, or in this case the EU) and the municipal (*the local*, or in this case the Member States). Therefore, this book wishes to analyse and discuss *the federal legality of the EU setting of economic governance* by assessing the normative validity of the EU's authority regarding the economic autonomy of national governments, considering the principles of federal respect (equilibrium of political authority) set out in the federal compact of the polity (i.e., the Treaties).

The innovation of the present book is twofold. First, it provides for a comprehensive legal analysis of the many forms of obligation that Member States are subject to due to EU rules on economic governance. Second, the work considers the extent and strength of the EU's authority regarding national economic policy autonomy from the perspective of federalism, that is: from the perspective of the balance of political authority constitutionally established between the EU and the Member States in the EU Treaties.

The legal literature discussing the subject of "euro-crisis law" has identified many of the abovementioned risks for the political equilibrium of the EU. A recent strand in the literature has considered the constitutionality of economic governance from the lens of the rule of law, including analysis of issues related to division of competences.[18] However, the findings of the literature do not provide a clear analysis of the problem of authority and also do not engage with federalism. A clear and comprehensive response to Professor Centeno's statement on the limits of the EU's powers *vis-à-vis* the Member States and the effects of such powers in the distribution and equilibrium of political authority in the EU constitution is still lacking.

This book attempts to provide such response, believing that the problem with the current system of economic governance (spoiler alert) lies with its intergovernmental character. In other words, it is the insufficient constitutional status of economic

[18] Dermine 2022, pp. 6–9.

governance that makes the EU powers in this policy area either completely ineffective and inexistent or, on the contrary, supremely dangerous for the EU's federal order, allowing for the dominium of some Member States by others. By "constitutional status" I mean the existence of sufficient legal and institutional safeguards for establishing a balance in the decision-making and accountability processes of economic governance between the different interests at stake: the interests of the Member States (national governments), the interests of the peoples of the Member States (in their vests as national peoples), and the peoples of EU (the peoples of the Member States considered together, as the EU's *demoi*).

1.4 Structure of the Book

Without structure, ideas and arguments can be charming, but unpersuasive.[19] The (research) method should follow the (research) object.[20] Therefore, the following work is organized into six chapters.

Chapter 2 presents a historical description of the legal framework of economic governance in the EU and its evolution. The purpose of the chapter is to identify the main dynamics and legal-institutional characteristics of the framework of economic governance, as well as to critically assess the merits of its evolution and design.

Chapter 3 analyses the current legal framework of economic governance in place. The chapter considers the constitutional purpose of economic governance, as well as the structure and capacities of the three types of powers of economic coordination—powers of definition of national economic policy, powers of supervision of economic policy implementation, and powers of financial assistance—and their respective institutional features and dynamics.

Chapter 4 discusses the normative character of EU powers of economic coordination. The chapter considers the legal force of such acts from an abstract and practical perspective and discusses the different types of legal rules and acts that the EU can produce, and their justiciability. The chapter closes by answering the first research question and offering an interim conclusion to this work: to what extent can the EU and its institutions legally direct the development of national economic policies?

Chapter 5 moves the conversation from the field of EU law to the realm of public law theory to discuss the political and normative concept of federalism as the framework for discussing the modes of organization of political authority in a compound polity. The chapter considers the concept of federalism and its convoluted meaning and presents an argument on how to understand it better and use it as an analytical tool. The chapter concludes by presenting three principles of political equilibrium in a federation, that can be called principles of federal "balance", federal "order", or federal "respect": integrity, loyalty, and adjudication.

---

[19] A small twist on a sentence by Rachel Cusk: "Without structures, events are unreal". Cusk 2016, p. 24.

[20] Lucas Pires 1988, p. 22.

Chapter 6 then discusses the EU as a federal polity. The purpose of the chapter is to consider the EU from the analytical lens of federalism and to understand the scope and meaning of the three political principles of federal balance in its legal order.

Building upon such conceptual work, Chap. 7 considers the fundamental issue of this work by analysing the EU's powers of economic coordination in light of the principles of federal balance set in the EU Treaties. The chapter concludes with an answer to the question of the problematic character (from the point of view of federal balance) of EU authority regarding economic policy autonomy by its Member States.

The book ends in Chap. 8, reflecting on the findings of the previous chapters, followed by a prospective analysis on the future of the political and legal "theatre" that is EU economic governance. The concluding thought of the work might be summed in this verse by the American novelist and songwriter John Darnielle: *I hope the fences we mended / fall down beneath their own weight.*[21] The following chapters shall explain why.

A small note—this book does not discuss powers of economic assistance provided through the Next Generation Fund. Although there are very important questions of economic governance involved, the impact of this scenario for the future of the EU's federal settlement is still unknown, despite some opinions on its significance.[22] Furthermore, and for the same reasons, monetary policy and its governance by the ECB is excluded from the scope of this work.

Finally, and for the sake of the argument, when making references to the capacity of Member States' governmental institutions to make decisions with macroeconomic effects, this book shall use the terms "economic policy" and "fiscal policy" interchangeably.

References

Cusk R (2016) Outline. Penguin

Dermine P (2022) The New Economic Governance of the Eurozone: A Rule of Law Analysis. Cambridge University Press

Dermine P (2023) Le plan de relance 'Next Generation EU' – de l'Union européenne – Analyse constitutionnelle d'une initiative historique. Bruylant, Brussels

Fatsis L (2015) The Greek crisis illustrates both the poverty of Syriza's ideology and the flaws in the EU's balance-sheet approach to decision-making. LSE Blog, 2 July. Available at: https://blogs.lse.ac.uk/europpblog/2015/07/02/the-greek-crisis-illustrates-both-the-poverty-of-syrizas-ideology-and-the-flaws-in-the-eus-balance-sheet-approach-to-decision-making/ accessed 15 August 2025

Lucas Pires F (1988) Teoria da Constituição de 1976: A Transição Dualista. Coimbra

Mayer F (2020) To boldly go where no court has gone before: the German Federal Constitutional Court's ultra vires decision of May 5. German Law Journal 21:1116–1127

Menéndez ÁJ (2012) La Mutación Constitucional de la Unión Europea. Revista Española de Derecho Constitucional 96:41–98

[21] The Mountain Goats "No Children" https://www.youtube.com/watch?v=fqGKZ3fzN1M&pp=ygUebm8gY2hpbGRyZW4gdGhlIG1vdW50YWluIGdvYXRz accessed 15 August 2025.

[22] Dermine 2023.

Menéndez ÁJ (2014) Editorial: A European Union in constitutional mutation? European Law Journal 20: 127–141

Moury C et al (2021) Capitalising on constraint: Bailout politics in Eurozone countries. Manchester University Press

Mudde C (2017) Syriza: The Failure of the Populist Promise. Palgrave Macmillan

Ramalho T (2025) Legitimating Austerity: The Politics of Crisis in Southern Europe. Bloomsbury Academic

Teixeira P (2022) The Legal History of the European Banking Union: How European Law Led to the Supranational Integration of the Single Financial Market. Hart Publishing

Chapter 2
History and Evolution of the Legal Framework of EU Economic Governance

Contents

Abstract This chapter provides a comprehensive historical and legal account of the evolution of EU economic governance, from the Treaty of Rome to the post-crisis reforms of the 2010s and beyond. It traces the development of EU economic governance as a supportive—but increasingly central—component of European integration, analysing how the original intergovernmental and technocratic framework gradually gave way to a more rule-based, supranational model, particularly after Maastricht. The chapter critically assesses the Stability and Growth Pact, the Eurozone sovereign debt crisis, and subsequent legal reforms, questioning the effectiveness and legitimacy of EU powers in the fiscal domain. It concludes by highlighting a persistent gap between legal form and political substance in the EU's economic governance architecture.

Keywords EU economic governance · Stability and Growth Pact · Maastricht Treaty · Sovereign debt crisis · Economic policy coordination

M. Lucas Pires, *The Federal Legality of EU Economic Governance*,
https://doi.org/10.1007/978-94-6265-747-2_2

2.1 Foundations of EU Economic Governance in the EEC Treaty

EU economic governance refers, basically, to the coordination of (macro)economic policy at an EU level.[1] Economic policy concerns all government action that has to do with the economy's performance as a whole (and not at an individual or sectoral level).[2] In this sense, economic coordination concerns the set of rules, procedures, and institutional structures in place for different governments to cooperate on issues of economic policy. The purpose of economic coordination is to deal with policy issues among interdependent economies, and to maintain growth while safeguarding financial stability (that is, the performance and resilience of their economic situations) when reacting to business cycle events.[3]

The two main economic policy instruments are fiscal and monetary policy. Fiscal policy refers to governments' tax and spending policies,[4] while monetary policy concerns decisions by central banks "to influence the cost and availability of money in an economy".[5] Both can be used for achieving economic objectives, although the objectives of monetary policy tend to be narrowly defined (e.g., in the US, the Federal Reserve's mandate is to achieve full employment, price stability, and moderate long-term interest rates;[6] in the EU, the ECB's mandate is to pursue price stability).[7]

Fiscal policy serves as the basis for all government action and planning. All spending and taxation must be established in a budget law approved yearly, representing deliberate choices of specific economic policies (such as public investment projects and social contributions). The budget establishes the predicted yearly expenses and incomes of a State, thus defining the financial capacity of a government to adopt and develop such policies.[8] In a nutshell: *the government's budget (and respective amendments that might be enacted during its execution) is the central instrument of fiscal policy.*

Monetary and fiscal policy influence one another and must ideally be developed in coordination.[9] As Karlo and Klaus Tuori put it: "[F]or monetary stability, fiscal policy is the crucial non-monetary field of economic policy".[10] In the EU, for example, monetary policy supports general EU economic policies for full employment and

[1] See, on this, and on conceptual discussions of fiscal policy more broadly Amtenbrink and Markakis 2023, pp. 173–176.

[2] Romer 2018, p. 1; Williamson 2018, 23.

[3] Frankel et al. 1990, pp. 10–16.

[4] Romer 2018, p. 660.

[5] ECB (2023) What is Monetary Policy?, available at https://www.ecb.europa.eu/ecb/educational/explainers/tell-me/html/what-is-monetary-policy.en.html accessed 15 August 2025.

[6] Federal Reserve Act 1977, Section 2a.

[7] According to article 127(1) TFEU.

[8] Ippolito 2003, p. 2.

[9] de Grauwe 2018, pp. 17–19; Laurens and de la Piedra 1998, p. 5.

[10] Tuori and Tuori 2014, p. 48.

economic growth.[11] However, monetary policy and economic governance are two distinct fields in the EU constitutional framework, where the competences and institutions responsible for each are different, as we shall see. Furthermore, monetary policy management usually holds a more technocratic character (it is the competence of politically independent institutions and officials appointed by the government) compared to the more politically charged matters of economic policy (enacted by institutions composed of democratically elected officials, like Parliaments).[12]

Economic governance has been a feature of European integration since its inception.[13] The two main objectives of the EEC were the creation of a common market and the approximation ("rapprochement", according to the French version of the Treaty) of the economies of its Member States to achieve welfare and stability.[14] Coordination of Member States' economic policies through centralized procedures was one of the activities the EEC would pursue to achieve its objectives, according to article 3 TEEC. However, it was not of the main objectives, occupying a secondary position in comparison with the primacy provided to integration mechanisms for the common market (the "microeconomic" constitution).[15] We can infer this from the eight place occupied by economic governance in the list of activities pursued by the EEC in article 3 TEEC (following the activities for the abolishment of customs duties, establishment of common tariffs and common commercial policy, abolishment of restrictions to freedoms of movement, the establishment of a common agricultural and transport policies and a regulatory system for the application of competition rules), and from the text of article 6 TEEC, establishing that coordination of Member States' economic policies should be done "to the extent that is necessary to attain the objectives of this Treaty" and that the institutions of the Community should act in a way that was not prejudicial to "the internal and external financial stability of the Member States."

Rules of economic governance were established in Part Three, Title II, Chapter I of the Treaty of Rome. The first rule was article 103 TEEC on conjectural policy. According to this rule, Member States should regard their economic policies as a matter of common concern and consult with each other and the Commission on these matters. The Council could decide (by unanimity) on a proposal by the Commission to adopt measures related to matters of conjunctural policy. "Conjunctural" means a set of circumstances that happens at a given moment, within a specific context.[16] Conjunctural policy measures were temporary measures that the Council

---

[11] Article 119(2) TFEU and Article 127(1) TFEU.

[12] Although the line between technocracy and political management is thin—if it exists at all. See Habermas 2015, pp. 3–7; Adamski 2018, pp. 46–49. See an example of the tensions between technical expertise and political control regarding central banking design in James 2012, pp. 27–28.

[13] Mourlon-Druol 2012, pp. 21–23 and 2020, pp. 17–19; Everling 1964, p. 576; Majone 2014, pp. 22–23; Borger 2020, pp. 83–84; Tuori and Tuori 2014, pp. 19–21.

[14] Article 2 TEC.

[15] Tuori and Tuori 2014, pp. 17–18.

[16] Because of the difficulty finding the meaning for the word in English, we used the French definition of *conjoncturel*, found in Larousse Dictionary https://www.larousse.fr/dictionnaires/francais/conjoncturel/18249 accessed 15 August 2025.

could take if they appeared necessary to safeguard the Treaty's objectives at a particular moment, according to the CJEU.[17] Most of the measures enacted on this legal basis concerned situations where there were difficulties in products' supply (such as energy, for example).[18]

Article 104 TEEC established four objectives and obligations that national governments had to follow when enacting their respective economic policies: they should "ensure the equilibrium of its overall balance of payments and […] maintain confidence in its currency, while ensuring a high level of employment and the stability of the level of prices." According to article 105 TEEC, the purpose of economic coordination was to facilitate the achievement of the objectives set in article 104. To pursue such goals, Member States should "institute a collaboration" among them at the level of their administrations, to discuss issues of fiscal policy, and central banks, to discuss issues of monetary policy. Furthermore, a Monetary Committee was set up to promote coordination in monetary policy. According to article 105(2) TEEC the Monetary Committee supervised financial and monetary developments in the Member States and the Community and provided reports and opinions on such matters to the Council and the Commission.

Articles 106 and 107 concerned rules on liberalization of payments and exchange rates, respectively, which are matters of monetary and market policy. More interesting for the purposes of this book is article 108 TEEC, establishing a mechanism of financial assistance, The EEC could, in the event of a Member State facing difficulties or overall disequilibrium of its balance of payments that threatened either the "functioning of the Common Market" or the establishment of the common commercial policy, recommend a plan of action or provide mutual assistance. Such mutual assistance could consist of "concerted action in regard to any other international organizations" or measures necessary to prevent "diversions of commercial traffic", or of the granting of limited credits by the other Member States, if previously agreed by the beneficiary Member State. In case a decision is not immediately taken, article 109(1) TEEC allowed the Member State concerned to take protective measures.

Considering the rules, it is possible to say that economic coordination in the EEC Treaty had very defined objectives and purposes, such as price stability and balance of payments equilibrium. It included an institutional system of supervision of national economic developments, the Monetary Committee and a mechanism for facing economic difficulties in the event of a balance of payments crisis. We can draw four conclusions based on this framework:

- The first conclusion is that economic *equilibrium* (i.e., stable prices and balanced payments) was already considered a matter of common interest of the Member States in the start of European integration, to support the establishment of the common market. Economic governance (or better: economic *coordination*) was a way to achieve and maintain such equilibrium, thus also supporting the establishment of the common market.

[17] CJEU, Balkan Import v. Hauptzollamt, 1973, Case 5-73, para 17.

[18] Article 103(4) TEC. See also Pintat 1977, p. 17.

- The second conclusion is that the normative modes for coordination consisted of administrative collaboration between the national executives and national central banks. The EEC could not legislate in this field, except regarding conjunctural (i.e., temporary) measures to solve temporary (urgent) issues, according to article 103 (1) and (2) TEEC.
- The third conclusion is Member States' powers of fiscal policy definition did not have any EEC limits, except in what concerned the implementation of custom duties and restrictions on freedom of movement. Also, monetary policy was more restricted due to the rules applicable to the definition of the exchange rate of national currencies.
- The fourth conclusion is that the EEC could provide assistance to Member States in certain circumstances. However, such assistance required the agreement of all Member States.

2.2 From the Treaty of Rome to the Treaty of Maastricht

Despite its secondary status in the EEC's original political and legal architecture, economic governance quickly became one of the most pressing matters in European politics in the first decade of the Treaty of Rome. During this period, three Member States—Germany, Italy, and France—suffered economic adjustment problems due to monetary and balance of payment crises.[19] Only France requested assistance from the EEC: Germany and Italy requested support from the IMF and the World Bank. As Francesco Martucci pointed out, the three crises showed how Member States tended to find solutions for monetary and economic issues outside the framework of the Treaty.[20] It became clear to the EEC and its Member States that, on the one hand, the level of economic governance in place was insufficient, and, on the other hand, that the casual linkage between monetary and fiscal policies made it necessary for some form of cooperation going beyond liberalization of payments and exchange rate controls to exist.

Progress in the legal framework of economic governance occurred in the intergovernmental logic and institutional practice established in the EEC, with the Council setting up several advisory committees composed of national officers in the field of economic policy (the Short-Term Policy Committee, the Medium-Term Policy Committee, the Budgetary Committee, and the Conjunctural Committee)[21] and in the field of monetary policy, with the creation of the Committee of Governors of the Central Banks of the EEC.[22] The escalation of monetary integration to an official objective of the EEC in the Hague Summit of Heads of State in 1969 indicated that the framework of economic governance was now an objective of the EEC and had to

[19] James 2012, pp. 45–46, 50–51 and 59–61; Mourlon-Druol 2020, p. 18.

[20] Martucci 2022, pp. 432–433.

[21] Mourlon-Druol 2020, p. 19.

[22] James 2012, pp. 52–55.

be to be developed.[23] The Werner report of 1970, the first official document analysing the modes for the realization of the EMU, emphasized the importance of economic convergence and integration among the Member States to complete a successful monetary union, to the point where "the essential features of the whole of public budgets, and in particular variations in their volume, the size of balances and the methods of financing or utilizing them, will be decided at the Community level".[24] Such integration, according to the Werner report, required three developments: definition of common economic policies, establishment of fiscal policy coordination, and tax harmonization.[25]

The implementation of the EMU as suggested by the Werner report did not occur due to the currency fluctuation crisis that took place after the fall of the Bretton Woods system (another economic crisis that demonstrated the importance of advancing monetary integration to achieve the objective of price stability established in the TEEC). The next decade and a half saw the enactment of several measures in the monetary field, first with the creation of the "snake" (an agreement among the Member States on the margin of fluctuation of exchange rates between EEC currencies)[26] and, afterwards, with the creation of the European Monetary System ("EMS"), an exchange rate system based on a unit of account (the European Currency Union or "ECU") supported by a basket of EMS currencies.[27] The only development in economic governance integration during this period was the creation of a new advisory committee, the Economic Policy Committee, which had limited effects in promoting enhanced convergence between national economies.[28]

Although the period after the entry into force of the Treaty of Rome showed how important it was for EEC economic governance to exist, the development of the framework of economic coordination continued by the same intergovernmental modes established in 1957, that is: through informal consultation bodies with no binding powers. Therefore, economic coordination remained limited to "soft" modes of political cooperation at a technical-administrative level. The EEC Member States preferred to adopt "harder" modes of integration regarding monetary policy due to the pressing challenges of international exchange rate fluctuation.

It is therefore interesting to note that, despite being established in 1957, the legal framework of economic coordination lagged behind the development of the framework of monetary integration, an objective only formally adopted as a community project a decade after the Treaty of Rome entered into force. There are three reasons

---

23 Communiqué from the heads of State or Government of the Member States of the EEC at the Hague December 1969, available at https://www.cvce.eu/obj/final_communique_of_the_hague_summit_2_december_1969-en-33078789-8030-49c8-b4e0-15d053834507.html accessed 15 August 2025.

24 Report to the Council and the Commission on the realization by stages of Economic and Monetary Union in the Community, p. 12, available at https://ec.europa.eu/economy_finance/publications/pages/publication6142_en.pdf accessed 15 August 2025.

25 Ibid., pp. 26–29.

26 Mourlon-Druol 2020, pp. 23–24; James 2012, pp. 96–102.

27 James 2012, pp. 146–188.

28 Barattieri and Thomas 1975, p. 504.

that explain this discrepancy. First, economic policy coordination and definition was a sensitive subject for the Member States, since the development of this area would necessarily affect the fiscal and political autonomy of States, to which many governments did not agree.[29] Second, the monetary challenges of the seventies provoked by the fall of the gold standard required a prompt response, making it necessary for mechanisms of collaboration of monetary policy to be put in place ahead of other forms of economic cooperation, such as fiscal policy coordination. Third and final, monetary policy was understood as a more technical, less political affair than economic policy definition. It was therefore easier for the Member States to establish a more binding legal framework for collaboration between specialized, technocratic institutions, such as central banks, rather than to establish a centralized legal framework for making decisions on common grounds of fiscal policy.[30]

2.3 The EMU and the Maastricht Model

The European integration project regained a new political impetus in the eighties, with the signing of the ESA and the launching of the objective of achieving a single market by 1992. Talks regarding the development of monetary integration as a necessary complement to the single market came again to the fore, with a new report produced by a committee chaired by Jacques Delors, president of the Commission, setting a blueprint for discussion.[31]

In the Delors report, monetary integration would consist of "complete freedom of movement for persons, goods, services, and capital, as well as irrevocably fixed exchange rates between national currencies and, finally, a single currency", with the EMU being the "final result of the process of progressive economic integration in Europe",[32] which gave a "messianic" feeling to the process of monetary integration.[33] However, to maintain the necessary political autonomy and respect the political, social, and cultural diversity of Member States, "an innovative and unique approach" would need to be developed, one that did not exist in federal states and that would be adequate to the Community's specific character.[34] Like the writers of the Werner

[29] Everling 1964.

[30] James 2012, pp. 2–5; Barattieri and Thomas 1975, p. 502.

[31] Committee for the study of Economic and Monetary Union (1989) Report on Economic and Monetary Union in the European Community, available at https://eurocid.mne.gov.pt/sites/default/files/repository/paragraph/documents/27448/report-economic-and-monetary-union-european-gpeudorpdfa1bcb5689401enc001.pdf accessed 15 August 2025.

[32] Ibid., p. 17.

[33] In line with messianic ends to EU integration. See Weiler 2011; Somek and Rendl 2023, pp. 147–159.

[34] Committee for the study of Economic and Monetary Union (1989) Report on Economic and Monetary Union in the European Community, p. 17, available at https://eurocid.mne.gov.pt/sites/default/files/repository/paragraph/documents/27448/report-economic-and-monetary-union-european-gpeudorpdfa1bcb5689401enc001.pdf accessed 15 August 2025.

report, the writers of the Delors' report understood that such unique approach needed to acknowledge the necessary links between the economic union and monetary union as two parts of the same phenomena.[35]

What would this innovative approach consist of? According to the Delors report, Member States would need to confer more powers to the EEC in the field of monetary policy and to establish some form of economic "management".[36] How? While monetary policy definition would be centralized in a supranational institution, economic policy definition would remain a prerogative of Member States, that had to be exercised within a common legal framework, with "procedures and rules" for defining a common "policy stance for the Community as a whole" to reduce differences in borrowing costs (debt levels) between the Member States and, finally, prevent the running of large-size budget deficits.[37]

The report would then conclude on a "monetarist" note by recommending that monetary integration be established in parallel with economic union. This moved contrary to other views, considered as "economist" views, that would have preferred that economic union and stronger economic convergence were achieved before advancing to the centralization of monetary policy.[38] Monetarists won, since the Delors report greatly influenced the making of the Treaty of Maastricht, which formally introduced monetary integration into the EC treaty framework.[39] In the Treaty, monetary policy was established as an exclusive competence of the EU, while the competences concerning economic policy would be limited to measures of coordination of national economic policies.[40] Such a division meant that monetary policy was entrusted to a specific institutional framework, the European System of Central Banks ("ESCB"), composed of a new EU institution, the ECB, and by the national central banks of the Member States (the governors of which were also part of the Governing Council of the ECB).[41] The primary objective of EU monetary policy (hence, the primary task of the ESCB) was to maintain price stability, with the support of general economic policies being its secondary purpose.[42]

Norms on economic policy coordination established in the Treaty of Rome suffered significant amendments. The first amendment established that economic policy should be conducted under two sets of criteria. The first set of criteria consisted of guiding policy principles, such as commitment to an open market economy with free competition, opting for an efficient allocation of resources, and achievement

[35] Ibid., p. 18.

[36] Ibid.

[37] Ibid., pp. 20–25, 28–29.

[38] Ibid., p. 32. For an explanation of the monetarist versus economist debate, see James 2012, p. 93; de Grauwe 2018, pp. 73–75.

[39] See Dermine 2022, pp. 27–34. For a history and explanation of the making of the Treaty of Maastricht, see Dyson and Featherstone 1999, pp. 19–33.

[40] Articles 3a(1) and 103 TEC (Maastricht Revision).

[41] Articles 105 and 106 TEC (Maastricht Revision).

[42] Articles 3a(2) and 105 TEC (Maastricht Revision).

and maintenance of stable prices, sound public finances, sound monetary conditions, and a stable balance of payments.[43] The second set of criteria was the Broad Economic Policy Guidelines ("BEPGs") issued by the Council, under the proposal of the Commission and after approval by the European Council.[44] The BEPGs were non-binding acts proposing general policy orientations for the Member States to follow. Contrary to the previous framework, there was now a structure dedicated to the convergence of national economic policies following not only the objectives of the Treaty but also centralized policy orientations issued by Community institutions.

The second significant amendment was the setting of a system for supervising economic developments in the Member States and monitoring economic convergence. This system, the Multilateral Surveillance Procedure ("MSP"), was managed by the Commission and the Council to assess the conformity of national fiscal policies with the BEPGs and check if there was any risk for the "proper functioning" of the EMU.[45] If a case of disconformity or deviation with the BEPGs were to happen, the Council (under the proposal of the Commission) could issue recommendations to Member States on economic policy measures and make them public.[46]

The third significant amendment concerned the definition, in the Treaty, of fiscal policy obligations for Member States. Member States had now the duty to have sound public finances, which meant avoiding excessive government deficits, according to article 104c of the amended TEEC. To avoid excessive government deficits meant limiting the ratio of budget deficits to GDP to 3% maximum and limiting the ratio of government debt to GDP to 60% maximum.[47] If a Member State threatened to fail or failed to fulfil one of these criteria, the Commission would assess the situation and communicate its opinion to the Council, which could declare the existence of an excessive deficit.[48] The Council would then recommend a corrective course of action for the affected Member State.[49] If the affected Member State did not comply with the recommendation, then the Council could request the Member State to take other actions to reduce the deficit within a specific timeframe. Continued failure to comply with the Council's requests could lead to the application of one or more of such sanctions: an obligation to publish additional information before issuing bonds and securities, an invitation to the European Investment Bank ("EIB") requesting reconsideration of its lending policy, the payment of a non-interest-bearing deposit, and the imposition of fines.[50]

The fourth significant amendment concerned the framework of financial assistance to Member States facing economic distress. In the Maastricht framework, assistance

---

[43] Article 102(a) TEC (Maastricht Revision).

[44] Article 103(2) TEC (Maastricht Revision).

[45] Article 103(3) TEC (Maastricht Revision).

[46] Article 103(4) TEC (Maastricht Revision).

[47] The reference values were set in Article 1 of the Protocol to the Treaty on the Excessive Deficit Procedure.

[48] Article 104c(6) TEC (Maastricht Revision).

[49] Article 104c(7) TEC (Maastricht Revision).

[50] Article 104c(11) TEC (Maastricht Revision).

could be provided, under certain conditions, when a Member State faced difficulties due to exceptional circumstances that were out of the Member State's control (e.g., in the event of a natural disaster).[51] However, outside of this scope, the Community and the Member States could not be liable for the financial commitments of other Member States.[52] Moreover, the ECB was prohibited from providing any credit facility to the Member States and purchasing Member States' debt instruments.[53] Assistance in the case of balance of payments disequilibrium and currency issues remained on similar terms as the ones set in 1957.[54]

The fifth and final significant amendment brought by the Treaty of Maastricht was the setting of convergence criteria for joining the single currency.[55] The EMU would be achieved in three stages: the first between 1992 and 1994, the second from 1994 to 1996 or, at best, 1999, and the third (with the adoption of the euro as a single currency) after 1999.[56] There were four criteria for the Member States to comply with by the end of the second stage: high degree of price stability, sustainability of budgetary finances of national governments, observance of the normal fluctuation margins of the EMS, and, finally, the durability of economic convergence achieved by the Member States.[57]

All in all, there were continuity lines between 1957 and 1992 since some basic structural features of the Rome model remained in place. An institutional system for monitoring and assessing the evolution of national economic situations continued to exist, and there were still rules for supporting Member States through balance of payments assistance. The two main economic policy principles remained: price stability and balance of payments equilibrium. Economic coordination continued to be a supportive competence, supporting in 1952 the establishment of the common market and, in 1992 supporting the establishment of monetary integration. Finally, the definition of economic policy, despite the developments with the BEPGs and the MSP, remained a competence of the Member States, with the latter still enjoying a high degree of political autonomy in its definition, to be exercised within the limits set by the Treaty.

There were also some crucial differences between the two models. The Maastricht model gave more importance to economic governance than the Rome model did. In Maastricht, economic governance had a more sophisticated legal and institutional framework, with new objectives and duties for the Member States (sound public finances, an open market economy, and sound monetary conditions), together with the establishment of common convergence criteria for economic policy definition. Informal institutions and *ad hoc* committees of experts and national officers were replaced by the Commission, the Council, and the European Council in the definition

[51] Article 103a(2) TEC (Maastricht Revision).

[52] Article 104b(1) TEC (Maastricht Revision).

[53] Article 104(1) TEC (Maastricht Revision).

[54] Article 109h TEC (Maastricht Revision).

[55] de Grauwe 2018, pp. 122–129.

[56] The move from one stage to another was set out in Articles 109c–109m TEC (Maastricht Revision).

[57] Article 109j(1) TEC (Maastricht Revision).

and supervision of economic policy coordination, thus granting these institutions a more significant political (and not only technocratic) status.

Arguably the most significant change in the legal framework of economic governance was the setting of binding rules to prevent the Member States from running excessive deficits. For the first time in the constitutional order of the EU, the Member States were subject to fiscal policy obligations. The purpose was to guarantee that Member States would not use the benefits of being in a monetary union (basically, lower borrowing costs in financial markets) to increase their expenses in an unsustainable manner and put the stability of the EC at risk.[58] Moreover, the limitation of EU financial assistance to interfere only in the event of unexpected and uncontrollable situations prevented the idea that non-compliant States could be bailed out, and dispelled fears of moral hazard and free riding.[59]

The EMU became a *rules-based* area,[60] but the establishment of rules on budgetary discipline was not without political and technical controversy. There were strong discussions among Member States in the making of the Treaty of Maastricht about what kind of EMU should exist, if a "harder" EMU with automatic application of sanctions for non-compliance, or if a more flexible EMU with sanctions dependent on an evaluation and confirmation by both the Commission and the Council.[61] The latter prevailed. However, the open terms used in article 104c TEEC (an excess declining "substantially and continuously," that is "exceptional and temporary," or with a ratio "sufficiently diminishing and approaching the reference value at a satisfactory pace") gave EU institutions some discretion to apply the rules. The margin of interpretation chosen by the institutions could minimize the rule's strength to the point of the rules becoming mere orientations or best-practice principles, which some Member States preferred.[62]

On the other hand, economists criticized the rules for what they considered an arbitrary definition of the reference values for an excessive deficit.[63] While agreeing that economic convergence was necessary for the success of monetary integration, and that fiscal equilibrium played a crucial role in such a situation, they doubted that such rules would substantially guarantee budgetary balance at the national level. With monetary sovereignty handed to the Community, fiscal policy limited by EC rules, and no adequate transfer mechanisms for shock absorption at the EC level, Member States could see their capacity for expansionary policies limited and become more exposed to economic shocks. The emergence of economic crisis could put in question compliance with the no-bailout clause set in the Treaties.

---

[58] de Grauwe 2018, pp. 137–138; Gros 1996, pp. 246–249. Critically, Adamski 2018, pp. 20–22.

[59] A fear shared by Germany, for example. See Dyson and Featherstone 1999, p. 789. See also Brunnermeier et al. 2016, pp. 98–100.

[60] On the debate between rules and flexibility in enacting Maastricht, see Brunnermeier et al. 2016, pp. 84–96.

[61] Dyson and Featherstone 1999, pp. 672–676.

[62] Ibid.

[63] Priewe 2020; Buiter et al. 1993, p. 62; de Grauwe 2018, pp. 127–128; Eichengreen 2023, p. 24; James 2023, pp. 59–60.

It is also important to mention how monetary integration became a priority and an existential target of the European project in Maastricht.[64] The move to a single currency was the most important change in a Treaty reform that intended to transform the EC in a political union with more competences, a Parliament with more decision-making powers, and an enhanced legal status for the peoples of the Member States through EU citizenship.[65] The completion of the single market plan by 1992 led to the launch of a new stage of integration that would require a higher degree of political and social commitment. The Member States considered the euro irreversible, and established 1 January 1999 as the date for starting the third stage of the EMU. The Community (the Union) would not be the same afterwards.

2.4 Post-Maastricht Blues and Reform of the SGP

The bigger the step, the greater the impact—and the greater the fall. Maastricht marked a before and after in EU integration, not only in terms of the Community growing politically and institutionally, but also because it was the first time that significant differences in the degree of legal integration between the Member States appeared. The EMU (with the opting out of Denmark and the United Kingdom) was no exception.[66] The rise of differentiated membership forms led to necessary discrimination in status and rules between the Member States that had adopted the euro and those that had not (known as "non-participating Member States").[67] The division would continue in subsequent EU enlargements (1995, 2004, and 2008). The consequence of this division was that the legal framework of the EMU did not apply to all Member States, although economic governance rules still did, to a certain extent.

After Maastricht, the Member States needed to prepare for the third stage of the EMU to fulfil the convergence criteria for the single currency.[68] The debate over the strength and effectiveness of the legal framework of economic governance and the rules on budgetary discipline returned. Although the Council set reporting obligations on planned and estimated government deficit and debt for four years,[69] some Member States believed that more was necessary as the third stage approached and the budgetary situation of Member States remained divergent. After a series of discussions, the Member States agreed in 1997 to increase their political and legal

---

[64] Fratzscher 2018, pp. 139–154.

[65] Craig and de Búrca 2015, pp. 11–12; Schütze 2016, pp. 22–27.

[66] Curtin 2020, pp. 11–12.

[67] As per article 7(1) of Council Regulation (EC) 1466/97 of July 7 1997 on the strengthening of the surveillance of budgetary positions and the surveillance and coordination of economic policies [1997] OJ L209/1.

[68] On the concept of convergence and its role in EMU policy, see Simón 2024.

[69] Council Regulation (EC) 3605/93 of 22 November 1993 on the application of the Protocol on the excessive deficit procedure annexed to the Treaty establishing the European Community [1993] OJ L332/7.

commitment to budgetary discipline by adopting a resolution on the Stability and Growth Pact ("SGP").[70]

The goal was for the SGP to reinforce the rule-based character of the framework of economic governance through the improvement of national fiscal policy supervision.[71] It represented a joint commitment by the Member States, the Commission and the Council to follow and apply the rules set out in the Maastricht framework. Member States would avoid running excessive deficits and would take all corrective measures necessary in case an excessive deficit occurred, while the Commission would exercise supervision and provide all studies and opinions on the application of the framework's rules. As for the Council, it would implement, in a rigorous and timely manner, all the elements of the SGP and comply with its duties of supervision of national policies.[72]

The SGP was composed of a resolution of the European Council and two Council regulations.[73] While the resolution reaffirmed the importance of budgetary equilibrium, the regulations set rules for improving the coordination of economic policies and surveillance of budgetary status. In other words, the Member States were completing the Treaty framework of MSP and EDP and detailing it through secondary legislation for preventing and deterring non-compliance with centralized fiscal policy rules and objectives.

Regarding the MSP, Council Regulation No 1466/97 established the obligation for the Member States to submit information, on an annual basis, to the Council and the Commission (in the form of programs) on their economic and budgetary situation and performance in the short and medium term.[74] Such programs would include, for example, an indication of budgetary and government debt targets through the setting of Medium-Term Objectives ("MTO"), assumptions concerning economic variables such as growth, employment, and expenditure and how they can affect the budgetary and debt position, and descriptions of budgetary and economic policies enacted). Member States adopting the single currency would have to submit stability programs, while non-participating Member States would submit convergence programs, but the information provided was essentially the same.[75] The Council would assess such programs and comment on their adequacy regarding the Union's objectives. The Council could also ask the Member States to adjust the programs when necessary. The Council, the Commission, and the Monetary Committee (an advisory body set in article 109c TEEC) would then monitor the execution of the programs, and the former could make recommendations when it was considered necessary to apply

[70] Resolution 97/C 236/01 of the European Council on the Stability and Growth Pact [1997] OJ NoC236/1.

[71] Amtenbrink and de Haan 2006, pp. 403–404; Estella 2018, pp. 134–147.

[72] See Point IV of Resolution 97/C 236/01.

[73] Council Regulation (EC) 1466/97 and Council Regulation (EC) 1467/97 of July 7 1997 on speeding up and clarifying the implementation of the excessive deficit procedure [1997] OJ L209/6.

[74] Articles 3(1) and 4 of Council Regulation (EC) 1466/97.

[75] Ibid., Article 7.

corrective measures.[76] There was no sanctioning mechanism for failure to comply with the recommendations.

As for the EDP, Council Regulation No 1467/97 clarified that a deficit should be considered exceptional and temporary[77] when the deviation from the reference value resulted either from an unusual event outside the control of the Member State concerned or from a severe economic downturn. An exceptionally severe economic downturn concerned an annual fall in real GDP of at least 2%; however, Member States could argue to the Council about the exceptionality of the downturn by using other evidence. The provision also set timings for decisions to be issued by the participating institutions in the EDP while detailing conditions for applying sanctions.[78] It was further established that the EDP would be held in abeyance every time a Member State acted in compliance with the recommendations made by the Council to correct the situation.[79]

The idea that the SGP was a way to strengthen the rules of economic governance seems incorrect in hindsight. What the SGP effectively did was to establish a legal framework for preventing budget deficits, consisting of fiscal and economic data disclosures to EU institutions. Clarification of the rules of the EDP was minimal, and the new provisions did not make the corrective procedure more stringent and automatic than before.[80] For example, in the case of understanding compliance with recommendations for holding the procedure in abeyance, it was not clear what the burden of proof was for assessing compliance. If the scope of the burden of proof accepted was broad, then the EDP would always be held in abeyance as soon as a non-compliant Member State started to take any form of corrective measure, whether in line with the recommendation or not. In such cases, sanctions would never apply unless the Member State flagrantly and explicitly disobeyed the corrective recommendation and continued to not comply with the Treaty and SGP rules. Moreover, the decision to acknowledge the existence of an excessive deficit and apply sanctions remained with the Council, and consequently with the Member States. Given the lax history of Member States confronting each other's through EU mechanisms,[81] there were strong reasons for being sceptical about the effectiveness of this model.

In 2003, the Commission and the Council declared the existence of excessive deficits in Germany and France (Germany's budget deficit amounted to 3.5% of GDP while France's deficit amounted to 3.1% of GDP).[82] Following an opinion by the Commission, the Council issued recommendations to both Member States, under

[76] Articles 6(3) and 10(3) of Council Regulation (EC) 1466/97.

[77] Article 2(1) of Council Regulation (EC) 1467/97.

[78] Ibid., Articles 3–8; concerning sections, see Articles 11–16.

[79] Ibid., Article 9(1).

[80] Amtenbrink and de Haan 2006, pp. 404–407.

[81] Adamski 2018, pp. 43–44.

[82] For Germany, see Council Decision (EC) 2003/89 of 21 January 2003 on the existence of an excessive deficit in Germany — Application of Article 104(6) of the Treaty establishing the European Community [2003] OJ L34/16; for France, see Council Decision (EC) 2003487 of 3 June 2003 on the existence of an excessive deficit in France — Application of Article 104(6) of the Treaty establishing the European Community [2003] OJ L165/29.

article 104(7) TEEC, to adopt corrective measures. Later, when evaluating compliance with the recommendations, the Commission found that both Member States would continue to run excessive deficits in 2004, and that their debt levels would also increase. Although the Commission acknowledged that Germany followed the recommendations of the Council in taking measures to reduce the deficit by 1%, the fact that the steps taken did not have the desired effect, together with the expectation that the 2004 deficit would increase along with the debt ratio was sufficient for declaring non-compliance with EU rules.[83] In the case of France, the Commission considered that the Member State did not take the actions requested to reduce the deficit and therefore was failing to comply with the fiscal rules.[84]

Upon receiving the Commission's opinions under the EDP procedure, the Council held a vote to decide on making the recommendations to France and Germany public under article 104(8) and to give notice to both Member States to remedy the situation, under article 104(9). No decision was adopted, for there was no qualified majority; furthermore, in the voting, France voted against the decisions regarding Germany and vice-versa.[85] Instead, the Council concluded the process by deciding to hold the EDP in abeyance for both countries to comply with new commitments and targets to correct their respective deviations from the rules, while further reaffirming the Council's commitment to the SGP and undertaking to improve and reinforce budgetary discipline in the Eurozone.[86]

The Commission was not satisfied with the outcome, declaring that the Council did not follow the spirit nor the letter EU Economic Governance rules, stating that "[o]nly a rule-based system can guarantee that commitments are enforced and that all Member States are treated equally".[87] The Commission then lodged an action for annulment with the CJEU of the Council's decisions to not follow the procedures of Article 104(8) and (9) TEEC and of the conclusions holding the process in abeyance.[88] In essence, the Commission was seeking to make the Council liable for not complying with the norms and procedures of the SGP on budgetary discipline.

The CJEU ruled in favour of the Council regarding the annulment of the decisions of non-adoption. The Court considered that there had been no decision, just a failure to reach the necessary majority to decide. Therefore, the action of the Commission was inadmissible because there was no act to annul, and the Commission—which had

[83] See European Commission (2003) Recommendation for a Council Decision establishing, in accordance with article 104(8) of the EC Treaty, that the action taken by Germany in response to the recommendations made by the Council pursuant to article 104(7) of the Treaty is proving to be inadequate.

[84] European Commission (2003) Recommendation for a Council Decision establishing, in accordance with article 104(8) of the EC Treaty, whether effective action has been taken by France in response to the recommendations made by the Council pursuant to article 104(7).

[85] Council (2003) Conclusions of the 2546th Council Meeting of Economic and Financial Affairs, pp. 15–21, available at https://data.consilium.europa.eu/doc/document/ST-14492-2003-REV-1/en/pdf accessed 15 August 2025.

[86] Ibid., pp. 21–22.

[87] Ibid., p. 22.

[88] CJEU, Commission v. Council, 2004, Case C-27/04.

argued that what existed was an implied decision *not to apply* the EDP procedure—should have brought its claim under the action of failure to act.[89]

The discussion on keeping the process in abeyance was also focused on its admissibility. The Council had argued that the conclusions were acts of political nature and did not have legal effects: the decision to hold the EDP in abeyance was an automatic consequence of the failure to vote on the Commission's recommendations. The Commission contested such arguments and stated that the conclusions were "*sui generis* measures whose main legal effect is to free the Council and the Member States concerned from the binding legal framework" of the Treaty and the SGP and to replace such rules with new guidelines and framework for monitoring excess deficits of the Member States concerned.[90] The Court noted that the Council's decision to hold the EDP in abeyance was conditional to the concerned Member States complying with specific commitments, which precluded the automatic character of abeyance.[91] The Court considered that the Council's amendment of the content of previously adopted recommendations in the scope of the EDP was another evidence of the intention of the Council to have the conclusions produce legal effects. The act, therefore, could be annulled.[92]

Regarding the substance of the act, the Court found that the Council's conclusions infringed article 104 TEEC, since the decision to hold the process in abeyance was not based on valid legal grounds but rather on the condition that unilateral commitments made by the Member States would be complied with.[93] Furthermore, the Court considered that the Council had also infringed the EDP when amending its previous recommendations to Germany and France without having a previous recommendation by the Commission for that purpose.[94] The conclusions were annulled, but no further consequences were established.

The case of *Commission v. Council* proved the sceptics of the framework of the rule-based system of economic governance right in a brutal fashion.[95] The case was a high-stakes situation, particularly for the Commission, given that the non-compliant actors were the Germany and France, the two biggest Member States. A more ironic twist is that Germany and its lawmakers had been staunch supporters of the rule-based system since day one.

The Commission was stringent in the application of the rules, given that the deficits for Germany and France were in excess, respectively, of 0.1% and 0.5% of the reference values (the excess of debt ratio increase was also minimal, at least by today's standards: 61% in Germany and 62% in France). However, the fact that both countries did not take measures to balance their budgetary situation in the short to medium term shows that they did not perceive the rules and attached consequences

[89] Ibid., paras 33–35.

[90] Ibid., para 43.

[91] Ibid., paras 47–48.

[92] Ibid., paras 50–51.

[93] Ibid., paras 88–89.

[94] Ibid., paras 94–96.

[95] Adamski 2018, pp. 38–40; Jones 2020, pp. 77–78.

as sufficiently binding and deterrent. Additionally, both countries managed to protect one another in the Council, which showed how difficult it was going to be to make States comply coercively with the framework of EU Economic Governance.

The case also shows the challenges the CJEU faces in exercising effective judicial control of the framework of EU economic governance. The arguments of the Council and the Commission on the character of the rules and of the procedures of the EDP (e.g., political and not legal decisions; *sui generis* procedures to override laws) demonstrate the problem with the legal character of the rules of economic governance and the role politics plays in their effectiveness. On one hand, the Court acknowledged that the rules on national budgetary discipline must be interpreted as fully effective, given the importance of the EU's political process.[96] On the other hand, however, the Court recognized the political discretion of the Council in taking decisions in the EDP,[97] which seemed to justify German and France's actions.

The bottom line of the case, therefore, *is that a Member State can do whatever it wants as long as the other Member States allow it.* The more capable a Member State is of convincing other Member States to vote against the implementation of the procedure, the less strength the rules have. In other words, the rule-based framework of EU Economic Governance was paradoxically fragile because it could be appropriated and manipulated by national governments. Moreover, judicial control did not lead to the automatic application of the procedure. The Court's decision had no practical effects: the Council continued without deciding on the application of sanctions under the EDP, and the procedures were effectively closed two and half years after the Court's decision.[98] All in all, this saga showed how little, in practice, the SGP added to the framework of EU economic governance.

To add more irony to the situation, the following legal reform of the economic coordination framework made the application of the SGP more flexible and adaptable to national situations.[99] The objective was to "enhance the governance and the national ownership" of the framework of fiscal coordination and to reinforce the preventive and corrective arms of the pact.[100] The reform consisted of two regulations, amending the previous provisions related to the MSP and the EDP.[101] Regarding the MSP, the new rules provided a new definition of MTO that opened the door for more flexibility for national action, allowing the Member States to present divergent MTOs close to

---

[96] CJEU, Commission v. Council, 2004, Case C-27/04, para 74.

[97] Ibid., paras 76–80.

[98] Regarding Germany, see Council Decision 2007/490/EC of 5 June 2007 abrogating Decision 2003/89/EC on the existence of an excessive deficit in Germany [2007] OJ L183/23; regarding France, see Council Decision 2007/154/EC of 30 January 2007 abrogating Decision 2003/487/EC on the existence of an excessive deficit in France [2007] OJ L68/3.

[99] See Estella 2023, pp. 152–156.

[100] Council Regulation (EC) 1055/2005 of 27 June 2005 amending Regulation (EC) No 1466/97 on the strengthening of the surveillance of budgetary positions and the surveillance and coordination of economic policies [2005] OJ L 174/1, Recital (2).

[101] Council Regulation 1055/2005, (n 116) and Council Regulation (EC) 1056/2005 of 27 June 2005 amending Regulation (EC) No 1467/97 on speeding up and clarifying the implementation of the excessive deficit procedure [2005] OJ L 174/5.

balance or surplus position.[102] What is more, the new rules allowed Member States to revise the MTO when implementing a structural reform ("measures that change the fabric of an economy, the institutional and regulatory framework in which businesses and people operate"[103]) or every four years. The changes thus granted the Member States more autonomy in adapting their economic policies to changes in the business cycles.[104] The Council would also consider structural changes adopted by Member States and their economic impact in this new framework, when performing assessments of compliance.

Regarding the EDP, the new rules broadened the set of criteria the Commission and the Council had to consider when verifying the existence of an excessive deficit; such new criteria included the impact of structural reforms, the achievement of European policy goals, contributions to foster international cooperation, among others.[105] The new rules also allowed, in what seems like an influence of the CJEU's decision in the *Commission v. Council* case, for the Council to present a revised recommendation under article 104(7) TEEC whenever the Member States complied and took adequate action to correct the deficit but then became suddenly faced with unexpected adverse economic events.[106]

In sum, these amendments made the SGP more accommodating to Member States' different needs and concerns while making the application of sanctions more difficult. It did not, however, make the framework of EU Economic Governance more effective, since Member States' compliance with the rules did not improve.[107] It also raised doubts as to the commitment (and belief) of Member States to the framework of EU Economic Governance.

2.5 The Sovereign Debt Crisis and Its Effects

The SGP and the CJEU decision on *Commission v. Council* were, in essence, the most significant developments in the legal framework of EU Economic Governance between Maastricht and the Eurozone crisis. The three Treaty reforms—Amsterdam, Nice, and Lisbon—did not significantly alter the framework of economic coordination and fiscal surveillance. The structure of the MSP and the EDP remained largely intact, as well as the rule-based system and the SGP.[108] The political and legal model

---

[102] Article 1(1) of Council Regulation 1055/2005 introducing article 2a to Regulation 1466/1997.

[103] European Central Bank, 2017, What are structural reforms?, available at https://www.ecb.europa.eu/explainers/tell-me/html/what-are-structural_reforms.en.html accessed 15 August 2025.

[104] Brunnermeier et al. 2016, p. 136.

[105] Article 1(1) of Council Regulation 1056/2005, amending article 2(2) and (3) of Regulation 1467/1997.

[106] Ibid., Article 3(b) amending Article 3(4) of Regulation 1467/1997.

[107] Adamski 2018, pp. 40–42.

[108] See Declaration by the Member States on article 126 of the TFEU, annexed to the Treaty of Lisbon.

and its underlying philosophy were still the same as in Maastricht, even after the decision of the CJEU. The SGP clarified the Treaty rules to a limited extent, and such clarification did not add much; instead, it only confirmed the highly political and technical nature of economic governance and the fragile legal character of its construction.

Such fragility became unavoidably evident with the financial crisis that started in 2008.[109] The crisis severely affected the sovereign bonds of eurozone Member States that, due to their economic vulnerability (e.g., budgetary imbalances, lower growth rates, and high levels of public debt), were incapable of resisting the pressure of financial markets and were facing increasing borrowing costs.[110] Such a situation demonstrated how ineffective the framework of economic governance and budgetary discipline was while showing the disadvantages of entering a monetary union without any instrument capable of reacting to asymmetric shocks. The risk that such States would become insolvent, and that the Eurozone could break led to a highly contentious period of political action and turmoil and to the enactment of urgent measures and reforms that had not been seen before in the history of EU integration.

The crisis—its causes and effects, dynamics, and many complexities—has been extensively covered in the academic literature, making a recapitulation here both repetitive and unnecessary.[111] Suffice to say that the EU's response occurred on two fronts: a corrective, short-term front and a preventive, medium-term front. Regarding the first level, the EU had to act immediately to calm the pressure on financial markets and guarantee the stability of the Eurozone. The path chosen consisted of bailing out the most affected Member States—Greece, Ireland, and Portugal—in exchange for the latter adopting economic reforms to correct their respective debt and deficit imbalances. Member States provided the bailout funds through facilities external to the EU framework to counter the prohibition of the no-bailout clause set in the TFEU. The IMF also participated in the intervention to offer expertise and support.

Regarding the second level of response, Member States enacted a comprehensive package of legal reforms to correct the deficiencies of the previous framework of EU economic governance. Such reforms occurred both within and outside the scope of EU law, through the enactment of secondary law (the six-pack[112] in 2011 and

[109] See, on the financial crisis, Tooze 2018, pp. 91–118 and 319–446.

[110] For a description of the crisis see Hadjiemmanuil 2020, pp. 1265–1326; Tuori and Tuori 2014, pp. 61–84; Markakis 2020, pp. 18–65; Tuori 2022, pp. 129–138; and, critically, Chiti and Teixeira 2013, pp. 683–708.

[111] For a recap of the legal and political bibliography of the eurozone crisis, see Beukers 2015 and Martinico 2014, pp. 247–280.

[112] The six-pack is composed of Regulation (EU) 1173/2011 of the European Parliament and of the Council of 16 November 2011 on the effective enforcement of budgetary surveillance in the euro area [2011] OJ L306/1; Regulation (EU) 1174/2011 of the European Parliament and of the Council of 16 November 2011 on enforcement measures to correct excessive macroeconomic imbalances in the euro area [2011] OJ L306/8; Regulation (EU) 1175/2011 of the European Parliament and of the Council of 16 November 2011 amending Council Regulation (EC) No 1466/97 on the strengthening of the surveillance of budgetary positions and the surveillance and coordination of economic policies

the two-pack[113] in 2013, comprising in total seven regulations and one directive) and with the signing of two treaties and one pact: the Treaty on Stability, Coordination and Governance in the EMU ("TSCG", also known as "Fiscal Compact"), the Treaty establishing the European Stability Mechanism ("ESM Treaty"), both signed in 2012, and the Euro Plus Pact (an initiative of Member States to foster economic competitiveness) agreed in 2011.[114] The SGP was amended, with Member States reaffirming (once more) the commitment to sound budget policies and setting out new obligations in the field of fiscal policy. Furthermore, the reforms created new procedures for monitoring and correcting economic developments (the Excessive Imbalance Procedure or "EIP") and established institutional mechanisms for future economic assistance with the European Stability Mechanism ("ESM").

There was another element to the EU's response, with the rise of the ECB as a principal institutional player. Often viewed as a mostly technocratic body, the ECB presented itself as the principal responsible for guaranteeing the stability of the Eurozone, going as far as proposing to use its monetary policy mandate to support economic developments in the affected Member States.[115] Such actions proved contentious and a major source of tensions between constitutional courts regarding the competence of the ECB and the limits of economic versus monetary policy powers, as we shall see in the next chapter.

2.6 Post-crisis Developments

In terms of the structure of the framework of EU economic governance, the financial crisis was the last moment of reform. Afterward, there were proposals for improvements and changes to enhance the EMU's capacity and legitimacy. A critical reflection came from a report produced by the presidents of the five EU institutions (Commission, Council, Eurogroup, ECB, and the Parliament).[116] The report covered several areas for further political and regulatory integration to improve the

[2011] OJ L306/12; Regulation (EU) 1176/2011 of the European Parliament and of the Council of 16 November 2011 on the prevention and correction of macroeconomic imbalances [2011] OJ L306/25; Council Regulation (EU) 1177/2011 of 8 November 2011 amending Regulation (EC) No 1467/97 on speeding up and clarifying the implementation of the excessive deficit procedure [2011] OJ L306/33; and Council Directive 2011/85/EU of 8 November 2011 on requirements for budgetary frameworks of the Member States [2011] OJ L306/41.

113 The two-pack is composed of Regulation (EU) 472/2013 of the European Parliament and of the Council of 21 May 2013 on the strengthening of economic and budgetary surveillance of Member States in the euro area experiencing or threatened with serious difficulties with respect to their financial stability [2013] OJ L140/1; and Regulation (EU) 473/2013 of the European Parliament and of the Council of 21 May 2013 on common provisions for monitoring and assessing draft budgetary plans and ensuring the correction of excessive deficit of the Member States in the euro area [2013] OJ L140/11.

114 See European Political Strategy Centre (2025) The Euro Plus Pact.

115 See Beukers et al. 2022, pp. 7–22; Tuori 2022, pp. 261–295.

116 Juncker et al. 2015.

EMU, suggesting proposals such as transforming the ESM into a European Monetary Fund, establishing a centralized budgetary mechanism for fiscal transfers between the EU and the Member States (the BICC)[117] and instituting a new figure (a European Minister) for taking care of economic and financial governance issues. There was also a proposal for a regulation instituting the BICC and an amendment to the ESM Treaty.

The emergence of the Covid-19 pandemic led to new developments in the EMU. On the one hand, the rules of the TSGP were suspended to allow the Member States more margin of action to support their economies and social systems.[118] On the other hand, the EU established a system of fiscal transfers through a series of instruments, such as the European instrument for temporary Support to mitigate Unemployment Risks in an Emergency ("SURE"), and the programs within NextGenerationEU, namely the Recovery Facility Fund ("RFF"). The RFF consists of a facility of 723.8 billion euros inserted into the EU budget to support reforms and investments of EU countries, half in the form of grants and the other half in the form of loans.[119] To receive the payments, Member States must submit a recovery plan to the Commission and the Council for the latter to approve and set out the binding targets and deadlines to be met. The Commission shall then monitor compliance and disbursement of the funds.

Finally, the last development of economic governance was the reactivation of fiscal rules, and their reform to facilitate growth and investment. In the words of the Council:

> The reform's overall objective is to reduce debt ratios and deficits in a gradual, realistic, sustained and growth-friendly manner, while protecting reforms and investments in strategic areas such as digital, green or defense. At the same time, the new framework will provide appropriate room for counter-cyclical policies and help address existing macroeconomic imbalances.[120]

From an operational perspective, the reform consisted in the enactment of three legal acts: Regulation (EU) 2024/1263 of 29 April 2024 of the European Parliament and the Council on the effective coordination of economic policies and on multilateral budgetary surveillance and repealing Council Regulation (EC) No 1466/97, Council Regulation (EU) 2024/1264 of 24 April 2024 amending Regulation (EC) No 1467/97 on speeding up and clarifying the implementation of the excessive deficit procedure

---

[117] On the BICC and other proposed reforms, see Dermine 2019, pp. 7–9.

[118] Council of the EU (2020) Statement of EU ministers of finance on the Stability and Growth Pact in light of the COVID-19 crisis, available at https://www.consilium.europa.eu/en/press/press-releases/2020/03/23/statement-of-eu-ministers-of-finance-on-the-stability-and-growth-pact-in-light-of-the-covid-19-crisis/ accessed 15 August 2025.

[119] For an analysis of the measures, see Schram et al. 2022, pp. 1–11. The constitutionality of these measures regarding the treaties is open to question. See de Witte 2021; Leino-Sandberg and Ruffert 2022, pp. 433–472.

[120] Council of the EU (2024) Council adopts reform of fiscal rules, available at https://www.consilium.europa.eu/en/press/press-releases/2024/04/29/economic-governance-review-council-adopts-reform-of-fiscal-rules/.

and Council Directive(EU) 2024/1265 of 24 April 2024 amending Directive 2011/85/EU on requirements for budgetary frameworks of the Member States.

In general, these measures aim to incorporate elements of the TSCG in the legal framework of the EU by establishing a new preventive arm of the SGP while updating its corrective arm. Member States are now required to prepare medium-term fiscal structural plans spanning 4-5 years. Countries with high debt or deficits will receive a reference expenditure trajectory from the Commission, which must respect safeguards on debt sustainability and deficit resilience. The framework also updates the excessive deficit procedure, incorporating an allegedly more nuanced approach to debt and deficit assessments. Furthermore, Member States committing to key structural reforms and investments may extend their adjustment period to seven years, with a focus on green, digital, energy, and defence priorities. To add more flexibility, Member States now have two escape clauses from complying with targets, whenever an unprecedented situation affects them individually or the whole of the eurozone. The opinion on the rules has, thus far, not been very positive.[121]

2.7 The EMU in Historical Perspective: Short Comment

EU economic governance has been ever-present in EU Treaties. However, it was never a top political priority, serving instead as necessary support for the creation of the common market (until 1968) and, once that goal was reached, for the prosecution of monetary integration (from 1970 onwards). Member States remained protective of their respective economic and fiscal disciplines, limiting the EEC's role to an inter-governmental and technical forum for collaboration and reflection, but without their own substantive regulatory powers. The fact that the supervision of economic developments was in the hands of *ad hoc* committees composed of national officers, of the executive body of EU officers that is the Commission, and that the Council took the decisions on economic governance were Member States' *de facto* rulers sat, is sufficient proof of such national intentions.

The event of the single currency with Maastricht, based upon the success of the single market and the collaboration in monetary policy matters, led to change in the framework. The definition of economic policy became more centralized with the enactment of EU guidelines for national economic policy definition and the enactment at Treaty and legislative level of EU standard rules of national budgetary discipline. The Commission grew in competences, particularly regarding surveillance and corrective procedures, and the intergovernmental committees were incorporated into the EMU framework. There was a clear commitment to avoid financial bailouts and to limit inter-State solidarity in the realm of monetary integration.

However, the structure proved weak, because the decisive power remained firmly with the Council (consequently, with the Member States). The Council had the last word on how to act in economic policy, both in its preventive and corrective arms.

[121] Pench 2025.

The unfortunate event of Germany and France not complying with the EDP rules and with the SGP showed how the formal development brought by Maastricht did not materialize in a decisive change of political dynamics. Member States would ultimately continue to pursue their economic and fiscal policies based on national preferences despite the EU integration rules and objectives they must abide by. Such a fact was problematic, given the importance of convergence and collaboration in fiscal and economic matters for the success of the monetary union. While EU Treaties recognized the importance of economic collaboration as an essential feature of monetary integration, such importance (or at least the terms in which such importance was characterized in the Treaties) was not subsequently acknowledged by the Member States in equal form. It can be argued that, given the asymmetric level of economic convergence among them, they could never have done so realistically speaking and that the technical and political expectations set in Maastricht were, at best, too naïve to be successful.[122]

The last batch of reforms enacted during the financial crisis aimed to correct the shortcomings of the EU framework of economic governance. The path chosen was, once again, to centralize more competences at a supranational level regarding the definition, supervision, and correction of economic policies. Unfortunately, the correction overfocused on revamping the rule-based system and less (at least in the first stage) on improving the EU's capacity to deal with asymmetric shocks. Moreover, the system's governance continues to remain largely intergovernmental and executive based. There is a sense that form and substance (that *law and power*) are somewhat disconnected or at odds within the framework of economic governance, which opens the question: did such a reform dramatically change the political dynamic of economic governance in the EU, or are we still within a legal system of economic governance that is incapable of producing order?

References

Adamski D (2018) Redefining European Economic Integration. Cambridge University Press

Amtenbrink F, de Haan J (2006) Reforming the stability and growth pact. European Law Review 31:402–413

Amtenbrink F, Markakis M (2023) Never Waste a Good Crisis: On the Emergence of an EU Fiscal Capacity. In: Hinarejos A, Schütze R (eds) EU Fiscal Federalism: Past, Present and Future. Oxford University Press, pp. 171–205

Barattieri V, Thomas A (1975) Monetary and Economic Co-Operation in the EEC. International Affairs 51:499–517

Beukers T (2015) Legal Writing(s) on the Eurozone Crisis. EUI Working Paper 2015/11. Available at: https://cadmus.eui.eu/bitstream/handle/1814/35418/LAW_2015_11.pdf?sequence=1&isAllowed=y accessed 15 August 2025

Beukers T et al (2022) Introduction: the New European Central Bank. In: Beukers T et al (eds) The New European Central Bank: Taking Stock and Looking Ahead. Oxford University Press, pp. 1–26

[122] A view shared by Adamski 2018, pp. 22–33.

Borger V (2020) The Currency of Solidarity: Constitutional Transformation During the Eurocrisis. Cambridge University Press
Brunnermeier MK et al (2016) The Euro and the Battle of Ideas. Princeton University Press
Buiter W et al (1993) Excessive Deficits: Sense and Nonsense in the Treaty of Maastricht. Center Discussion Paper, No. 674, Yale University. Available at https://www.econstor.eu/bitstream/10419/160596/1/cdp674.pdf accessed 15 August 2025
Chiti E, Teixeira PG (2013) The constitutional implications of the European responses to the financial and public debt crisis. Common Market Law Review 50:683–708
Craig P, de Búrca G (2015) EU Law – Text, Cases and Materials. Oxford University Press
Curtin D (2020) From a Europe of bits and pieces to a union of variegated differentiation. EUI Working Paper RSCAS 2020/37. Available at: https://cadmus.eui.eu/bitstream/handle/1814/67047/RSCAS%202020_37.pdf?sequence=1&isAllowed=y accessed 15 August 2025
de Grauwe P (2018) Economics of Monetary Union. Oxford University Press
de Witte B (2021) The European Union's COVID-19 recovery plan: The legal engineering of an economic policy shift. Common Market Law Review 58:635–682
Dermine P (2019) The Commission's December Package 18 months later. CERiM Online Paper 2/2019. Available at: https://papers.ssrn.com/sol3/papers.cfm?abstract_id=3500755 accessed 15 August 2025
Dermine P (2022) The New Economic Governance of the Eurozone: A Rule of Law Analysis. Cambridge University Press
Dyson K, Featherstone K (1999) The Road to Maastricht: Negotiating Economic and Monetary Union. Oxford University Press
Eichengreen B (2023) Conceptual Foundations of Economic and Monetary Union: The Economic Dimension. In: Adamski D et al (eds) The Cambridge Handbook of European Monetary, Economic and Financial Integration. Cambridge University Press, pp. 19–32
Estella A (2018) Legal Foundations of EU Economic Governance. Cambridge University Press
Estella A (2023) EU Fiscal Coordination: Past and Present. In: Hinarejos A, Schütze R (eds) EU Fiscal Federalism: Past, Present and Future. Oxford University Press, pp. 139–170
Everling U (1964) Les aspects juridiques de la coordination de la politique économique au sein de la Communauté Economique Européenne. Annuaire Français de Droit International 10: 576–604
Frankel JA et al (1990) The Rationale for, and Effects of, International Economic Policy Coordination. In: Branson WH et al (eds) International Policy Coordination and Exchange Rate Fluctuations. The University of Chicago Press, pp. 9–62
Fratzscher M (2018) The Germany Illusion: Between Economic Euphoria and Despair. Oxford University Press
Gros D (1996) Towards a credible excessive deficit procedure. In: Torres F (ed) Monetary Reform in Europe: An Analysis of the Issues and Proposals for the Intergovernmental Conference. Universidade Católica Portuguesa Editora
Habermas J (2015) The Lure of Technocracy. Polity Press
Hadjiemmanuil C (2020) The Euro Area in Crisis: 2008–2018. In: Amtenbrink F, Herrmann C (eds) The EU Law of Economic and Monetary Union. Oxford University Press, pp. 1252–1362
Ippolito DS (2003) Why Budgets Matter: Budget Policy and American Politics. Pennsylvania University Press
James H (2012) Making the European Monetary Union. Harvard University Press
James H (2023) Monetary Union and the Single Currency. In: Adamski D et al (eds) The Cambridge Handbook of European Monetary, Economic and Financial Integration. Cambridge University Press, pp. 51–68.
Jones E (2020) The Politics of Economic and Monetary Union. In: Amtenbrink F, Herrmann C (eds) The EU Law of Economic and Monetary Union. Oxford University Press, pp. 53–96
Juncker JC et al (2015) Completing Europe's Economic and Monetary Union, available at https://commission.europa.eu/publications/five-presidents-report-completing-europes-economic-and-monetary-union_en accessed 15 August 2025

Laurens B, de la Piedra EG (1998) Coordination of Monetary and Fiscal Policies. IMF Working Paper 98/25
Leino-Sandberg P, Ruffert M (2022) Next Generation EU and its constitutional ramifications: A critical assessment. Common Market Law Review 59:433–472
Majone G (2014) Rethinking the Union of Europe Post-Crisis: Has Integration Gone Too Far? Cambridge University Press
Markakis M (2020) Accountability in the Economic and Monetary Union: Foundations, Policy and Governance. Oxford University Press
Martinico G (2014) EU Crisis and Constitutional Mutations: A Review Article. Revista de Estudios Políticos 165:247–280
Martucci F (2022) Les racines historiques et théoriques de l'Union économique et monétaire. Legal History Library 61:427–457
Mourlon-Druol E (2012) A Europe Made of Money: the Emergence of the European Monetary System. Cornell University Press
Mourlon-Druol E (2020) History of an Incomplete EMU. In: Amtenbrink F, Herrmann C (eds) The EU Law of Economic and Monetary Union. Oxford University Press, pp. 12–36
Pench L (2025) European Union fiscal rules: it's already time to reform the reform, Bruegel, https://www.bruegel.org/analysis/european-union-fiscal-rules-its-already-time-reform-reform accessed 15 August 2025
Pintat JF (1977) Report drawn up on the behalf of the Committee on Energy and Research. European Parliament 309/77
Priewe J (2020) Why 60 And 3 Percent? European Debt and Deficit Rules – Critique and Alternatives. IMK Study 66:1. Available at: https://www.boeckler.de/pdf/p_imk_study_66_2020.pdf accessed 15 August 2025
Romer D (2018) Advanced Macroeconomics. McGraw Hill
Schram L et al (2022) Building 'Next Generation' after the pandemic: The implementation and implications of the EU Covid Recovery Plan. Journal of Common Market Studies 60:114–124
Schütze R (2016) EU Constitutional Law. Cambridge University Press
Simón GA (2024) Opening the Black Box of 'Convergence' in the European Monetary Union: A Discursive Analysis. Journal of Common Market Studies 63:1119–1137
Somek A, Rendl J (2023) Messianism, Exodus, and the Empty Signifier of European Integration. In: Komárek J (eds) European Constitutional Imaginaries: Between Ideology and Utopia. Oxford University Press: 147–159.
Tooze A (2018) Crashed: How a Decade of Financial Crises Changed the World. Viking
Tuori K (2022) The European Central Bank and the European Macroeconomic Constitution: From Ensuring Stability to Fighting Crisis. Cambridge University Press
Tuori K, Tuori K (2014) The Eurozone Crisis: a Constitutional Analysis. Cambridge University Press
Williamson SD (2018) Macroeconomics. Pearson
Weiler J (2011) 60 Years since the First European Community – Reflections on Political Messianism. EJIL Talk! available at https://www.ejiltalk.org/60-years-since-the-first-european-community-%E2%80%93-reflections-on-political-messianism/ accessed 15 August 2025.

Chapter 3
Rules and Powers of EU Economic Governance

Contents

Abstract This chapter analyses the EU's economic governance framework as a constitutional arrangement, focusing on the scope, structure, and limits of the Union's competence in shaping national economic policy. It outlines the distinction between competence and power, and organizes EU action into three categories: definition, supervision, and assistance. By examining key legal bases such as Articles 121 and 136 TFEU, the chapter evaluates the EU's ability to impose economic constraints on Member States while remaining within its coordination mandate. Special attention is given to corrective mechanisms and financial assistance procedures, notably the EDP and the ESM.

Keywords Economic policy competence · Article 121 TFEU · Article 135 · Excessive deficit procedure · European Stability Mechanism

3.1 Economic Governance as a Constitutional Issue

The purpose of the EU's constitutional competence of economic governance is to arrange and manage the organization and definition of national economic policy in line with the objectives of the EU.[1] More specifically, economic governance

[1] Article 119 TFEU.

M. Lucas Pires, *The Federal Legality of EU Economic Governance*,
https://doi.org/10.1007/978-94-6265-747-2_3

is a necessary tool for achieving the objective of financial stability of the Eurozone.[2] Therefore, it is expected that the constitutional framework of EU economic governance regulates procedures for monitoring, assessing, and reacting to economic developments in the Member States.

It is possible to divide the EU competence of economic governance into three different sets of powers. The first power is the power of *defining* economic policies by setting common economic targets and objectives for the Member States to comply with. The second power is the power of *supervising* economic developments. This power concerns the EU's capacity to assess the economic situation of its Member States and to monitor its evolution, while checking States' compliance with EU economic policy rules, procedures and objectives. This power can be further divided into two sub-sets of powers: powers of *preventive supervision*, which are powers to monitor the progress of Member States and provide orientations on EU economic targets and objectives, and powers of *corrective supervision*, which are powers to propose and apply remedies, and to sanction deviations with EU economic policy rules and objectives. Finally, the third power of economic governance is the power of *providing economic assistance*. It concerns the capacity to provide financial support to the Member States that are under severe economic distress.

The constitutional issue with economic governance concerns the limits of EU legitimate intervention in national economic policy definition. Assessing such limits is a complex issue for many reasons.

The first reason is that the *locus* of political authority remains with the Member States, meaning that it is up to them not only to decide on economic policy choices but also to implement them within their respective jurisdictions.[3] A second reason is that, because of the first reason, the EU has limited scope for intervention since it cannot direct nor command the definition of national economic policies. The EU only has what can be described as a procedural competence, where powers are limited to establishing institutional and normative platforms with incentives for the Member States to organize among themselves coordinated measures of economic policy. At the same time, the EU can, within the scope of coordination, intervene to a certain extent in national government's autonomy, particularly in situations of financial instability or situations where a Member State is not complying with the rules (and, therefore, risks provoking financial instability). Finally, a more formal reason for the complexity of the EU constitutional framework of economic governance is that its procedures are established in different legal sources: the TFEU, EU secondary legislation, and international treaties (the TSGP and the ESM Treaty). The institutions competent to act are part of the EU framework, but some institutions belong (at least formally) to an international law framework (the ESM). Furthermore, not all EU institutions act (relevantly) in economic governance, with the European Council limited to the preparation and approval of the conclusions of BEPGs and the European Parliament enjoying a reduced, *ex-post*, supervisory role. The powers of judicial review of the CJEU are also limited.

[2] On the definition of financial stability, see Lo Schiavo 2017, pp. 11–32.

[3] Amtenbrink 2023, p. 72.

The current constitutional framework of economic governance remains identical, in its form, to the one set up during the financial crisis of 2009–2013. The inherent (and, it must be noted, purposefully built) tension between the *formal structure* and the *practical operation* of the framework animates its dynamic. As Uwe Puetter writes, "This framework reflects both economic conviction and political reality. Decision-makers widely believe in the sustainability and advantages of national discretion within the boundaries of a limited set of rules."[4] It is also this complexity that makes the constitutional framework of economic governance so problematic from a normative perspective. Any analysis of this framework must consider both its structure, set out in the rules of economic coordination, and the practical operation of applying and adjudicating such rules, respectively, by the EU executive and judicial bodies.

Given the complexity of this legal and institutional mosaic, the subsequent analysis is organized in the following manner. In the first part, this chapter discusses the meaning and scope of the EU's constitutional competence of economic governance, identifying the basic guiding parameters of EU action in this regulatory field. In the second part, this chapter analyses the framework of economic governance according to the different types of power (powers of definition, supervision, and assistance). In this second part, the chapter discusses each power of economic governance and its respective scope and legal basis, as well as its institutional setting and procedures. The chapter concludes with a general comment on the constitutional character of the EU framework of economic governance.

3.2 The Scope of the EU's Competence of Economic Governance

According to the principle of conferral, the EU can only act within the scope of competences the Member States conferred on it in Treaties.[5] According to the latter, economic policy coordination means that "The Member States shall coordinate their economic policies within the Union. To this end, the Council shall adopt measures, in particular broad guidelines for these policies."[6] The article further stresses that "[s]pecific provisions shall apply to those Member States whose currency is the euro." A first, immediate thought is that EU action in this policy field in limited when compared to other policy areas where the EU has exclusive or shared competence (such as monetary policy, for example) but seems broader than in areas where it only has what the Treaty calls "complementary and coordination" competences.

When acting within a coordinating competence, EU institutions can only produce legislative acts to set up procedural structures for the Member States to interact

[4] Puetter 2006, p. 166.

[5] Article 4(1) TEU. Craig 2004, p. 324; Schütze 2015, pp. 76–77.

[6] Article 5(1) TFEU.

with one another.[7] According to Robert Schutze, the EU's powers are limited to the provision of "'arrangements' for the Member States to exercise their competence in a coordinating manner".[8] This means that the main political actors in the field of economic coordination are the Member States: it is they who hold ultimate decision-making power.[9] Consequently, the EU cannot replace the Member States when acting in those policy areas.[10]

Although such an understanding is non-controversial in EU law,[11] the question of what coordination competences allow for has proved confusing in EU constitutionalism.[12] This is more so in the case of economic governance, which "stands out as a particularly fragmented and indeterminate field of competence",[13] where the EU can address legally binding acts to the Member States. It is therefore necessary to understand what the scope of the EU's competence of economic governance is.

An historic analysis of the problem of competence delimitation in the EU reveals a functional underpinning in its definition: competences were "established according to objectives to be achieved and means for achieving those objectives".[14] The functional basis of coordination powers refers to the "the process of organizing people or groups so that they work together properly and well" and to the "harmonious functioning of parts for effective results".[15] Therefore, literally speaking, coordination is a form of organization among different units to achieve something in common. In other words, *coordination is a collective effort whereby individual units must structure their respective actions in a certain way so that all actions combined help them converge to a single end*. In this sense, individual actions do not need to be *identical*; instead, they should be *identically* ordered and directed at attaining a common goal. Coordination, thus, is like a sports team effort such as football, where all players must organize themselves (following the orders of a coach) as a team and structure their efforts when playing to help the team win.

Policy coordination can be looser, leaving individual actors more autonomy, or stricter, with more centralized action from the part of the coordinating institution. Robert Putnam and Randall Henning, in their seminal contribution to the study of international economic coordination, proposed five modes of policy coordination, ranging from the loosest to the strictest. Their modes are: unilateral adjustment (actors consider their counterparts' actions and react accordingly), consultation

[7] CJEU, Federal Republic of Germany and others v. Commission, 1987, Joined cases 281, 283, 284, 285 and 287/85.

[8] Schütze 2016, p. 242.

[9] Puetter 2006, p. 38.

[10] Bieber 2014, p. 89.

[11] CJEU, Thomas Pringle v. Government of Ireland and Others, 2012, Case C-370/12, para 64, and General Court of the European Union, Alexios Anagnostakis v. Commission, 2015, Case T-450/12, para 58.

[12] Craig 2004, pp. 338–340; Schütze 2015, p. 87.

[13] Dermine 2022, p. 147.

[14] Konstadinides 2009, p. 9.

[15] Merriam-Webster Dictionary, available at https://www.merriam-webster.com/dictionary/coordination accessed 15 August 2023.

(actors engage with each other to negotiate the adoption of a policy pact), reinforcement (actors try to impose their national policy choices to others via supranational means), package deals (actors negotiate and agree on binding policy agreements for all to implement) and supranational integration (policies are set at the supranational level by supranational institutions).[16] Unilateral adjustment, consultation, and reinforcement do not need formal agreements, while package deals and supranational integration do, making these modes of policy coordination typical of frameworks where informal policy deliberation play a more prominent role.[17] Normative harmonization, on the other hand, is a formal mode of policy coordination, where the setting of common regulatory standards is the instrument for structuring and ordering the conduct of social actors.[18]

In the policy areas that are part of exclusive and shared competences, the EU can legislate and produce normative harmonization (although the level of harmonization can vary from policy area to policy area[19]). In the policy areas that are part of complementary competences, the EU is explicitly prohibited from producing measures destined to harmonize national laws.[20] Regarding coordinating competences, there is no similar prohibition stated in the Treaty. Therefore, it is constitutionally admissible for the EU to harmonize laws in the field of economic coordination *to some degree*.[21] The historical argument also supports this view since the drafters of the Treaty of Lisbon decided to differentiate the coordinating competences of article 5 TFEU from the coordinating and complementary competences of article 6 TFEU.[22]

The EU constitutional framework of economic governance is, therefore, composed of informal and formal modes of policy cooperation. An example of the former is that the EU's powers to establish a structure for Member States to consult with one another, enabling (as we shall see below) reinforcement modes of coordination. An example of the latter is the existence of package deals—the SGP, the TSGC—and the existence of a minimum degree of supranational integration through normative action, such as the SGP or the golden rule on excessive deficits, and, more significantly, articles 121(6) and 136(1) TFEU.

According to article 121(6), the Parliament and the Council can enact regulations detailing rules for the MSP. Therefore, they are competent only to enact binding rules on *procedural cooperation* but not on *policy integration*; they can enact by law frameworks for coordination but cannot enact binding rules with economic policy choices for the Member States to follow. Notwithstanding this interpretation, the article has served as the legal basis for enacting regulations and other legally binding acts concerning several other procedures that do not have to do with the MSP itself,

[16] Putnam and Henning 1989, pp. 14–16.

[17] Puetter 2006, p. 29.

[18] The degree of harmonization can vary—see Snell 2017, pp. 335–337.

[19] Craig 2004, p. 333.

[20] See Article 2(5) TFEU and Schütze 2016, pp. 242–243.

[21] Ibid., pp. 241–242; Craig 2004, p. 340.

[22] Ibid., p. 338; Schütze 2015, p. 87.

such as the EDP, and rules concerning normative standards for national budgetary frameworks.[23]

As for article 136(1) TFEU, it allows the Council (without the Parliament) to adopt measures specific to those Member States whose currency is the euro "to strengthen the coordination and surveillance of their budgetary discipline". The article has served as the legal basis for the enactment of measures concerning supervision of economic policy developments. More specifically, it was used as legal basis for Council decisions concerning individual measures on fiscal policy targets and policies applicable to the Member States under assistance programs,[24] during the financial crisis. Although some scholars consider the norm a form of enhanced cooperation that facilitates "within the euro area the use of existing Union competences" and, therefore, an additional provision to articles 121(6) and 126 TFEU,[25] EU institutions have used it differently, as the basis for adopting measures that, according to some, "could not have been adopted otherwise", such as the EIP[26] (this argument, however, is not accurate: the legal basis for the EIP was article 136(1) and article 121(6) TFEU for Regulation 1174/2011, and article 121(6) TFEU solely for Regulation 1176/2011). Therefore, articles 121(6) and 136(1) TFEU seem to open the door for legislative intervention in the definition of national economic policy. This has led to the suggestion that the scope of article 136(1) TFEU is "actually much wider" than what the majority of the literature considers it to be.[27]

How should one interpret articles 121(6) and 136(1) TFEU? According to the principle of proportionality established in article 5(4) TEU, the scope of EU normative action must be adequate to the function and purpose of the specific policy area.[28] The aim of EU economic governance is to enhance cooperation and convergence among Member States in the field of economic and fiscal policies to guarantee the stability of the eurozone. According to the article 119 TFEU, EU economic governance must support the achievement of the objectives of Article 3 TEU, as well as respecting the principles of an open market economy with free competition, stable prices, sound public finances, monetary conditions and a sustainable balance of payments. While pursuing such goals, EU institutions should respect the autonomy of Member States to define their own fiscal policies: EU economic governance measures should not (*de jure* and *de facto*) pre-empt Member States' powers in enacting their respective fiscal policies. Member States should enjoy a high degree discretion in fiscal policy definition according to the Treaties. Such a degree of discretion would be abused if EU institutions could, based on articles 121(6) and 136(1) TFEU, decide on the

---

[23] Keppenne 2020, p. 847.

[24] Council Decision 2010/320/EU of 5 June 2010 addressed to Greece with a view to reinforcing and deepening fiscal surveillance and giving notice to Greece to take measures for the deficit reduction judged necessary to remedy the situation of excessive deficit [2010] OJ L145/6.

[25] Keppenne 2020, pp. 845–846; Flynn 2019, pp. 1320–1321; Ohler 2022a, pp. 507–509.

[26] Keppenne 2020, p. 846.

[27] Dermine 2022, p. 157.

[28] Schütze 2015, pp. 96–101.

content of national budgets or command Member States to follow EU-defined fiscal policies.

Therefore, articles 121(6) and 136(1) TFEU should be read considering "the specificities of economic policy and their organization on the lines of policy coordination".[29] Fiscal policy definition is the ultimate competence of the Member States, which shall define it according to their respective preferences while respecting the obligations of EU law established in the Treaties, such as the rules prohibiting the running of excessive deficits.[30]

In this sense, the enactment of measures on the establishment of supranational legal frameworks for cooperation among Member States on matters of economic policy is in line with the teleological objective of articles 121(6) and 136(1) TFEU. Measures to support or complement such legal frameworks to make cooperation more effective (for example, establishing regular reporting duties on economic policy indicators for Member States, or uniformizing statistics and data frameworks) are also within the EU's scope of competence in the field of economic governance. It is also constitutionally compatible with the teleological scope of the competence of economic governance the setting of supervisory procedures to monitor certain elements of the economy based on pre-determined sets of economic indicators (such as macroeconomic imbalances, however one defines them).[31]

However, it is constitutionally problematic to include, within the competence of economic governance, the enactment of corrective supervisory procedures that enable the application of sanctions for failure to comply with legal, non-Treaty criteria of economic performance. That is the case, for example, of the NCP and the EIP.[32] The only corrective procedure in the Treaties is the EDP, which refers to a special constitutional commitment regarding financial stability of the monetary union. To establish another corrective procedure is to excessively limit the autonomy of Member States regarding fiscal policy and therefore seems incompatible with the coordinating nature of the EU's economic governance competence.

Regarding powers of financial assistance, the Treaty revision enacted in 2012 made it possible for Member States to establish a stability mechanism, the ESM.[33] It is questionable whether the EU needed to revise the Treaties to enact the ESM, particularly after the decision of the CJEU in *Pringle*.[34] However, the approval and amendment of conditions of financial assistance through article 136(1) TFEU does not seem compatible with the scope and telos of the norm. The measures go beyond

---

29 Dermine 2022, p. 158.

30 Puetter 2006, p. 41.

31 On the question of economic policy supervision and the definition of economic indicators see Bénassy-Quéré and Wolff 2020, pp. 10–11.

32 Both procedures are discussed in the present chapter.

33 European Council Decision 2011/199/EU of 25 March 2011 amending Article 136 of the Treaty on the Functioning of the European Union with regard to a stability mechanism for Member States whose currency is the euro [2011] OJ L91/1.

34 Timmermans 2014, p. 165.

the purpose of strengthening coordination and supervision of national fiscal discipline; instead, they establish an imperative condition for the adoption of a specific policy measure (for example, "a reduction of the Easter, summer and Christmas bonuses and allowances paid to civil servants"[35]). Such measures are out of the scope of Article 136(1) TFEU: they ought to be enacted in the scope of the EFSM framework[36] or in the scope of the ESM framework.[37]

In sum, the scope of EU competences in economic governance should be restricted to policy coordination, meaning that: consultation, policy package agreements, and a minimum degree of supranational integration. This degree should allow for the enactment of rules and procedural structures to complement the powers already established in the Treaties and international agreements (such as definition of BEPGs, supervision of economic developments, application of corrective measures regarding excessive deficits, and provision of financial assistance) but should not be used to impose specific economic policy measures on the Member States. It is this level of intervention that makes this type of coordination competences—in contrast with the *other type of* coordinating competences set in article 6 TFEU—a *sui generis* type of competence.[38]

3.3 EU Powers of Economic Governance

One thing is competence: the purpose and delimitation of EU's action in a specific policy field. Another thing is power: the specific set of actions the EU can take within that competence—the EU powers regarding economic policy definition by the Member States. We shall consider three sets of powers: powers of economic policy definition, economic policy supervision, and economic assistance.

3.3.1 Economic Policy Definition

When discussing the power to define economic policies, we can refer to two different forms of power. In the first sense, the power of definition can mean the power to authoritatively decide on a specific course of fiscal policy choices. It is, in this sense, a power to *command*, to order the enactment and adoption of a specific set of fiscal policies. In the second sense, the power of definition is the power to propose policy

---

[35] Article 2(1)(f) of Council Decision 2010/320/EU.

[36] For example, through Article 3(7) or Article 4(3) of Council Regulation (EU) 407/2010 of 11 May 2010 establishing a European financial stabilization mechanism [2010] OJ L118/1.

[37] The legal basis for Council Decision 2010/320/EU was articles 136(1) and article 126(9). The use of the latter is difficult to explain since it concerns measures to react to non-compliance by Member States with Council recommendations within the EDP. Why is a norm regarding corrective supervision being used as legal basis for a measure detailing conditions for financial assistance?

[38] Bieber 2014, p. 90.

orientations without binding character. In this sense, it is the power of *guidance* to provide directions to policymakers based on common objectives to be achieved.

The definition in this section refers to the latter. That is the only meaning that the power of definition of economic policy has in the constitutional setting of EMU, considering what has been discussed so far regarding the scope of EU competence of economic governance. Given the constitutional primacy of the Member States in fiscal policy definition, the function of definition powers is to guide Member States' actions so that they ultimately achieve the EU's economic policy objectives and targets. It is a form of package deal coordination in the framework proposed by Putnam and Hedding: an act produced by consultation and deliberative procedures at the inter-governmental and executive levels.

The legal basis for the EU power of definition of economic policy is set in articles 5(1), 121(2), and 136(1)(b) TFEU. The EU can issue broad economic policy guidelines (BEPGs). Such guidelines have the legal format of a recommendation: they are non-binding acts according to article 288 TFEU. The guidelines should serve as an element for the Member States to consider and follow when drafting their respective fiscal and structural policies.[39] The BEPGs include, among other things, proposals on investment, job creation, and sustainability of public finances.[40] Recommendations are general in scope and aspirational in purpose: they set broad policy targets without specifying the policy measures and actions to be enacted. Consider, for example, the following guideline:

> Information and communication technologies and the digital economy are important drivers of productivity, innovation and growth in all sectors of the economy. Promoting private investment in research and innovation should be accompanied by in-depth reforms to modernize the research and innovation systems, to enhance cooperation between public institutions and the private sector, and to improve the broader framework conditions for companies to become more knowledge-intensive. Raising the quality and efficiency of public investments in research and innovation will continue improving the quality of public finances and could improve the long-term sustainability of public finances.[41]

The Council issues the BEPGS on a recommendation from the Commission, following the European Council's conclusions. The European Parliament is informed of the recommendation. Whenever the Member States execute policies that are incompatible (to borrow the word of the Treaty) with the guidelines, or that can endanger the functioning of the EMU, the Council (acting on a recommendation by the Commission) can recommend to the Member States to take a corrective course of action.[42]

---

[39] Article 121(3) TFEU. According to article 3(2) (ab) of Council Regulation (EC) 1466/97 (amended by Regulation 1175/2011 of the Parliament and the Council), a stability program shall present "information on the consistency of the stability program with the broad economic policy guidelines and the national reform program".

[40] See, for example, Council Recommendation (EU) 2015/1184 of 14 July 2015 on broad guidelines for the economic policies of the Member States and of the European Union [2015] OJ L192/27.

[41] Ibid., 4–5.

[42] Article 121(4) TFEU.

Finally, powers of definition include enacting economic policy guidelines specifically for eurozone Member States.[43] Such guidelines have the same form (non-binding acts), logic (orientations but not commands), and procedure (Council recommendation acting on a Commission proposal and including the conclusion of the European Council, according to the cross-reference in article 136(1) to the "relevant procedure from among those referred to in Articles 121 and 126") as BEPGs.

In this sense, EU powers of economic policy definition are powers of orientation of national economic policies, whereby Member States consult with one another and the Commission to agree on the guidelines. Final agreement on the BEPGs is reached at the European Council, thus guaranteeing that the BEPGs are approved at the highest political level by the heads of national governments.

3.3.2 Economic Policy Supervision

Supervision of economic policy developments refers to the systematic surveillance by the Commission and the Council of the economic situation of Member States. The purpose is to follow their progress and assess if there is, on the one hand, convergence with the targets set in the BEPGs, and on the other, compliance with EU fiscal discipline rules. Such supervision is exercised from November until October of the following year,[44] in the European Semester (hereinafter referred to as "the Semester").[45]

The Semester is an upgrade to the SGP, providing a structured time frame for the Member States to exchange information with the Council and the Commission concerning their respective economic performances, budgetary policies, and medium-long term economic projections, as well as allowing EU institutions to provide assessments and recommendations.[46] All information is made public on the Commission's website, making it available for all Member States and EU citizens, enabling (and inviting) horizontal surveillance and peer pressure (inter-State and intra-State).

There are five supervisory procedures at work simultaneously during the Semester. Two of these procedures are *preventive*, for they consist in the monitoring and assessment of economic developments to prevent the emergence of problematic situations. The other three procedures can be considered *corrective* because they aim to remedy deviations from targets and rules identified in the procedures of preventive supervision. In corrective procedures, the application of sanctions can take place.

---

[43] Article 136(1)(b) TFEU.

[44] A timeline and documentation of the European Semester is available in the website of the European Commission at https://ec.europa.eu/info/business-economy-euro/economic-and-fiscal-policy-coordination/eu-economic-governance-monitoring-prevention-correction/european-semester/european-semester-timeline_en accessed 15 August 2025.

[45] Article 3 of Regulation 2024/1263 of the European Parliament and of the Council.

[46] See Recitals (4) to (9) of Regulation 1175/2011 of the Parliament and the Council.

The procedures of preventive supervision are the MSP, the Annual Budgetary Framework ("ABF"), and the Enhanced Surveillance Procedure ("ESP"), while the procedures of corrective supervision are the NCP, the EDP and the EIP. Their respective analysis shall be divided according to their preventive or corrective character. The EIP has preventive and corrective features, but this work shall consider only the corrective part.

3.3.2.1 Preventive Supervision: MSP and ABF

The MSP is a procedure of economic policy supervision based on Article 121(3) TFEU and Regulation 2024/1263 of the European Parliament and the Council. Within the MSP, Member States must submit their national medium-term fiscal-structural plans for the Commission to assess its compliance with EU rules. According to article 16 of Regulation 2024/1263, the Commission shall evaluate whether the proposed net expenditure path ensures that the general government debt is placed on, or maintained along, a plausibly downward trajectory by the end of the adjustment period or remains at prudent levels below 60% of GDP. It shall also assess whether the government deficit is brought below, and sustained under, the 3% of GDP threshold over the medium term. For Member States that have received a reference trajectory, the Commission shall further verify compliance with the specific requirements. The Commission shall also see if the national medium-term fiscal-structural plan sets out a multiannual net expenditure path, underpinned by economic assumptions and fiscal-structural measures demonstrating compliance with the applicable fiscal requirements. The plan must also include the Commission's reference trajectory or technical data and, where it proposes a higher expenditure path, provide sound, evidence-based justification, and it should explain how planned reforms and investments respond to country-specific recommendations and advance common Union priorities, including the green and digital transitions, social and economic resilience, energy security, and, where necessary, defence capabilities. The plan must also address macroeconomic imbalances, justify any proposed extension of the adjustment period, and assess the fiscal impact of past reforms. It shall further include key budgetary assumptions, contingent liabilities, investment forecasts, and information on parliamentary consultations and consistency with cohesion and recovery instruments. This is according to article 13 of Regulation 2024/1263 of the European Parliament and of the Council.

Based on the results of the assessment, the Council can issue (on a proposal from the Commission) guidance to each country (through the Country Specific Recommendations or "CSRs") that summarizes their findings and assessments, while proposing the endorsement of the plan, or its revision.[47] Therefore, in the MSP, the powers of EU institutions are limited to enacting non-binding acts.

The second procedure of preventive supervision is the ABF, based on Regulation473/2013 of the European Parliament and of the Council. According to the ABF, eurozone Member States shall make their medium-term fiscal plans public and

[47] Articles 17 and 18 of Regulation 2024/1263 of the European Parliament and of the Council.

submit draft budgetary laws to the Commission and the Eurogroup.[48] The former shall assess the plans and provide an opinion to the Member States concerned and to the Eurogroup; the latter shall assess them considering the whole of the Eurozone's economic perspectives (the Eurogroup can decide to make the assessment public).[49] Like the MSP, the powers of EU institutions are limited to enacting non-binding acts of assessment of national policies.

The third procedure is the ESP, established in Regulation 472/2013 of the European Parliament and of the Council. The ESP applies to two situations: when the Member States are facing severe financial difficulties that can have spill-over effect to the eurozone, and when a Member State is under a financial assistance program.[50] It is up for the Commission to decide on the application of the ESP to a Member State, considering the former's financial situation; if a Member State does not require financial assistance, the Commission shall have to provide additional justification for putting the Member State under the ESP).[51] Under this procedure, the Commission can order Member States to submit reports concerning their financial status and economic developments and to monitor progress and compliance with recommendations made under other supervisory procedures.[52] The Commission can also request that Member States enact stress tests on significant financial institutions and communicate them to the ECB.[53] In the end, the Commission can propose to the Council to recommend the adoption of precautionary measures or of a Macroeconomic Adjustment Program ("MEAP")[54] by the Member States, which is the step before initiating a procedure of financial assistance. In this sense, unlike in the other two procedures of preventive supervision, EU supervisory powers in the ESP are of an executive, binding nature and allow the Commission to command the Member States to provide more detailed information regarding their financial situation.

3.3.2.2 Corrective Supervision: EDP and EIP

During a preventive supervisory procedure, if the Commission or the Council find that Member States' actions are diverging with the pre-defined targets of the Treaty, the TSCG, and BEPGs, the Commission can initiate a procedure for the Member States to correct the discrepancies and return to compliance with economic governance rules. There are three corrective procedures in place, concerning different types of economic divergences.

---

[48] Articles 4(1) and 6(1) of Regulation (EU) 473/2013 of the European Parliament and of the Council.

[49] Ibid., Article 6(3) and (4).

[50] Article 2(1) and (3) of Regulation 472/2013 of the European Parliament and of the Council.

[51] Ibid.

[52] Ibid., Article 3(1).

[53] Ibid.

[54] Ibid., Article 3(7).

The first corrective procedure and the most important one, is the EDP, concerning the identification and application of corrective measures and enhanced monitoring for Member States running an excessive deficit.[55] The basic structure of the EDP is in article 126 TFEU and in Council Regulation 1497/97 (as amended by Regulation 2024/1264 of the European Parliament and the Council. The regulation establishes the elements of data and economic developments that are to be taken into account by the Commission when assessing the existence or risk of an excessive deficit situation in a Member State and establishes the timeframes for the Commission, Council and Member States to act in the context of the EDP.[56] The reform of the framework in the six-pack introduced two amendments, consisting, on the one hand, in making fines the main sanction applicable for failure to comply with EDP recommendations (with the other sanctions established in the TFEU working as additional sanctions)[57] and, on the other hand, in giving powers to the Commission to make monitoring missions to the Member States within the procedure.[58] The 2024 reform, on the other hand, established new criteria for assessing the existence of a deficit and new monitoring obligations for the Commission and the Council.[59] The reference values for maximum deficit and government debt remain unchanged since the creation of the EDP.

The second corrective procedure is the EIP, concerning corrective measures and enhanced monitoring of the Member States whose economic situation is considered "unbalanced". The EIP is, arguably, the most important innovation (and the most controversial one too, from a legal perspective) brought by the six-pack reform.[60] Its purpose is to facilitate the identification and correction of economic developments that "are adversely affecting, or have the potential adversely to affect, the proper functioning of the economy of a Member State or the economic and monetary union, or of the Union as a whole".[61] An alert mechanism with a scoreboard with economic and financial indicators allows EU institutions to identify internal and external imbalances in the Member States.[62] The Commission shall use the result of its assessment of the scoreboard to produce an annual report on financial and economic imbalances that will then present to the European Parliament, the Council, and the European

[55] Article 126(7) to (14) TFEU and Council Regulation (EC) 1467/1997 (as amended by Regulation 2024/1264 of the European Parliament and the Council).

[56] Seikel 2016, pp. 1403–1404. See also articles 2–4 of Council Regulation (EC) 1467/1997 (as amended by Regulation 2024/1264 of the European Parliament and the Council).

[57] Article 11 of Council Regulation (EC) 1467/1997 (as amended by Regulation 2024/1264 of the European Parliament and the Council) and Article 6(1) of Regulation 1173/2011 of the European Parliament and the Council.

[58] Article 10a(1) of Council Regulation (EC) 1467/1997 (Regulation 2024/1264 of the European Parliament and the Council).

[59] See recitals 8–20 of Regulation 2024/1264 of the European Parliament and the Council.

[60] See Hodson 2018, pp. 1610–1611; Scharpf 2011, pp. 188–189.

[61] Article 2(1) of Regulation 1176/2011 of the European Parliament and the Council.

[62] Ibid., Articles 3 and 4.

Economic and Social Committee.[63] The Council shall discuss and analyse the report within the MSP.

If under this analysis, or due to urgent events and after an in-depth review of the Commission, EU institutions consider that a Member State is experiencing excessive economic imbalances, a corrective procedure is put in place, similar to the EDP. Under this procedure, EU institutions can impose on the affected Member State the obligation to adopt a corrective plan based on the Council's recommendations.[64] The Commission shall then monitor and assess the implementation of the corrective plan. If the Commission considers that the Member State did not take corrective measures as recommended by the Council, it will issue a report and advise the Council to declare non-compliance.[65] This can lead to the imposition of an interest-bearing deposit with the Commission and the application of annual fines.[66]

A small note should be made here regarding the NCP. The NCP[67] concerns non-compliance by the Member State with the form and content of national medium-term fiscal-structural plan submitted in the European Semester, within the MSP. In this procedure, the Council (acting on a recommendation by the Commission) can recommend that the Member State, in certain situations, adopts the reference trajectory issued by the Commission as its net expenditure path,[68] or, in the case of failure to comply with investment and reform commitments, recommend a revised net expenditure path with a shorter adjustment period.[69] "Unsatisfactory" implementation of these commitments shall lead to special consideration of the Member State in assessments regarding the EIP.[70] Therefore, no sanctions are applied in the NCP procedure.

The NCP replaced the Significant Deviation Procedure ("SDP"); in the latter, what was at stake was the correction of a deviation from the medium-term objective set out in the stability and convergence programs (the antecedents of the medium-term fiscal-structural plan) submitted by the Member States in the European Semester. If the deviation was not corrected after a recommendation by Council was issued, then the procedure would be the following: the Commission would issue a warning that could be followed by a Council recommendation (acting on a recommendation by the Commission) establishing measures to correct the divergences. If the Member State did not correct the deviations, the Council could issue a decision establishing that no

---

63 Ibid., Article 3(4). The scoreboard data and reports can be read here: https://economy-finance.ec.europa.eu/economic-and-fiscal-governance/macroeconomic-imbalances-procedure/scoreboard_en#:~:text=Macroeconomic%20imbalance%20procedure%20scoreboard,-The%20analysis%20in&text=The%20scoreboard%20is%20designed%20to,indicators%20of%20high%20statistical%20quality accessed 15 August 2025.

64 Article 8 of Regulation 1176/2011 of the European Parliament and the Council.

65 Ibid., Article 10.

66 Article 3 of Regulation 1174/2011 of the European Parliament and the Council.

67 Articles 18 of Regulation 2024/1263 of the European Parliament and of the Council and Article 4 of Regulation 1173/2011 of the European Parliament and the Council.

68 Ibid., Article 19.

69 Ibid., Article 20.

70 Article 31(1) of Regulation 2024/1263 of the European Parliament and of the Council.

effective action had been taken, acting upon a recommendation by the Commission and voted under reverse qualified majority. After enacting a decision, the Commission could propose a sanction (consisting of the provision of a non-bearing deposit with the EU) to be applied by the Council, under Regulation 1173/2011.

With the repeal of Regulation 1466/97 by Regulation 2014/1263, and the lack of amendment to Regulation 1173/2011 establishing an explicit cross-reference to the new Regulation,[71] the connection between failure to comply with the medium-term fiscal-structural plans and the enactment of a corrective procedure is unclear. A teleologic reading of the framework made the connection possible, considering that the purpose of Regulation 2024/1264 is to replace Regulation 1467/1997 with a similar monitoring procedure of fiscal and economic developments in the Member States, with an obligation remaining for the latter to devise economic projections and trajectories that should be followed after their approval by the Council, while the purpose of 1173/2011, on the other hand, remains the same: to enable the imposition of sanctions for Member States that fail to comply with pre-established rules and targets on fiscal and economic monitoring (which includes not deviating from targets established in articles 16(2), (3) and 13 of Regulation 2024/1264). However, it is established in Regulation 2024/1276 that failure to comply with guidelines and recommendations issued under the Regulation shall result in further recommendations, a warning pursuant to article 121(4) TFEU, or measures under the EDP and the EIP.[72] In this sense, the Regulation excludes the applicable of sanctions established in Regulation 1173/2011 and thus de facto revoking the provisions of the latter that were applicable in the context of Regulation 1466/1997. Therefore, failure to comply with the NPC shall not lead to financial sanctions under a specific procedure, only in the context of the EIP or the EDP.

3.3.3 Economic Policy Assistance

There are two instruments of financial assistance available to eurozone Member States within the framework of economic governance: the EFSM and the ESM.[73] During the crisis there was a third instrument, the EFSF, a private law vehicle incorporated in Luxembourg with the eurozone Member States as shareholders.[74] The EFSF has been discontinued, with its facilities assumed by the ESM; therefore, it will not be considered.

---

71 Reference is still made, in articles 2(1) and 4(1), to Council Regulation (EC) 1466/1997.

72 Article 4(3) of Regulation 2024/1263 of the European Parliament and of the Council.

73 For non-eurozone States there is a third instrument, the Balance of Payments Assistance Facility, set in Article 144(1) TFEU and Council Regulation (EC) 332/2002 establishing a facility providing medium-term financial assistance for Member States' balances of payments [2002] OJ L53/1.

74 On the EFSF, see Ruffert 2011, pp. 1780–1781; Pereira Coutinho 2016, pp. 112–115.

The first instrument of assistance, the EFSM, was created under Article 122(2) TFEU, via Council Regulation (EU) 407/2010.[75] The EFSM consists of a credit line facility provided to Member States; to access it, Member States must agree to execute a MEAP and sign a MoU with the Commission (on behalf of the EU).[76] The conditions for receiving assistance, established in the MoU, are previously prepared by the Commission, while the Council decides on granting the assistance (acting on a proposal of the Commission).[77] The Commission shall organize disbursements of the instalments of the loan or credit line following the progress made by the Member State in executing its adjustment program.[78] The Commission and the affected Member State can agree to amendments regarding the MoU; however, the Council has to approve the amendments for them to be effective.[79]

The second instrument of financial assistance is the ESM. The TESM was an agreement signed by the Member States, whose currency is the euro, to create a contingency instrument for the Eurozone. The purpose of the ESM is "to mobilize funding and provide stability support under strict conditionality",[80] and "to be activated if indispensable to safeguard the stability of the euro area as a whole".[81] The ESM is, therefore, an international financial institution whose purpose is to provide financial assistance to its members when they face severe financing problems.

The ESM is ruled by a board of governors composed of the finance ministers of the contracting States, which means that the ESM is effectively ruled by the Eurogroup.[82] Financial assistance can be provided through loans, credit lines, or bond purchases in the primary or secondary market. All assistance is subject to the setting of policy conditions to be followed by the aided Member State in a MEAP (an act of EU law that must be accepted by the Council under the ESP Regulation)[83] and in a MoU.[84] The purpose is for the ESM to be the recourse of last resort, with the TSCG and the framework of EU economic governance being the "first line of defence against confidence crisis affecting the stability of the euro-area".[85] The ESM only has the power to provide financing: it neither negotiates the conditions for support with the financially distressed Member State nor monitors compliance with the assistance program. These tasks are entrusted to the Commission.[86]

---

[75] Council Regulation (EU) 407/2010 of 11 May 2010 establishing a European financial stabilisation mechanism [2010] OJ L118/1.

[76] Ibid., Article 3(3).

[77] Ibid., Article 3(3)(b).

[78] Ibid., Article 4.

[79] Ibid., Article 3(6) and (7).

[80] Article 3 TESM.

[81] Consideration number (2) of the TESM.

[82] Article 5(1) TSM. The President of the Euro Group is the chairperson of the ESM's board of governors, an option made by the Board in accordance with article 5(2) TSM.

[83] Article 7(1) of Regulation (EU) 472/2013 of the European Parliament and the Council.

[84] Article 12 of the TESM.

[85] Recital number (4) TESM.

[86] Ibid., Article 5 (6)(g) TESM.

The constitutionality of creating assistance mechanisms to support Member States in financial distress is controversial.[87] Within the legal framework of the Treaties, the EU can only provide financial assistance to the Member States in the event of natural catastrophes or exceptional and uncontrollable situations and under certain conditions. In other cases, the no-bailout clauses of articles 123 and 125 TFEU should apply. These norms prohibit the provision of credits and the buying of Member States' government debt by the ECB and national central banks, as well as the assumption of Member States' financial liabilities by the EU and its institutions.[88] The purpose of the norms is to establish the rules of market discipline: the Member States are free to choose and define their fiscal policies, but they should also be aware that they are responsible for their financial situation. The *telos* of the rules was that the EU would not support the Member States nor establish a transfer union for fear of generating moral hazard and supporting fiscal profligacy. In the words of the CJEU: "The prohibition laid down in Article 125 TFEU ensures that the Member States remain subject to the logic of the market when they enter into debt since that ought to prompt them to maintain budgetary discipline."[89]

However, because of how some Member States were affected by the financial crisis, given their specifically vulnerable economic situations, the EU found it urgent to devise a form of supporting such States to guarantee the stability of the single currency. The provision of financial assistance turned into a complex political problem, for it put into question not only a fundamental principle of EMU's *telos*, the principle of market discipline, but also led to the establishment creditorship relations between the EU and its Member States.[90] From a constitutional point of view, there was the problem of how articles 122(2) and 123–125 TFEU should be understood, and if they could allow for some sort of assistance mechanism to be put in place.

A literal reading of the above-mentioned norms indicates that the Treaty legally permits the provision of financial assistance to the Member States facing economic difficulties. Article 122(2) TFEU allows for financial assistance to be provided on an *ad hoc* basis in the event of specific situations and with conditions attached. Article 125 TFEU does not prohibit financial assistance; rather, it prohibits the EU or its institutions from assuming a Member State's legal and financial liabilities (that is: to be assigned the debts of the Member States), as confirmed by the CJEU.[91] Therefore, according to the Court, if there is no legal transfer of risk—meaning: the EU does not assume the Member State's debts as its own—between the EU and the Member States, financial assistance is possible in terms of Treaty law.[92] According

---

[87] Peers 2013, pp. 37–72; Tuori and Tuori 2014, pp. 119–136; Hinarejos 2020, pp. 1377–1388; Van Malleghem 2013, pp. 141–168; Deters 2014, pp. 204–218.

[88] On article 125, see Ohler 2022b, pp. 181–192.

[89] CJEU, Thomas Pringle v. Government of Ireland and Others, 2012, Case C-370/12, para 135.

[90] A complicated situation as described by Dyson 2014, pp. 61–65.

[91] CJEU, Thomas Pringle v. Government of Ireland and Others, 2012, Case C-370/12, paras 130–132.

[92] Ibid., para 146.

to Darius Adamski, "pursuant to *Pringle* no temporary bailout in the Eurozone is legally problematic, as long as it works and the assistance is paid back".[93]

How do the assistance instruments comply with this constitutional understanding? Although the EFSM is still in force, it was only used to provide a temporary solution during the financial crisis. In this interpretation, the EFSM had limited use, and does not seem to go against EU law. Furthermore, it is unclear to what extent the EFSM will be used again, with the ESM now firmly established as the main stability facility in the EMU—the Commission even proposed to incorporate the ESM into the EU legal framework and rename it to a European Monetary Fund.[94]

Unlike the EFSM, the ESM is not a temporary solution but a permanent body that can assist States in financial distress, which makes it a more complex constitutional case. However, the CJEU found that the creation of the ESM was not in violation of EU law because it did not constitute an instrument for the Member States to circumvent the provisions of article 125 TFEU. The Court considered that the ESM is a distinct legal entity from the EU and the Member States, which means that it is liable for its actions that (from a legal perspective) do not bind the Member States.[95] Furthermore, according to the CJEU, as long as financial assistance is provided with conditions that "prompt [the beneficiary] Member State to implement a sound budgetary policy",[96] such action is not prohibited by article 125 TFEU. Therefore, article 125 TFEU should be read as normative reinforcement of Article 119(3) TFEU regarding the duty for Member States to pursue fiscal policies that are balanced and sound, in line with EU policy goals.

A more interesting question concerns the categorization of the EMS as a mere "financing" instrument but not as an instrument of economic governance. According to the CJEU, signing the ESM Treaty does not affect the EU's competence in economic coordination because the ESM aims to "mobilize funding and to provide financial stability support to ESM Members who are experiencing, or are threatened by, severe financing problems".[97] The Court then adds that conditionality attached to ESM assistance does not constitute an instrument of policy coordination but only a guarantee that financial assistance complies with the *telos* of article 125 TFEU (i.e., a guarantee of sound fiscal policies) and with coordinating measures "adopted by the Union".[98] However, the argument of the CJEU is unconvincing, since the purpose of conditionality is to ensure that the beneficiary Member States adopt sound budgetary policies. One of the three principles of economic conduct that EU economic governance efforts must comply with is also sound budgetary policies, according to article 119(3) TFEU. Therefore, *the purposes of conditionality in financial assistance and economic governance are the same*, partaking in the same objective: to guarantee

93 Adamski 2018, p. 83.

94 See European Commission (2017) Proposal for a Council Regulation on the establishment of the European Monetary Fund.

95 Article 8(5) TSM.

96 CJEU, Thomas Pringle v. Government of Ireland and Others, 2012, Case C-370/12, para 137.

97 Ibid., para 110.

98 Ibid., para 111.

financial stability in the Eurozone. In this sense, there is no way that *financial assistance is not, also, an instrument of economic governance* (one might even add that financial assistance is arguably the most effective mechanism of coordination, from a legal perspective, as we shall discuss later). Therefore, ESM affects EU competence in economic governance matters.

Since it is an international law body, there were also questions regarding the application of EU law to the EMS and its acts (such as the MoUs establishing the conditions for financial assistance).[99] Steve Peers points out that as "a matter of principle, it would be problematic if the EU institutions could escape the constraints of the Charter [and of other EU legal principles] merely because they happen to be acting pursuant to treaties between member states, rather than EU law".[100] In the case of *Ledra Advertising*, the CJEU accepted that EU law applies to EU institutions that play crucial roles in the ESM's tasks, like the Commission and the ECB.[101] By acknowledging that EU institutions are bound to EU law and its principles within the framework of the EMU, the Court strengthened the connection between the ESM framework and the constitutional principles of EU law. Furthermore, in the *BPC Lux 2 Sàrl* case, the CJEU ruled that the MoUs enacted within the EFSM were EU law acts.[102] Although ESM MoUs are formally outside the scope of EU law, they must be "fully compatible" with the MEAP that is negotiated with EU institutions.[103] Since MEAPs must be approved by the Council and are, therefore, acts of EU law, there is a connection (even if indirect) between ESM law with EU law.[104] Finally, it is unclear to what extent Member States are bound to EU law principles (such as loyal cooperation and equality) when *acting outside* the scope of EU Treaties but while *taking actions that can affect* the implementation of the Treaties. In any case, EU law seems to apply, even if indirectly, to the ESM's activity.

The ESM represents a tremendous shift in the EU economic governance framework established in Maastricht. As Kaarlo and Klaus Tuori aptly argue, the centre of the economic constitution is no longer the purpose of price stability but financial stability,[105] with the ESM playing the role of the respondent of last resort, providing "lifelines" for reacting against the dramatic consequences of asymmetric economic shocks. The Maastricht model of State liability for financial affairs was severely affected, although not completely broken, due to the setting of conditionality measures in the assistance programs to guarantee fiscal policy compatibility with EU targets. However, this evolution emptied the application of the no-bailout clause,

[99] Peers 2013, pp. 46–52.

[100] Ibid., 53.

[101] CJEU, Ledra Advertising Ltd and Others v. Commission and ECB, 2016, Joined Cases C-8/15 P to C-10/15 P, paras 55–56.

[102] CJEU, BPC Lux 2 Sàrl and others v. Banco de Portugal and others, 2022, Case C-83, paras 29–30.

[103] Article 8(2) of Regulation 472/2013 of the European Parliament and the Council.

[104] Peers 2013, p. 53.

[105] Tuori and Tuori 2014, p. 134. See also Lo Schiavo 2017, pp. 85–88.

which nowadays serves more as a guiding principle for the setting of conditionality assistance than a binding constitutional rule of the Treaty.

That is not to say that the ESM does not help achieve substantive EU law goals being, in that sense, compatible in substance with the EU law normative framework. It is, in some respects, an instrument of solidarity between States.[106] It is debatable, however, how solidary such an instrument is, considering the political and social burden caused by conditions of assistance.[107] On a more technical level, the ESM supports compliance with the objective of sound public finances, as the CJEU states, which is the second objective of economic and fiscal policy.

3.4 Conclusion

When defining their respective fiscal policies, the Member States are subject to the limits set out in the Treaties. National fiscal policy must be developed in line with the constitutional objectives of EU Treaties and following economic and monetary objectives defined by EU institutions, while avoiding excessive deficits. Additionally, Member States must coordinate their economic policies at the EU level, which means that they should converge in a way that supports the achievement of common goals. Outside of these limits, Member States are free to define their economic policies. According to the principle of conferral, the EU cannot enact measures that impose specific policy choices on the Member States.

According to the Treaties, the EU has a coordination competence regarding economic policy governance. It can enact coordinating measures, which include acts setting institutional and temporal structures for consultation among national governments and acts that complement, enhance, or support such structures of coordination. There can be some degree of normative harmonization, but only if it serves the purpose of coordination and, once again, does not impose fiscal policy obligations on the Member States.

The leading institutions in the policy area of economic coordination are the Commission, the Council, the European Council, the ECB, and the EMS. The Commission serves as the administrator, exercising supervisory functions and proposing policy guidelines (both collective and individual) to be adopted by the Council and, in the case of the BEPGs, the European Council. The Council is the ultimate decision-maker, putting national governments in charge of the matters of economic supervision and assistance. The intergovernmental character of EU economic governance is reinforced by the informal role played by the Eurogroup in policy coordination. The European Parliament does not play any decisive role in this field.

Regarding the extent and scope of the powers, the EU cannot impose fiscal policy choices on the Member States, but it can nevertheless monitor their compliance with

[106] See for example Ciornei and Ross 2021, pp. 209–214.

[107] A critique of this view comes from Kilpatrick 2015, pp. 333–345.

EU rules on fiscal policy definition and issue recommendations on their status and prospects. Furthermore, in procedures of economic policy supervision, the EU has powers to sanction the Member States for failure to correct excessive deficits, deviations from their stability programs, and failure to correct economic imbalances. Within this form of "corrective" monitoring, the EU can, by using sanctions mechanisms, request that the Member States adopt specific measures to achieve sound budgetary policies. Additionally, within financial assistance procedures, EU institutions have the power to request that a beneficiary Member State implements policy measures in exchange for the disbursement of funds. Such conditions guarantee the implementation of sound budgetary policies in line with EU goals and objectives and, therefore, help advance the objectives of EU economic governance.

In sum, the powers of EU institutions in the policy area of economic governance seem to be wide-ranging, especially the powers of corrective supervision and the powers of assistance. To what extent do they comply with the coordination character of the EU's competence in this field? That is the subject of the next chapter.

References

Adamski D (2018) Redefining European Economic Integration. Cambridge University Press

Amtenbrink F (2023) On the Misalignment of Monetary, Economic, and Political Integration in European Economic and Monetary Union. In: Adamski D et al (eds) The Cambridge Handbook of European Monetary, Economic and Financial Integration. Cambridge University Press, pp. 69–86

Bénassy-Quéré A, Wolff G (2020) How has the macroeconomic imbalances procedure worked in practice to improve the resilience of the euro area? IPOL Economic Governance Support Unit, available at https://www.bruegel.org/sites/default/files/wp-content/uploads/2020/03/IPOL_STU2020645710_EN.pdf accessed 15 August 2025

Bieber R (2014) The Allocation of Economic Policy Competences. In: Azoulai L (ed) The Question of Competence in the European Union. Oxford University Press, pp. 86–100

Ciornei I, Ross MG (2021) Solidarity in Europe: From Crisis to Policy? Acta Politica 56:209–219 https://link.springer.com/content/pdf/10.1057/s41269-021-00195-7.pdf?pdf=button accessed 15 August 2025

Craig P (2004) Competence: Clarity, Containment and Consideration. European Law Journal 29:323–344

Dermine P (2022) The New Economic Governance of the Eurozone: A Rule of Law Analysis. Cambridge University Press

Deters H (2014) National Constitutional Jurisprudence in a Post-National Europe: The ESM Ruling of the German Federal Constitutional Court and the Disavowal of Conflict. European Law Journal 20:204–218

Dyson K (2014) States, Debt, and Power: 'Saints' and 'Sinners' in European History and Integration. Oxford University Press

Flynn L (2019) Article 136. In: Kellerbauer M et al (eds) Commentary on the EU Treaties and the Charter of Fundamental Rights. Oxford University Press, pp. 1320–1321

Hinarejos A (2020) The Legality of Responses to the Crisis. In: Amtenbrink F, Herrmann C (eds) The EU Law of Economic and Monetary Union. Oxford University Press, pp. 1363–1399

Hodson D (2018) The Macroeconomic Imbalance Procedure as European integration: a legalization perspective. Journal of European Public Policy 25:1610–1628

Keppenne J-P (2020) EU Fiscal Governance on the Member States: The Stability and Growth Pact and Beyond. In: Amtenbrink F, Herrmann C (eds) The EU Law of Economic and Monetary Union. Oxford University Press, pp. 813–849
Kilpatrick C (2015) On the Rule of Law and Economic Emergency: The Degradation of Basic Legal Values in Europe's Bailouts. Oxford Journal of Legal Studies 35:325–353
Konstadinides T (2009) Division of Powers in European Union Law: The Delimitation of Internal Competence between the EU and the Member States. Wolters Kluwer
Lo Schiavo G (2017) The Role of Financial Stability in EU Law and Policy. Wolters Kluwer
Ohler C (2022a) Article 136. In: Siekmann H (ed) The European Monetary Union: A Commentary on the Legal Foundations. Hart Publishing, pp. 505–514
Ohler C (2022b) Article 125. In: Siekmann H (ed) The European Monetary Union: A Commentary on the Legal Foundations. Hart Publishing, pp. 181–192
Peers S (2013) Towards a New Form of EU Law? The Use of EU Institutions outside the EU Legal Framework. European Constitutional Law Review 9:37–72
Pereira Coutinho F (2016) Austerity on the loose in Portugal: European judicial restraint in times of crisis. Perspectives on Federalism 8:105–132 http://webarchive-2009-2021.on-federalism.eu/attachments/249_download.pdf accessed 15 August 2025
Puetter U (2006) The Eurogroup. Manchester University Press
Putnam RD, Henning CR (1989) The Bonn Summit of 1978: A Case Study in Coordination. In: Cooper RN et al (eds) Can Nations Agree?: Issues in International Economic Cooperation. Brookings Institute Press: 12–140
Ruffert M (2011) The European debt crisis and European Union law. Common Market Law Review 48:1777–1805
Scharpf FW (2011) Monetary Union, Fiscal Crisis and the Pre-emption of Democracy. Journal for Comparative Government and European Policy 9:163–198
Schütze R (2015) EU Competences: Existence and Exercise. In: Chalmers D, Arnull A (eds) The Oxford Handbook of European Union Law. Oxford University Press, pp. 75–102
Schütze R (2016) EU Constitutional Law. Cambridge University Press
Seikel D (2016) Flexible Austerity and Supranational Autonomy: the Reformed Excessive Deficit Procedure and the Asymmetry between Liberalization and Social Regulation in the EU. Journal of Common Market Studies 54: 1398–1416
Snell J (2017) The Internal Market and the Philosophies of Market Integration. In: Barnard C, Peers S (eds) European Union Law. Oxford University Press, pp. 310–338
Timmermans C (2014) ECJ Doctrines on Competences. In: Azoulai L (ed) The Question of Competence in the European Union. Oxford University Press, pp. 155–167
Tuori K, Tuori K (2014) The Eurozone Crisis: a Constitutional Analysis. Cambridge University Press
Van Malleghem P-A (2013) Pringle: A Paradigm Shift in the European Union's Monetary Constitution. German Law Journal 14: 141–168

Chapter 4
The Legal Strength of EU Powers of Economic Governance

Contents

Abstract This chapter analyses the legal strength of the European Union's powers in economic governance, focusing on the extent to which Member States are bound by EU rules and economic coordination mechanisms. It proposes a methodological framework to assess the binding nature of legal acts, distinguishing between their internal (degree of obligation) and external (enforcement in practice) dimensions, and applies it to both hard and soft law instruments. Special attention is given to the pervasive use of soft law—particularly recommendations—in economic governance, whose formal non-binding nature contrasts with their practical and sometimes sanction-linked effects. The analysis covers EU primary and secondary law, as well as international frameworks such as the TSCG and ESM, highlighting variations in legal force across preventive, corrective, and assistance procedures. While corrective mechanisms like the EDP and EIP display stronger normative and enforcement capacity, preventive tools such as the MSP rely mainly on political pressure. Ultimately, the chapter concludes that EU economic governance operates

M. Lucas Pires, *The Federal Legality of EU Economic Governance*,
https://doi.org/10.1007/978-94-6265-747-2_4

in a constitutionally intergovernmental field, where legal obligations can significantly constrain national fiscal autonomy, but enforcement remains subject to political discretion—except in financial assistance contexts, where compliance is more strictly compelled.

Keywords EU economic governance · Legal strength · Soft law · Fiscal policy coordination · Enforcement mechanisms

4.1 The Constitutional Complexity of EU Economic Governance

The present chapter proposes an analysis of the EU powers of economic governance and their respective legal character, that is, the level of normative obligation they generate for their subjects (i.e., Member States). The chapter wishes to answer the following question: to what extent are Member States bound to follow EU rules and powers of economic governance?

The constitutional framework of EU economic governance is legally puzzling, for it is an area of law in which there is a constant tension between the form and the substance of the legal acts adopted. Such a conundrum generates confusion about the nature and force of EU norms of economic governance and the extent to which Member States are compelled to follow them.

The confusion starts with the variety of legal sources from where EU acts of economic governance emanate (some acts have their legal basis in EU law, others in international law, and some also in national law[1]) and the different normative characters of rules, with different levels of obligation being set for the Member States to follow. The EU legal framework of economic governance is set in EU primary law (TEU and TFEU) and secondary law (the six-pack and two-pack legislation). Both primary and secondary law sources grant powers to EU institutions to enact legal acts of a general and individual nature addressed to the Member States. Such acts can be binding (regulations, decisions, directives) and non-binding (such as recommendations, opinions, and warnings). This mix of hard law, guiding principles, and soft law makes it difficult to understand *what the obligation is to be complied with* and what legal expectations the Member States should comply with, without risking infringement and the consequent activation of sanctions. Moreover, there are several interpretative acts in place that delimitate the extension of EU competences and the use of EU powers of economic governance, such as guidelines and interpretative

[1] Given the obligation set out in the TSCG to transpose the Fiscal Compact into national law, and for Member States to create independent fiscal institutions. See, respectively, article 3(2) of the TSCG and article 5 of Regulation 473/2013 of the European Parliament and the Council.

instruments produced by the Commission (e.g., the Vade Mecum,[2] the guide on the flexibility of the SGP),[3] and CJEU decisions (particularly on the role of the ESM that define the meaning and scope of EU action (and, consequently, have an impact in the Member States' expectations on the level of obligation). Finally, there is also the problem of the effective implementation of the rules, powers, and principles of economic governance by EU institutions and the Member States. There are and, historically, there were, problematic discrepancies between the legal framework and its application to specific situations. These discrepancies make it more difficult to understand the real meaning and value of the rules and, one might add, the legal framework of economic governance in general.

The analysis in this chapter shall focus on assessing the legal character and strength of the rules and powers of EU institutions applicable to the Member States in the policy area of economic governance by looking at the source of these powers. Therefore, the first analysis shall consider the rules and powers of EU economic governance set in the EU Treaties and EU secondary law, while the second analysis shall consider the rules and powers set in international law. The chapter does not consider national law obligations, for they are outside of the scope of this work.

Before undergoing the analysis, it is necessary to adopt a methodological framework for assessing the normative strength of EU rules to understand to what extent they are binding and to identify the incentives for its addressees to comply with them. Such a method requires a jurisprudential analysis of the norms of the legal framework of EU economic governance, as well as an analysis of the legal mechanisms that are in place for applying, upholding, and reviewing the legality of these norms.

Hence, the first part of the chapter shall present the jurisprudential framework of analysis, with a more detailed focus on soft law acts in the EU legal order. The second part shall consider the rules and analyse them against the jurisprudential framework previously discussed. The third part shall conclude with an opinion on the legal strength of EU powers of economic governance.

[2] European Commission (2019) Vade Mecum on the Stability and Growth Pact – 2019 Edition, available at https://economy-finance.ec.europa.eu/publications/vade-mecum-stability-and-growth-pact-2019-edition_en accessed 15 August 2025.

[3] European Commission (2015) Making The Best Use Of The Flexibility Within The Existing Rules Of The Stability And Growth Pact, available at https://ec.europa.eu/economy_finance/economic_governance/sgp/pdf/2015-01-13_communication_sgp_flexibility_guidelines_en.pdf accessed 15 August 2025.

4.2 Assessing the Legal Strength of Normative Acts: An Analytical Proposal

4.2.1 Legal Character and Legal Operation of Norms

Law is a normative system concerned with setting social order (that is, with the organization of actions and expectations among social actors).[4] Law comprises norms, that is, statements that serve as imperative instruments that legal subjects should follow. Norms are the essence of law, holding a prescriptive character.

The two most important categories of norms in jurisprudential terms are principles and rules.[5] Principles are norms representing a fundamental, substantive objective of the legal order that serve as justifying reasons for deciding cases.[6] In this sense, principles are generic and less specific prescriptive declarations, with a different character than rules.[7] Principles represent a guiding idea or value that should orientate the applicant of the law when deciding the case, but do not call for an all-or-nothing application to the case.[8] Therefore, principles are more general and open than norms, and their boundaries and normative scope can vary depending on time and context. Principles involve pondering and balancing competing interests when considering the facts of the case. When applying principles, the applicant enjoys a higher degree of discretion than when applying rules.

As for rules, they are precepts that establish standards of conduct (proposing action or inaction, enabling, or prohibiting courses of conduct) that people ought to follow under penalty of sanction.[9] In a technical sense, rules establish, as Joseph Raz puts it, exclusionary reasons for people to adopt or refrain from adopting a specific behaviour.[10] By knowing that a rule is in place, law subjects became immediately aware of the risk of provoking a negative social judgment with practical consequences if the precept in question is not abided by. The law balances expectations among actors in society through rules: people understand what is permissible (what is legal) and what is not (what is illegal), and aptly organize their actions based on these assumptions.

Therefore, to assess the legal strength of a norm it is necessary to assess the latter's authority—its capacity to be followed by the normative subjects. The greater the capacity to generate obedience, the stronger the norm is. If a norm is often disregarded and ignored (i.e., not followed), its (practical) strength is weak. *Therefore,*

---

[4] Kelsen 1949, pp. 3–4 and 1967, pp. 24–27; Raz 1980, pp. 43–50 and 121–167; Luhmann 1988, pp. 12–35.

[5] Dworkin 1967, pp. 25–29; Kennedy 1976, pp. 1687–1689.

[6] Kennedy 1976, p. 1688; Cortês 2010, p. 10.

[7] Raz 1972, pp. 834–837.

[8] Dworkin 1967, pp 25–28.

[9] Lamond 2000, 20 pp. 41–45.

[10] Raz 1983, pp. 15–19. See also Besson 2005, pp. 461–465.

the normative force of a norm consists of their capacity to generate obedience—their degree of practical authority.

There are two dimensions to this character, one internal and another external. The internal dimension concerns the degree of obligation a norm sets *in substance.* Norms can set different forms and degrees of obligations and duties for people to follow. For example, a norm that establishes that diving in the river is prohibited provides, in the abstract, a stronger exclusionary reason not to dive than a norm stating that people should refrain from diving in the river. Additionally, a duty that is not possible (in practice or law) to be complied with also makes the obligation non-existent—*impossibilium nulla obligatio est*[11]—and, therefore, weak.

The external dimension concerns the implementation of the norm in practical life, that is, its regular application to daily events. Legal norms are social creations, generated and applied by a group that shares a common understanding of what is normatively binding (customary law) or by a governing power, that is, by an institutional setting entrusted with the ruling of a group of people within a specific territory.[12] In the latter case, legal norms are not only social creations but *political* creations, for they represent an act of self-government. The political character of law[13] consists not only of its production and enactment but of its application by governing institutions (typically, the bodies responsible for the administration of public affairs or the executive body) and its adjudication by judicial bodies: bodies that have the political function of deciding with final authority on legal disputes, i.e., disputes arising from the application or compliance with a set of norms.

In methodological terms, the notion of normative force (or of the "force of law"[14]) can both refer to the internal dimension of a norm (the inherently binding character of the obligation set in the legal statement)[15] or to the norm's external dimension—the capacity of that norm to be enforced in practice.[16] However, a realist perspective of the legal phenomenon must look at normative force as including both dimensions: the normative character that is internal to a norm and the effects of the norm's application in the world.[17] Although a legal norm does not lose its normative status when disregarded by its subjects,[18] the fact is that a "dead-letter" norm (i.e., a rule that exists as a legal statement but that is not followed by anyone nor enforced by anyone, be it public powers or individuals) has little to no practical significance.[19] In realist terms, a norm must be "living": it must be part of (or generally regarded as being part of) the precepts that are in force to be capable of being applied within the

[11] Mordechai Rabello 2010, pp. 346–358.

[12] See Unger 1976, pp. 49–52.

[13] Alexander 2019, p. 355.

[14] See Derrida 1992, pp. 5–16.

[15] See Schauer 2015, pp. 31–37.

[16] Ibid., pp. 1–10. See also Hagg 2018, pp. 21–22.

[17] Kennedy 1991, p. 348. See also McDougal 1952, p. 110.

[18] As Joseph Raz puts it, there is no obligation to follow the law, the law only provides exclusionary reasons for its subject to follow. See Raz 1983, pp. 227–243.

[19] McNeilly 1968, pp. 63–64.

community's social consciousness. A norm that, for whatever reason, is not applied nor followed fails to have any meaningful significance.

Therefore, when considering the strength of legal acts, it is essential to consider the normative force from both perspectives: from the internal perspective (the character of the obligation set by the rule and its capacity to generate obedience) and from the external perspective (the extent to which such rule is effectively followed and applied by—respectively—its addressees and administrative/judicial applicants and, if so, *how* it is applied and *where* is it applied). Usually, a presumption is that acts *formally* considered as binding acts will always be enforced. This analytical framework shall be followed throughout this chapter and particularly in Sects. 4.3 and 4.4 below.

Academic and practical discussions concerning the normative force of norms generally focus on their effectiveness, that is, their ability to be followed and applied in practice (in our framework this is the problem of the external dimension of normative force).[20] From a philosophical perspective, the question of the normative force of a norm (more specifically, of a rule) in the internal dimension can seem, in some ways, confusing. The essence of rules, what makes them essentially *rule-like*, is their prescriptive quality. They are rules because their statement is authoritative and generates obedience and respect. Obligations can be more stringent or flexible (for example, the norm can include conditions or exceptions in the event of a specific criterion). However, they always "bind" (i.e., provide exclusionary reasons) the addressee to follow them. When the normative statement does not claim obedience but merely suggests or warns (leaving the addressee with enough freedom to decide whether to follow the suggestion or warning or not), then it is not a real prescription. In other words, *it lacks the quality of a rule*. It is, at best, guidance, a suggestion, but nothing more: it does not ultimately put forward a claim on (or attempts *to bind*) the subject to act in a specific way. Therefore, talking about normative force of legal acts that are not rules, in this methodological sense, might seem paradoxical and contradictory—except for situations in which the legal statement itself puts forward conditions or caveats for the enforcement of the rule.

4.2.2 The Legal Strength of Soft Law Acts

There is, however, a phenomenon that challenges the concept of legal strength and the normative force of legal norms discussed in the previous paragraph: it is the phenomenon known as soft law.

Soft law consists of legal *instruments* (e.g., normative statements issued by government institutions) that cannot be considered entirely as law because they lack the binding character of norms.[21] However, they are not legally insignificant, as they do produce (or *intend* to produce) some normative effect, albeit weaker than norms. These instruments, while not purely prescriptive, still maintain a certain level of

[20] See Kelsen 1967, pp. 30–50; Raz 1983, p. 152.

[21] Wellens and Borchardt 1989, p. 274; Snyder 1993, p. 32.

authority.[22] As Linda Senden states, soft law instruments are "[r]ules of conduct that are laid down in instruments which have not been attributed legally binding force as such but may have certain (indirect) legal effects, and that are aimed and may produce practical effects".[23]

Soft law is generally a product of the executive branch of government, specifically the state administration, which includes departments, ministries, agencies, and regulators. The public administration typically possesses the authority to enforce existing laws but lacks legislative power. Furthermore, the ability to create legally binding acts is restricted by the principle of legality in administrative power.[24] The capacity to recommend and suggest benchmarks, standards, and guidance serves as an alternative means of establishing order and direction, compensating for the lack of legislative power. However, one might question the most crucial power of government in realist terms: whether it lies *in the power to legislate and establish regulations that apply to a broad range of actions*, or *in the power to apply and enforce the law, which involves authoritatively defining the scope and interpretation of the law in specific situations.*

Soft law allows legal subjects to exercise a considerable degree of autonomy in deciding how to adhere to and to what extent they follow the guidelines provided by administrative institutions.[25] In this sense, soft law is considered an appealing regulatory tool due to its flexibility and informality, providing drafters with various possibilities and safeguards the autonomy of legal subjects,[26] while its flexibility allows for effective governance in highly technical regulatory fields. However, along with this flexibility, there also comes a certain degree of risk for legal subjects and the stability of the legal system, for the proliferation of soft law instruments can generate confusion due to their hybrid, malleable, and informal nature. In some cases, soft law acts may be used as a desired method to enforce authoritative rules in situations where there is no competence for exercising binding powers.[27] Furthermore, it can be challenging to determine the extent to which addressees are obligated to follow soft law acts. Compliance with and obedience to such acts becomes a complex matter, as legal subjects must interpret the intentions and competences of the issuing institutions within the specific regulatory context. Judges, in particular, face challenges when conducting judicial review[28] as they need to grasp the "sentiment" of normativity or the "penumbra of the law", as Anne Peters described it.[29] This task is much more intricate than assessing compliance with a clearly defined prescriptive statement.

The (ab)use of soft law instruments carries significant risks to legal stability. It can disrupt the balance of powers between institutions, with the executive branch

22 Terpan 2015, pp. 70–71; Mahler 2021, p. 26.

23 Senden 2004, p. 112.

24 Chamon and Arriba-Sellier 2022, p. 287; Stefan et al. 2019, pp. 34–37; Peters 2011, pp. 30–31.

25 Daly 2021, pp. 8–9.

26 Senden 2004, pp. 23–25; Trubek et al. 2005, pp. 11–12.

27 Stefan et al. 2019, p. 26.

28 See Eliantonio 2021, pp. 283–301; Dermine 2022a, pp. 12–13; Gentile 2020, pp. 466–492.

29 Peters 2011, p. 23.

assuming a legislative role while being shielded from judicial challenges. Soft law, therefore, poses challenges to the accountability and legitimacy of institutions, which can affect the position of subjects of normative acts.[30] Ultimately, the rule of law and the balance of powers, with a potential shift towards a more executive-based form of authority, may be at stake.[31]

4.2.3 Soft Law in the E(M)U Context

Soft law plays a significant role in the EU legal order.[32] EU institutions extensively use guidelines, recommendations, and opinions in several policy areas, including competition law, health policy, and banking regulation, where technical and scientific expertise is crucial. The use of soft law is particularly prominent in the Open Method of Coordination (OMC), a hybrid form of governance introduced in 2000 as part of the Lisbon agenda. The OMC combines traditional legal and coercive instruments (hard law) with informal mechanisms for policy coordination and harmonization, such as political, scientific, or technical mechanisms.[33] Within the OMC, the EU acts as a benchmark, standard-setter, reviewer, and supervisor of practices among Member States, providing input, reports, and guidance to achieve specific policy objectives.[34] This method allows for decentralized policy development, granting Member States a higher level of autonomy compared to the traditional regulatory approach known as the Community Method, which is based on normative authorization.[35]

While Article 288 of the TFEU establishes the formal distinction between binding and non-binding acts (regulations, directives, and decisions being binding, and recommendations and opinions being non-binding), EU courts have acknowledged that this article alone does not provide a comprehensive understanding of binding acts.[36] The Court has recognized that certain legal instruments, despite not appearing "rule-like" in form or substance, can still have normative effects and impose de facto binding rights and obligations[37]—for example, in the Grimaldi case, the CJEU stated that recommendations "cannot be regarded as having no legal effect".[38] The Court understands that soft law acts can impact the legal position of their addressees, either

[30] Bobic 2024, pp. 61–65.

[31] Senden 2004, pp. 477–497; Stefan et al. 2019, pp. 34–38; Mendes 2019, pp. 6–10.

[32] Stefan et al. 2019, pp. 3–4; Eliantonio et al. 2021, pp. 1–3.

[33] For hybrid modes of governance in the EMU, see Maher 2007, pp. 682–688; Trubek and Trubek 2005, pp. 347–363.

[34] Dawson 2011, pp. 42–47.

[35] For an explanation of the community method, see European Commission (2001) European Governance: A White Paper, available at https://ec.europa.eu/commission/presscorner/detail/en/DOC_01_10 accessed 15 August 2025.

[36] Senden 2004, pp. 249–251.

[37] CJEU, Commission v. Council, 1971, Case C-22/70, para. 42 and Tridimas 2019, p. 47.

[38] CJEU, Salvatore Grimaldi v. Fonds des maladies professionnelles, 1989, Case C-322/88, para 18.

independently or by providing crucial supportive and interpretative criteria for other legal acts.[39] In some instances, the CJEU has annulled soft law measures, considering them binding and thus invalid for breaching EU primary law on the definition of competences.[40]

EU economic governance makes extensive use of the OMC,[41] being not only a politically sensitive area but also a framework that requires technical expertise to consider the complexities of economic and fiscal data necessary for providing appropriate guidance. In the EMU, EU competences are primarily limited to the definition and execution of monetary policy, while economic policy powers are focused on managing and enhancing the coordination of Member States' policy options, as discussed in Chap. 3. Due to the limitation of binding powers and the prevalence of executive administration powers, soft law becomes a crucial tool for providing guidance and setting guidelines to improve the coordination of national policies.

As a result, it is not surprising that soft law instruments constitute the majority of legal activity by EU institutions in the area of economic governance. There are several types of soft law instruments used by EU institutions in this field,[42] ranging from preparatory or informative instruments[43] to interpretative and decisional instruments,[44] as well as steering instruments such as recommendations, which are intended to guide the actions of their addressees.[45] These instruments serve both a "pre" and "post" legal function, as some are adopted to support the preparation of EU acts, while others are adopted to complement the implementation of EU policies or instruments.[46] Additionally, some soft law instruments can serve a quasi-legal function, being "structured in several respects in a comparable way to legal rules meaning that various principles of law can be applied to them by analogy".[47] This is the case of recommendations issued in procedures of economic supervision.

Among the variety of soft law instruments used, recommendations play a significant role in the EU economic governance framework. Recommendations are steering

---

[39] Senden 2004, p. 263.

[40] More recently in cases involving the EU's Banking Union: CJEU, BT v. Balgarska Narodna Banka, 2021, C-501/18, and Fédération bancaire française (FBF) v. Autorité de contrôle prudentiel et de resolution, 2021, C-911/19. See Chamon and Arriba-Sellier 2022; Gentile 2021, pp. 981–1005.

[41] Dawson 2011, p. 50; Hodson and Maher 2001, pp. 719–721.

[42] The classification of types of soft law acts is from Senden 2004, pp. 118–119.

[43] For example, the proposal by the European Commission (2022) for a Joint Employment Report from the Commission and the Council, available at https://commission.europa.eu/system/files/2022-11/COM_2022_783_1_EN.pdf accessed 15 august 2025.

[44] For example, the European Commission's Vade Mecum on the Stability and Growth Pact – 2019 Edition, available at https://economy-finance.ec.europa.eu/publications/vade-mecum-stability-and-growth-pact-2019-edition_en accessed 15 August 2025.

[45] For example, the European Commission's recommendations to the Council in the procedures of economic governance, such as European Commission (2022) Recommendation for a Council Recommendation on the 2022 National Reform Programme of Portugal and delivering a Council opinion on the 2022 Stability Programme of Portugal, available at https://commission.europa.eu/system/files/2022-05/2022-european-semester-csr-portugal_en.pdf accessed 15 August 2025.

[46] Senden 2004, p. 120.

[47] Daniel Thürer in Senden 2004, p. 120.

instruments that provide guidance to Member States on aligning their actions with fiscal rules and targets. The content of recommendations is not legally defined, allowing them to cover a wide range of policy areas and include suggestions for adopting measures or achieving policy targets, whether they are numerical or substantive.[48] Recommendations are used in five out of the six procedures of economic governance, with the exception being the AFB, where the actors are the Eurogroup and the Commission, and the adopted acts are opinions.[49]

In all procedures of economic governance, recommendations are issued by the Council, based on a recommendation from the Commission. The European Parliament does not have formal powers to address recommendations to Member States or supervise the implementation of national economic reforms. Its powers include fostering an "economic dialogue", which involves engaging with other institutions and Member States to monitor developments and the application of rules.[50] The 2024 reform of the fiscal rules sought to increase the accountability of the procedures of economic governance by the Parliament, with the Commission and the Council having now the duty to transmit to the Parliament not only the national medium-term fiscal-structural plans submitted by the Member States, but also other relevant information regarding economic governance supervision.[51] As good as that seems, the fact is that the Parliament continues to stand on the sidelines of authority-yielding in the economic governance area.

Non-compliance with Council recommendations issued in the EDP and EIP can result in financial penalties. The potential activation of sanctions in case of failure to comply with recommendations might suggest a strong legal character of this instrument, akin to being binding (as described by EU public officers who refer to CSRs as "politically binding", though they do not fully address the legal effects of such acts).[52] However, this is controversial, demonstrating a discrepancy between the form (recommendations being non-binding acts according to Article 288 TFEU) and the substance (as recommendations vary greatly in content, ranging from specific to broad, highly prescriptive to merely suggestive). Moreover, the application of sanctions for non-compliance with a soft law instrument is not automatic but subject to assessment by the Council, which means that there is significant degree of discretion attached to the application of sanctions, making it more difficult to understand what exactly is binding in the recommendation. This complex normative status of recommendations has sparked doctrinal debates, raising questions about the extent to which the rule-based system of EU economic governance possesses "rule-like" qualities.

---

[48] Generally, recommendations are composed by several, different sub-recommendations. Poiares Maduro et al. 2017, p. 20.

[49] Article 7(1) of Regulation 473/2013 of the European Parliament and the Council.

[50] See, for example, article 14 of Regulation 1176/2011 of the European Parliament and the Council, whose formulation is transcribed *ipsium verbis* in all the legal acts composing the six-pack. On the Parliament's role in economic dialogue, see Fromage 2018, pp. 281–294.

[51] See article 27 of Regulation 2024/1263 of the European Parliament and of the Council.

[52] See Angerer et al. 2020, p. 4.

Damian Chalmers, for instance, argues that due to their administrative nature and "lack of rule-like qualities", the normative force of recommendations in the field of economic governance remains "unclear".[53] Regarding the CSRs issued in the MSP, Frank Nispen considers them non-binding, yet Member States are expected to eventually comply with them to a certain degree.[54] Cristina Fasone notes that recommendations of the Commission on national stability programs were considered binding.[55] Päivi Leino and Thomas Saarenheimo argue that these instruments are not binding due to the highly political nature of fiscal governance at the EU level.[56] Finally, Fabian Amtenbrink and René Repasi posit that recommendations in the EIB and EDP are not legally binding; however, they acknowledge that non-compliance with recommendations triggers corrective procedures in the EIB.[57]

Taking a systematic approach to economic governance, Miguel Maduro, António Frada, and Pierluigi Pierdominici contend that Council recommendations are "unequivocally" binding as they serve a post-law function in light of TFEU and SGP obligations. According to their perspective:

> [w]hen EMU Treaty Provisions and SGP Regulations provide that national budgets have to be coherent with the recommendations adopted in the context of the SGP and that Member States must put in practice and comply with such recommendations, it is appropriate to consider that we are in the face of recommendations that, by virtue of those other rules, legally bind Member States to whom they are addressed.[58]

The three authors develop their argument when reviewing (and criticizing) the decision taken in 2014 by the Portuguese Constitutional Court ("PCC") on the national budget law during the period of financial intervention. The PCC took the view that it did not need to assess the binding character of Council recommendations addressed to Portugal in the context of the EDP, given that those instruments were only binding concerning the objectives and not the means, and therefore there was no need to review national budgetary measures in light of EU law rules.[59] The PCC's stance contrasts with the approach taken by the Slovenian Constitutional Court ("SCC"). In a 2012 judgment, the latter considered that "findings made in the EDP", which included Council recommendations, were relevant criteria for the SCC to conduct a constitutional assessment of a referendum request.[60]

The contrasting views on the normative force of these acts highlight the dangerous paradox between the legal form and legal force of soft law instruments that can

---

[53] Chalmers 2012, p. 683.

[54] van Nispen 2017, pp. 2 and 17.

[55] Fasone 2015, p. 4.

[56] Leino and Saarenheimo 2016, p. 15.

[57] Amtenbrink and Repasi 2017, pp. 156–164.

[58] Poiares Maduro et al. 2017, p. 23.

[59] Decision by the Portuguese Constitutional Court 574/2014 para 12, available at https://dre.pt/application/conteudo/56396778 accessed 15 August 2025.

[60] Bardutzky 2016, pp. 12–13.

generate problematic effects for the rights of Member States.[61] Therefore, it is necessary to understand these acts and their characteristics better to comprehend the legal strength of soft law acts in general in EU economic governance.

4.2.4 The Legal Character of Soft Law

The jurisprudential challenge posed by soft law lies in the tension between the content of the legal act and its formal force, which can generate doubts over its true potency. From a normative point of view, soft law instruments, to borrow a Portuguese expression, are "neither fish nor meat", but rather legal instruments that straddle the line between law and non-law. They tend to be, in general, political or technical declarations enacted to orient and guide behaviour without having a potent prescriptive scope. The existence of such a category can lead to confusion when distinguishing law from other forms of social and moral expressions of command, such as politics.[62]

It is thus essential to devise analytical and conceptual tools to measure the degree of binding force of these legal instruments to comprehend the full extent of their effects and risks, and to propose answers and solutions. The hybrid nature and heterogeneity of soft law instruments make their legal strength dependent on contextual analysis, using analytical criteria to measure how binding or non-binding an instrument is.

Different proposals for measuring and comprehending the normative force of soft law have been put forth.[63] Kenneth Abbot et al. proposed the seminal framework concerning the degree of legalization of institutions. In their paper, soft degrees of legalization were distinguished from hard degrees of legalization based on three characteristics of the legal act: obligation (whether or not the instrument states a rule of conduct), precision (the way the rule of conduct is stated, whether it is ambiguous or not), and delegation (whether it grants authority to third parties to enforce, interpret, apply, or decide on the enforcement and application of the rule.[64] The degree of normative force is classified into different dimensions. The legal instrument can be a clear non-legal norm or a binding rule (within the obligation dimension); it can be a vague principle or a precise and highly elaborated rule (within the precision dimension); or it can also be subject to diplomatic, informal modes of control or strict judicial control and adjudication (delegation).[65]

In EU law doctrine, two different analytical frameworks for assessing the "strength" of soft law acts have been proposed, respectively, by Linda Senden and Fabien Terpan. Senden proposes a test based on criteria of the CJEU to identify whether a given act was either a 'true'—non-binding—soft law act or an act with

[61] Dermine 2022a, pp. 8–12.

[62] Thürer 2009, pp. 159–178.

[63] See Trubek et al. 2005, pp. 9–17; Stefan et al. 2019, pp. 20–25.

[64] Abbot et al. 2000, pp. 401–402.

[65] Ibid., 404.

legally binding force.[66] This test has two prongs: the first is to understand whether the drafters of the act intended to make the latter binding upon its addressees, and the second is to understand whether the act created new legal effects or not. The intention of the drafters is evaluated by examining the "wording, terms and context" of the act. Terpan, on the other hand, proposes a variation of Abbot and others' framework to measure the legalization of legal instruments, in which the dimensions of delegation and precision are replaced by the dimension of enforcement, i.e., how the instrument is sanctioned, whether through coercive means or other forms (e.g., reputational means).[67] According to Terpan, these criteria "allow us to construct soft law as an autonomous category of norms" by looking at how "hard" its obligation and its enforcement are: if there are no obligations and no enforcement, then it is merely politics; if at least one of them exists, it is soft law; if both exist and are "hard", it is hard law.[68]

Fabian Amtenbrink and René Repasi offer a third proposal based on the literature on compliance to assess how Member States adhere to or do not adhere to the rules and legal acts issued in the area of economic governance. According to the authors, compliance should be seen from a dual perspective in terms of the reasons for non-compliance, whether voluntary or involuntary. Subsequently, it becomes necessary to distinguish between the mode of enforcing compliance—whether top-down (through ex-ante persuasion, ex-post monitoring and sanctioning, or ex-ante or ex-post management) or bottom-up (through the internalization of behaviours).[69] Their perspective concentrates on the legal strength of rules, specifically from the standpoint of their enforcement.

None of these classifications is ideal, as some authors recognize,[70] given the heterogeneity of soft law acts and the variety of contexts, institutional practices, and purposes in which they are used. It is also challenging to measure the degree of how binding a legal instrument is, and to find definitive criteria to assert that force. Nevertheless, these classifications are helpful in that they deconstruct the various dimensions in which legal strength can be measured, thereby allowing for the creation of a framework to analyse the normative force of atypical rules and legal instruments.

All previously proposed frameworks share two fundamental elements for measuring legal strength, even if they are discussed in different terms: obligation and enforcement. Obligation concerns the command, the prescription of the legal instrument, and the *rule's internal dimension*. It pertains to the definition of the rule (the precision of the rule) and its purpose (the institutional, political, and social order

[66] Senden 2004, p. 266.

[67] Terpan 2015, p. 73.

[68] Ibid., 74.

[69] Amtenbrink and Repasi 2017, pp. 148–151. Dermine also proposes a set of criteria for considering a recommendation judicially reviewable under EU law that is generally similar to the frameworks proposed by the authors abovementioned, focusing on the elements of form, content and enforcement. See Dermine 2022b, pp. 222–231.

[70] Ibid. See Abbot et al. 2000, p. 403.

that it wishes to establish—its regulatory intent). The more specific and defined the obligation, the more binding the instrument. Obligation can be assessed by examining the practice and intention of the institutions that issue such acts. In terms of enforcement, a legal act will be more binding if it has a greater potential for enforcement, with non-compliance generating effects on the legal status of the act's addressee (*the external dimension of the rule*). The dimension of enforcement is measured considering the ability of the instrument to affect its addressees, that is, to incentivize or deter them from adopting a specific conduct. Enforcement can be assessed by examining the legal basis of the act and understanding how sanctions are activated.

An analysis of the legal strength of Council recommendations in economic governance procedures must take into account the dimensions of obligation and enforcement. This involves understanding how specific, defined, and precise (in sum, how "unequivocal") the prescriptions set out in the legal instruments are, in relation to the legal basis of the instruments, their text, and purpose; and examining the consequences for non-compliance, and the type of burden that it places on the legal status of the addressee. The burden is evaluated in terms of how weak (e.g., purely reputational) or strong (e.g., financial penalty or other types of sanctions) the negative consequence for the addressee is.

Moreover, it is also important to add a third element to the analytical framework: an empirical assessment of the practical effects of recommendations. In other words, an overview of how recommendations are implemented (in the case of CSRs), complied with, and enforced (in the case of EDP and EIP) by the Member States. This analysis provides insight into the perception in EU law practice of recommendations in the economic governance procedures and aids in analysing legal strength using this methodological framework.

4.3 The Legal Strength of Rules and Powers of EU Economic Governance Based on EU Sources

4.3.1 Obligations of Member States Under EU Primary Law

The constitutional basis of the EU consists of the TEU, the TFEU, and the Charter of Fundamental Rights. From a legal perspective, the Treaties are international law agreements signed by the Member States. These Treaties set forth a series of goals for the Member States and the EU institutions to pursue; these goals are subsequently translated into a normative system comprising rules and principles that Member States (and the EU institutions) must comply with. If the Member States fail to adhere to Treaty rules, the EU and other Member States are entitled to initiate infringement procedures that can result in a judicial case in the CJEU and the application of sanctions.

Concerning economic governance, the obligations for the Member States are set out in Article 120 TFEU, which cross-references Article 3 TEU and Article 119 TFEU. Accordingly, Member States shall conduct their respective economic policies to contribute to the achievement of the Union's goals, as stipulated in Article 3 TEU (general objectives of the EU), guided by the principles of an open market economy and free competition. Moreover, Member States must coordinate their economic policies, observing guiding principles such as stable prices, sound public finances and monetary conditions, and a sustainable balance of payments. They should also favour efficient resource allocation.

The legal strength of these provisions is somewhat limited. There is not a normative commitment but merely a political one; in other words, there is not a legal obligation, only a statement of duty to pursue social and economic goals while adhering to general economic policy orientations. Primacy in matters of economic and fiscal policy remains with the Member States; their commitment to the EU is limited to a best-effort duty of conforming to the EU's economic benchmarks. The degree of obligation is imprecise due to the aspirational character of political and technical concepts such as "price stability", "sustainable balance of payments", and "free competition". Member States are obligated not to become "closed economies" with stringent protectionist policies, but apart from that, there is a considerable degree of political and legal discretion available.

The coordination of economic policies in the Council (as set out in Article 121 TFEU) does not encompass any legal obligation. There is no legal duty to follow the BEPGs issued by the Council—they are formally non-binding acts. In substance, they establish broad and general policy objectives that the EU recommends the Member States to pursue, making the obligation imprecise.[71] There is no normative character to such acts, just a best-effort duty to comply with them. Regarding enforcement, there is no "hard" mechanism for sanctioning non-compliance. If national economic policies diverge from the BEPGs, the Council can issue a recommendation to that state and make it public, potentially prompting market pressure from other states and market actors. However, recent developments in secondary law have established some legal obligations of disclosure within the SGP during the European Semester. These will be discussed further below.

The only explicit obligation of EU economic governance set in EU primary law pertains to the rules on balanced budgets and fiscal discipline. As per Article 126 TFEU, Member States must avoid excessive deficits, i.e., they should not diverge from the reference values of 3% for the deficit to GDP ratio and 60% for the debt to GDP ratio. The obligation is clear: there is a normative duty, not just a best-efforts duty. However, exceptions are allowed based on the fulfilment of one of three criteria: the excessive deficit must be decreasing both substantially and continuously and remain close to the reference value; the excessive deficit must be temporary or exceptional and stay close to the reference value; and the excessive debt level must

[71] Hodson 2011, pp. 78–91; Deroose et al. 2005, pp. 8–10.

be decreasing significantly.[72] These criteria—"exceptional", "temporary", "significantly", and "substantively and continuously"—are somewhat indeterminate and require the application of external interpretative criteria. Therefore, EU institutions (legislative, executive, or judicial) must provide an interpretation of their meaning to increase the norm's precision and its application's predictability.

Regulation 1467/1997 in the SGP, which was reformed in 2005, 2011 and 2024, provided some definitions. According to this provision, a deficit is considered exceptional when provoked by an "exceptional circumstances outside the control of the government" or when caused by a severe economic downturn.[73] Conversely, a deficit is deemed temporary if the Commission estimates that by the end of the exceptional event, the deficit will return to levels within the reference value.[74] As for a "significant decrease" in excessive debt, it means that the Member State is respecting the net expenditure path set by the Council under article 17 of Regulation 2024/1263 of the European Parliament and the Council.[75] Moreover, when preparing a report on the existence of an excessive deficit, the Commission must assess all relevant economic and fiscal dynamics and developments concerning the Member States (such as the enactment of structural reforms), as well as consider their opinions and concerns.[76]

Legal fulfilment of the criteria in the SGP did not eliminate the indeterminacy of some of its elements. For instance, it remains unclear what constitutes an "unusual and uncontrollable" event. At the same time, the SGP heavily relies on the Commission's forecasts on the evolution of the economic elements of the Member States. Depending on these forecasts, an exception to the EDP might be granted.[77] The Vade Mecum serves as an auxiliary document, applying rules and procedures laid down in primary and secondary legislation, thereby providing a measure of clarity and stability—i.e., a degree of precision. However, the Vade Mecum is a complex and potentially confusing document[78] that the Commission can modify at its discretion, as has occurred in the past.[79] Furthermore, the Commission issued a communication on flexibility within the SGP, which contributes to the confusion and subjectivity of

[72] Article 127(2)(a) and (b) TFEU.

[73] Article 2(1) of Regulation 1467/97 of the Council. See also Article 25 of Regulation 2024/1263 of the European Parliament and of the Council.

[74] Ibid.

[75] Article 2(1a) of Regulation 1467/97 of the Council.

[76] Articles 2(2) of Regulation 1467/97 of the Council.

[77] Ibid., Article 2(3) and (4).

[78] Ilzetzki 2021.

[79] The Vade Mecum was published in 2013 and yearly editions were published until 2019.

the rules.[80] Thus, the Commission enjoys a considerable degree of discretion in evaluating the circumstances of Member States under the EDP rules and in determining when an excessive deficit (or its risk) exists.

4.3.2 Obligations of the Member States Under EU Secondary Law

4.3.2.1 Acts of a General Nature

Secondary norms discussed in this subsection concern binding legal acts as established in Article 288 TFEU: regulations, directives, and decisions (the latter of a general scope).[81] Secondary law acts are presumed to be formally binding unless their provisions state otherwise.[82] Non-compliance with these acts can lead to an action for infringement against the non-compliant Member State, the potential consequences of which, if convicted, include the imposition of a fine.

The TFEU provides two legal bases for EU institutions to enact legal acts in the area of economic governance: Article 121(6) and Article 136(1). These acts have been analysed in Chap. 3, in the discussion concerning the scope of EU competence in economic governance. It is sufficient to say that both articles allow the EU to enact binding acts (decisions, regulations, and directives in the case of Article 121, and similarly under Article 136). Although their scope cannot exceed what is considered coordination (i.e., they cannot dictate Member State policy), the acts and powers that can be created bear strong normative force from a formal perspective. Non-compliance with such acts can therefore lead, in practice, to actions for infringement—for instance, failure to fulfil duties set out in the norms, such as the submission of stability programs.

In preventive supervision, Member States are required to define and submit their national medium-term fiscal-structural plan during the European Semester.[83] Member States must ensure that their budgetary procedures align with the rules and acts issued within the economic governance framework and must communicate to EU institutions their draft budget plan, their national medium-term fiscal plans, and their national reform plans. In the ABF, Member States must adopt or finalize their

---

[80] European Commission (2015) Communication From The Commission To The European Parliament, The Council, The European Central Bank, The Economic And Social Committee, The Committee Of The Regions And The European Investment Bank: Making the Best Use of the Flexibility Within the Existing Rules of the Stability and Growth Pact, available at https://eur-lex.europa.eu/legal-content/EN/TXT/PDF/?uri=CELEX:52015DC0012&qid=1428419309956&from=EN accessed 15 august 2025. On the confusing and subjective character of the framework, see Thygesen et al. 2018.

[81] On the division between decisions that are individual-scope or decisions that are general-scope acts see Schütze 2016, pp. 93–95.

[82] Ibid., pp. 90–93.

[83] Article 11 of Regulation 2024/1263 of the European Parliament and the Council.

budget for the upcoming year no later than 31 December (which can be extended if objective requirements are not met).[84] The draft budget plan must align with the recommendations issued under the SGP and the MSP, and include the information requested by Regulation 473/2013.[85] Member States subject to enhanced supervision under Regulation 472/2013 must comply with additional reporting and disclosure obligations.[86] Lastly, Member States are required to have independent fiscal bodies to monitor compliance with numerical fiscal rules.[87]

Secondary legislation also establishes legal obligations for Member States within the EDP and the new supervisory procedure for macroeconomic imbalances. In the EDP, Member States with an excessive deficit must submit a report detailing actions taken to correct the situation, and an economic partnership program adhering to the guidelines set by Regulation 473/2013.[88] Moreover, Member States under the EDP must report budgetary execution and development to the Commission and the Economic and Financial Committee.[89] Concerning the EIP, a Member State subject to it must submit a corrective action plan under the terms set in Regulation 1176/2011 to the Commission and the Council.[90]

Does secondary legislation create new obligations for the Member States beyond those established in primary law? It appears that the legal obligations defined by EU secondary law are essentially procedural obligations that supplement the norms of EU primary law without imposing new economic and budgetary targets on Member States. Secondary law rules primarily establish duties concerning manner, timing, and conditions for submitting information. Such obligations are essentially expansions of the general duties established in primary law regarding collaboration in defining economic policy and multilateral surveillance. The EIP acts as a warning system that does not inherently create any obligations for Member States. Therefore, these secondary law acts neither limit nor infringe upon the budgetary autonomy of Member States; they merely establish procedural standards for consultation among Member States and enhance the EU's oversight capacity for budgetary development.

Within the procedures of economic definition, EU institutions issue BEPGs, non-binding acts of a general nature. These do not impose specific obligations but set broad objectives and goals (e.g., "[improve] framework conditions and [ensure] that companies operate in a sufficiently competitive and attractive environment"), and the language is non-prescriptive ("Member States *should*…").[91] Moreover, there is no

---

[84] Article 4(3) of Regulation 473/2013 of the European Parliament and the Council.

[85] Article 6(1) of Regulation 473/2013 of the European Parliament and the Council.

[86] Article 3(2) of Regulation 472/2013 of the European Parliament and the Council.

[87] Article 5(1) of Regulation 473/2013 of the European Parliament and the Council.

[88] Article 9 of Regulation 473/2013 of the European Parliament and the Council.

[89] Article 10(3) of Regulation 473/2013 of the European Parliament and the Council.

[90] Article 8(1) of Regulation 1176/2011 of the European Parliament and the Council.

[91] The examples are taken form the BEPGs of 2008–2010. Council (2008) Recommendation of 14 May 2008 on the broad economic policy guidelines for the Member States and the Community (2008–2010) available at https://eur-lex.europa.eu/legal-content/EN/TXT/PDF/?uri=CELEX:32008H0390&from=EN accessed 15 August 2025.

enforcement mechanism to review Member States' implementation of the BEPGs. The Commission and the Council must assess the compatibility of stability programs with the BEPGs within the MSP and the ABF, but there are no sanctions for deviations from the targets. While the Commission can issue a warning and the Council may opt to make a recommendation to the respective Member State public, there are no further consequences.

4.3.2.2 Acts of an Individual Nature

Acts Enacted in the Procedures of Economic Policy Definition

There are two individual acts issued in the procedures of economic policy definition: warnings to Member States whose economic policies are incompatible with the Broad Economic Policy Guidelines (BEPGs), and individual decisions taken by the Council pursuant to article 136(1) of the TFEU. The significance of warnings and their legal strength were discussed earlier, as were the individual decisions issued under article 136(1) TFEU (for instance, in the context of the EFSF). While Article 136(1) TFEU empowers the Council to enact formally binding acts with a high degree of formal legal obligation, the Council's powers are, in essence, confined to coordination measures.

Acts Enacted in the Procedures of Economic Policy Supervision

EU institutions can make individual decisions in supervisory procedures. For example, the Council can decide on the existence of an excessive deficit or an economic imbalance and can decide on the application of sanctions for failure to correct economic imbalances,[92] or excessive deficit.[93] The Council can also decide on the application of sanctions concerning statistical manipulation.[94] Concerning the ESP, the Commission can decide whether to subject a Member State to enhanced surveillance. Individual decisions produce legal effects on their addressees, and their legal strength is considerable.

The issue of recommendations enacted in supervisory procedures, both corrective and preventive, presents a more complex analysis. The functions of such recommendations vary depending on the procedure in which they are issued, affecting their degree of obligation and enforcement capacity. Hence, the following subsections

[92] Article 3 of Regulation 1174/2011 of the European Parliament and the Council.

[93] Article 5(1) and 6(1) 1173/2011 of the European Parliament and the Council.

[94] Article 8(1) 1173/2011 of the European Parliament and the Council.

examine the legal strengths of recommendations within different supervisory procedures, using recommendations issued to Portugal within the MSP (between 2014 and 2019)[95] and the EDP (between 2009 and 2016)[96] as examples.

Council Recommendations Issued in the MSP

The MSP serves two intertwined objectives: to coordinate the economic situation of Member States for the creation of a common economic policy and to manage and control potential deviations from the goals, principles, and rules of EU economic coordination, as well as targets outlined in the economic programs submitted in the Semester and approved by EU institutions. In other words, the MSP has both a coordination and a prevention function. In the MSP, the Council may issue CSRs.

From 2014 to 2019, the CSRs addressed to Portugal included, on average, around five sub-recommendations each, primarily composed of policy targets. These targets ranged from specific measures such as, "[f]urther improve the evaluation of the housing market, including by setting up, by the end of 2014, a more systematic monitoring and reporting framework and issue a comprehensive report on the shadow economy",[97] to broad objectives like, "[i]mprove the efficiency of public employment services"[98] or "[s]tep up efforts to clean up the balance sheets of credit institutions (…)".[99] Quantitative targets, such as to "[e]nsure that the nominal growth rate of net primary government expenditure does not exceed 0,7 % in 2019, corresponding to an annual structural adjustment of 0,6 % of GDP",[100] were seldom set.[101] The CSRs also suggested the adoption of conducts, usually as a mean to achieve a given target,

---

[95] This timeframe was chosen because the first CSRs issued to Portugal (between 2011 and 2013) only recommended the implementation of Council Implementing Decision 2011/344/EU of 30 May 2011 on granting Union financial assistance to Portugal [2011] OJ L 159/88; from 2014 onward, CSRs started to cover other policy areas than the areas covered by the conditions of the program of financial assistance.

[96] This refers to the last EDP open against Portugal, closed in 2017; documentation is available here: https://economy-finance.ec.europa.eu/economic-and-fiscal-governance/stability-and-growth-pact/corrective-arm-excessive-deficit-procedure/closed-excessive-deficit-procedures/portugal_en accessed 15 august 2025.

[97] Council Recommendation 2014/C of 8 July 2014 on the National Reform Program 2014 of Portugal and delivering a Council opinion on the Stability Program of Portugal, 2014 [2014] OJ C 247/20, 107.

[98] Council Recommendation 2015/C of 14 July 2015 on the 2015 National Reform Program of Portugal and delivering a Council opinion on the 2015 Stability Program of Portugal [2015] OJ C 272/94, 97.

[99] Council Recommendation 2017/C of 11 July 2017 on the 2017 National Reform Programme of Portugal and delivering a Council opinion on the 2017 Stability Programme of Portugal [2017] OJ C 261/21, 107.

[100] Council Recommendation 2018/C of 13 July 2018 on the 2018 National Reform Programme of Portugal and delivering a Council opinion on the 2018 Stability Programme of Portugal [2018] OJ C 320/21, 96.

[101] Only the CSRs of 2018 and 2015 recommended the achievement of quantitative targets. The other CSRs—2014, 2016, 2017 and 2019—set only qualitative targets.

such as "[u]se windfall gains to accelerate the reduction of the general government debt ratio".[102]

Generally, recommended targets and conduct for the addressed State were aspirational and broad, such as "ensure that the minimum wage is consistent with the objectives of promoting employment and competitiveness across sectors",[103] or "[i]mprove the quality and labour-market relevance of the education system".[104] Yet, at times, they were quite precise, stipulating targets such as "[a]chieve the medium-term budgetary objective in 2020".[105] Furthermore, they would encompass several measures to be adopted.[106] The precision of the obligation varied across and within CSRs, and identical recommendations appeared in different CSRs.[107]

In terms of sanctions, Article 4(3) of Regulation 2024/1263 stipulates that failure by Member States to comply with recommendations and guidance on fiscal policy can lead to measures under the EDP and the EIP. Article 6(1) of Regulation 473/2013 further reinforces this obligation for Eurozone Member States, stating that their budgets must be consistent with the recommendations issued under the SGP. However, practice has shown that the repercussions of non-compliance, such as issuing further recommendations and warnings, are relatively mild from a legal perspective, leading primarily to reputational damage and political pressure.

What then, is the legal strength of CSRs? It is difficult to determine, given the variety of measures and their differing levels of precision. From an intent perspective, *the recommendations function as guiding instruments meant to influence rather than dictate* policy change. Some policy targets and measures are unambiguously defined, while others are not. Regarding enforcement, violations of CSRs do not result in financial sanctions, only administrative responses, such as further recommendations and warnings. Hence, it is fair to conclude that CSRs possess a weak legal force and do not bind the Member States due to the variable precision of their obligations and the non-stringent sanctions in place.

This perspective is supported by practical evidence. Assessing how effectively Member States implement recommendations can be challenging,[108] as many of the

---

[102] Council Recommendation 2018/C of 13 July 2018 on the 2018 National Reform Programme of Portugal and delivering a Council opinion on the 2018 Stability Programme of Portugal [2018] OJ C 320/21.

[103] Council Recommendation 2016/C of 12 July 2016 on the 2016 National Reform Programme of Portugal and delivering a Council opinion on the 2016 Stability Programme of Portugal [2016] OJ C 299/26, 113.

[104] Council Recommendation 2014/C of 8 July 2014 on the National Reform Program 2014 of Portugal and delivering a Council opinion on the Stability Program of Portugal, 2014 [2014] OJ C 247/20.

[105] Council Recommendation 2019/C of 9 July 2018 on the 2019 National Reform Programme of Portugal and delivering a Council opinion on the 2019 Stability Programme of Portugal [2019] OJ C 301/22, 134.

[106] This CSR included many measures, given that it was the first CSR addressed to the State after the period of financial assistance.

[107] For example, policies on the consistency of the minimum wage with employment promotion in the CSRs of 2014, 2015 and 2016.

[108] Alcidi and Gros 2017, p. 7.

targets and measures are broadly defined, policy assessment tends to be more qualitative than quantitative, and certain measures and targets need longer timeframes to be fully realized. Nonetheless, contributions from EGOV[109] and independent policy research centres such as Bruegel,[110] CEPS[111] and ETUI[112] provide insightful data and valuable assessments on how Member States receive recommendations.

The consensus[113] from these studies is that the implementation of CSRs is relatively low among Member States and has been declining since 2012. Implementation rates differ significantly not only among Member States but also among policy areas. The reasons posited for this low implementation rate are primarily political, with Member States resisting EU interference in their national matters,[114] particularly in politically sensitive areas such as social policy, which includes pension and employment reforms.[115] It appears that recommendations are more frequently implemented when Member States are experiencing economic downturns: the better the economic situation, the lower the implementation rates.[116] Cinzia Alcidi and Daniel Gros also propose a reason for the low implementation of CSRs, pointing out the lack of coercive mechanisms to enforce them.[117] These findings align with the jurisprudential analysis of this form of legal action.

Council Recommendations Issued in the EDP

The aim of the EDP is to correct a deviation from the deficit rules. Recommendations in this procedure are issued after the Council has determined that an excessive deficit exists, and the deviating Member States must take measures to rectify it.[118] The purpose of EDP recommendations is corrective.

EDP recommendations addressed to Portugal contained several numerical targets related to budget and structural deficits.[119] They also incorporated a blend of numerical targets and policy measures to achieve those targets. For instance:

> [taking] additional measures worth 0,3 % of GDP to confine the deficit to 5,0 % of GDP [that] include freezing some of the 2012 budget appropriations for investment projects not yet initiated, raising stamp duties on high-value properties and tax rates on investment income,

[109] Angerer et al. 2020. Information available regards only the CSRs for 2019, since no report regarding the implementation of the CSRs for 2020 and 2021 has been published—see Angerer and Grigaitė 2021, p. 2. See also, recently, Mariotto 2022, pp. 40–57.

[110] Efstathiou and Wolff 2019.

[111] Alcidi and Gros 2017.

[112] Al-Kadi and Clauwaert 2019.

[113] See, with other views, Bockhorst 2022; Eihmanis 2023, p. 296.

[114] Alcidi and Gros 2017, p. 5.

[115] Al-Kadi and Clauwaert 2019, p. 8.

[116] Efstathiou and Wolff 2019, p. 13.

[117] Alcidi and Gros 2017, p. 8.

[118] Article 126 TFEU.

[119] For this purpose, Council Recommendations of 30 November 2009, 2 October 2012 and 18 June 2013 with a view to bringing an end to the situation of an excessive government deficit in Portugal [2009], [2012] and [2013] were considered.

> frontloading some of the 2013 budget measures to reduce social benefits and applying other measures generating savings in intermediate consumption and revenue from sales.[120]

In the EDP recommendations issued to Portugal, there were also some general policy targets, like "streamlining and modernizing public administration, addressing redundancies across public sector functions and entities, improving the sustainability of the pension system (...)".[121] However, generally, measures were quite specific and well-defined, with measures set to achieve numerical objectives (e.g., level of debt and deficit reduction, cost of measures to be taken).

Given that most of the targets outlined in these EDP recommendations are quantitative, the obligations are precise and carry a high degree of normative strength. The strategies to achieve the targets are typically well-defined and specific. The drafters' intent is also clearly expressed in each recommendation's first subsection: the addressed Member State should rectify the excessive deficit situation within a predefined timeframe. Failure to rectify the excessive deficit can lead to a Council decision of non-compliance and the implementation of the following sanctions: publication of additional information before issuing bonds and securities (reputational sanction); re-evaluation of lending policy with the European Investment Bank (reputational/financial sanction); non-interest-bearing deposit and an annual fine (financial sanctions); and partial or total suspension of payments from European Structural Investment ("ESI") Funds.[122]

In terms of obligation criteria, the legal strength of EDP recommendations is considerable; targets and measures are unequivocally defined. The same holds true for the enforcement criteria, given the pressure put on a non-compliant Member State. Therefore, the overall legal strength of EDP recommendations is high.

However, it is unclear what exactly triggers the sanction. Is it non-compliance with the recommendation itself or the failure to rectify the excessive deficit? A literal interpretation of the TFEU indicates it is the latter. Policy recommendations are crucial in aiding the Member State comply with the deficit rules established in the Treaties and the SGP. This was evident in Council Decision 2016/1230, which found that Portugal had not taken measures to correct the excessive deficit. In that decision, the Council acknowledged Portugal's efforts to comply with policy targets but observed that numerical targets concerning deficit reduction were not met. The Council therefore concluded that "[t]he fiscal effort falls significantly short of what was recommended by the Council".[123] This statement reinforces the idea that EDP recommendations are post-legal, not para-legal, acts and serve to reinforce the hard law rules established in the Treaty.

[120] Council Recommendation of 2 October 2012, 14.

[121] Council Recommendation of 18 June 2013, 14.

[122] 126(11) TFEU and Article 23(9) of Regulation 1033/2013 of the European Parliament and of the Council.

[123] Council Decision 2016/1230, of 12 July 2016 establishing that no effective action has been taken by Portugal in response to the Council recommendation of 21 June 2013 [2016] OJ L 202/21.

Given that the excessive deficit rule is mandatory and unambiguous, recommendations serve to bolster the obligations outlined in the Treaties.[124] Therefore, in theory, Member States could choose not to follow the suggested targets and measures and still evade sanctions, if deficit correction is achieved. However, rectifying an excessive deficit without implementing some of the recommended measures or targets could prove challenging. It is also worth noting that sanctions are not automatically imposed:[125] the Council must decide that failure to take corrective action has occurred before implementing penalties. The introduction of reversed qualified voting for the application of sanctions may have diluted the Council's decision-making power, but it does not make the implementation of sanctions automatic.[126] Therefore, the question of causality becomes irrelevant because the decision to implement the sanction procedure will always depend on what the Council deems reasonable.

Compliance with EDP recommendations can then be assessed in two seemingly contradictory ways—a sort of "glass half full/empty" duality. The first is that fiscal discipline rules have been violated, given the number of EDPs initiated. The second is that currently, there are no open EDPs,[127] which suggests that when Member States have breached fiscal discipline rules, they have taken action to correct the situation and reverse the trajectory of deviation, at least to a level acceptable to the Council. Thus, considering that the primary objective of these instruments is to guide Member States to rectify excessive deficits, it is plausible to assert that the degree of compliance with EDP recommendations is high.

Enforcement comes into play when Member States fail to take corrective action, or when the action taken is insufficient, potentially leading to sanctions. The four known cases where the sanction application was considered involved Germany and France[128] first, and then Portugal and Spain.[129] In none of these cases sanctions were applied, primarily due to political reasons as the decision to impose sanctions lies within the Council's discretion. The closest instance of nearly applying EDP sanctions was with Hungary in 2012, where a freeze on the country's cohesion funds was contemplated but ultimately did not take place.

This reliance on political procedure may cast doubt on the effectiveness of enforcing corrective measures: Member States might believe that they can evade penalties for non-compliance with Treaty rules through political negotiations. Nonetheless, the threat of sanction enforcement does concern some (typically smaller) Member States. For example, in the previously mentioned SCC case, Slovenia's National Assembly argued for the importance of EDP recommendations,

---

[124] Poiares Maduro et al. 2017, p. 24.

[125] Amtenbrink and Repasi 2017, p. 162.

[126] Palmstorfer 2014, p. 188.

[127] According to the Commission, the number closed from 24 to none in eight years. Currently there is an EDP open against Romania. The data is available at https://ec.europa.eu/info/business-economy-euro/economic-and-fiscal-policy-coordination/eu-economic-governance-monitoring-prevention-correction/stability-and-growth-pact/corrective-arm-excessive-deficit-procedure/excessive-deficit-procedures-overview_en accessed 5 June 2023.

[128] Palmstorfer 2014, pp. 190–191.

[129] Leino and Saarenheimo 2016, p. 13.

citing the potential risk to the state's financial credibility should it fail to take corrective action and thus be subject to EDP sanctions.[130] Therefore, at least in some Member States, there is an understanding that non-compliance with EDP rules and recommendations can lead to unfavourable outcomes.

Council Recommendations Issued in the EIP

The primary objective of the EIP is to rectify excessive economic imbalances. Once the Council identifies an imbalance, it issues a recommendation proposing corrective measures to the impacted Member State.[131] The Council declares the imbalance in a recommendation, not a decision as in the EDP. The onus then lies with the affected Member State to present a corrective action plan, which the Council approves in another recommendation.[132] Recommendations are also issued when an affected Member State fails to enact corrective action after the plan's approval.[133] In such scenarios, the Council decides that there has been non-compliance with the suggested corrective action and sets deadlines for the Member State to rectify the situation.

At this point, no EIP has been initiated by EU institutions. As a result, there are no recommendations to analyse or assess in terms of how suggestions and targets are drafted. An interesting question that arises pertains to the potential precision of these guidelines, given the broad legal definition of what constitutes an economic imbalance, defined merely as any macroeconomic event or trend that negatively affects, or can affect, the normal functioning of national economies, EMU, or the EU.[134] Reference to the indicative thresholds of the economic indicators from the AMR[135] can provide clarity on the concept. Given the reliance on numerical indicators like the AMR, it is reasonable to assume that the content of EIP recommendations will mirror that of recommendations issued in the EDP and primarily consist of numerical targets and policy measures aimed at reaching those targets. The precision of their obligation remains to be seen; if it follows the precedent set by the EDP, it will be high.[136]

Sanctions in the EIP apply when Member States fail twice to submit a corrective action plan, and when, after the adoption of the corrective plan, Member States fail to comply with the action suggested by the Council.[137] Sanctions range from an interest-bearing deposit to an annual fine (if non-compliance is recurrent). Since

---

[130] Bardutzky 2016, p. 26.

[131] Article 7(2) of Regulation 1176/2011 of the European Parliament and of the Council.

[132] Ibid., Article 8(2).

[133] Ibid., Article 10(4).

[134] Ibid., Article 2.

[135] Ibid., Articles 3 and 4.

[136] See Dermine 2022b, p. 220.

[137] Article 3 of Regulation 1174/2011 of the European Parliament and of the Council. It is also applicable in these situations Article 23(9) of Regulation 1033/2013 of the European Parliament and the Council of 17 December 2013 laying down common provisions on the European Regional Development Fund, the European Social Fund, the Cohesion Fund, the European Agricultural Fund for Rural Development and the European Maritime and Fisheries Fund and laying down general provisions on the European Regional Development Fund, the European Social Fund, the Cohesion

the imposition of sanctions is directly connected with compliance with Council-recommended action and involves a financial penalty, the legal strength of the EIP recommendations, like in the EDP procedure, is high.

Council Recommendations Issued Under the ESP

The goal of the ESP is to bolster the supervision of Member States whose financial stability is threatened.[138] In the ESP, the Council issues recommendations when, following review missions conducted by the Commission to a Member State facing financial difficulties, further measures are necessary to avert adverse effects on the financial stability of the euro area or the Member States.[139] The recommendation may suggest that the surveilled Member State either adopt precautionary corrective measures or prepare a draft MEAP.

As of today, no recommendation has been issued in this procedure, making it impossible to evaluate the legal strength regarding obligation. However, considering enforcement, no sanctioning mechanisms are currently in force, which implies that the legal strength of the instrument is weak or non-existent.

4.3.2.3 Acts Enacted in the Procedures of Economic Policy Assistance

Acts issued in procedures of economic assistance consist of those enacted by the EFSM. The EFSM aids Member States in financial distress through a loan or a credit line. This mechanism can be activated by a Member State requesting the Commission and subsequently developing an adjustment program. The Council must approve the plan, doing so by issuing an implementing decision, which establishes the general economic conditions for the disbursement of financial assistance. The Commission and the Member State then negotiate a MoU detailing the economic policy conditions to be adopted. The Commission disburses the loan in instalments, according to the degree of compliance with the conditions set in the Council's decision. Access to a credit line also depends on the Commission's verification of the implementation of conditions by the Member State.

Conditions for the provision of financial assistance include obligations for fiscal consolidation of a specific value, commitments to enact policy reforms in certain sectors, such as the energy market, or implement labour market reforms.[140] Additionally, policy targets are set annually, encompassing duties to reduce fiscal expenditure and improve fiscal income, with measures addressing specific areas of state

Fund and the European Maritime and Fisheries Fund and repealing Council Regulation (EC) No 1083/2006 on suspension of ESI Funds.

[138] Article 2(1) of Regulation 472/2013 of the European Parliament and the Council.

[139] Ibid., Article 3(7).

[140] This work analyses the implementing decisions addressed to the two Member States assisted by the EFSM, Portugal and Ireland. See Council Implementing Decision 2011/77/EU of 7 December 2010 on granting Union financial assistance to Ireland [2011] OJ L 30/34 and Council Implementing Decision 2011/344/EU of 30 May 2011 on granting Union financial assistance to Portugal [2011] OJ L 159/88.

competence and organization such as the distribution of local administrative units like parishes and municipalities.

From a substantive perspective, the obligations set in the Council's implementing decisions approving assistance under the EFSM are generally precise and clear. Some are obligations of result, while others are obligations of means, such as the obligation to act upon a specific area or pursue a broadly defined policy objective. These targets must be achieved within a specified timeframe. The formulation of the conditions is also prescriptive: the assisted Member State "shall adopt the following measures". In the case of Portugal, there were prescriptive statements demanding the elimination of regulated tariffs in electricity and gas retail markets,[141] while for Ireland there were prescriptive statements calling for "a 10 % pay reduction for new entrants to the public service".[142]

From a legal standpoint, one might question the degree of obligation to which Member States are subjected. The Council's decision approving the plan is a binding act, as stipulated by Article 288 TFEU. Moreover, the CJEU has recently affirmed[143] that MoUs signed within the scope of the EFSM are acts of EU law.[144] Non-compliance can consequently lead to an infringement procedure for failure to uphold EU law. This procedure can ultimately result in an action in the CJEU and the imposition of financial penalties. Hence, there is a stringent sanction for non-compliant entities. However, the question remains whether the reliance on the Commission's discretionary initiative might impact on the effectiveness of infringement procedures as mechanisms of EU law enforcement.[145]

4.4 The Legal Strength of Rules and Powers of EU Economic Governance Based on International Law Sources

4.4.1 Obligations for Member States Under the TSGC Framework

The TSGC is an international treaty to which all EU Member States, except for the Czech Republic, have agreed. This Treaty strives to augment the economic framework of the EMU by setting new rules for signatory States to adhere to in the realm of economic governance. The Treaty emerged as a second-best solution; the original

---

[141] Article 3(6)(o) of Council Implementing Decision 2011/344/EU.

[142] Article 3(7)(a) of Council Implementing Decision 2011/77/EU.

[143] On the erratic jurisprudence of the CJEU concerning the application of EU law to financial assistance programs, see Lucas Pires 2022; Pereira Coutinho 2016. See also Violante 2023, pp. 240–266.

[144] CJEU, BPC Lux 2 Sàrl and others v. Banco de Portugal and others, 2022, Case C-83, para 30.

[145] See Variu 2012, pp. 400–420.

intention was to amend the Treaties, but the United Kingdom's resistance made this route unfeasible.[146] The Treaty's formal disconnection from the EU legal order positions it more akin to a "shareholders' agreement", that is, a system of rules of international law signed by joint enterprise parties dictating their actions and behaviour within the EMU legal framework.[147]

The primary obligation is stipulated in Article 3 of the TSCG. Signatory States are required to enact, preferably in constitutional law form, rules necessitating States to adhere to fiscal discipline: duties to maintain balanced budgets (with limited exceptions and deviations) and activate "correction mechanisms" in case of significant deviations from balanced budget targets.

The other provisions of the TSGC establish new rules concerning the execution of the EDP.[148] Such obligations for signatory States encompass duties regarding the speed of debt reduction, the requirement to present an economic partnership program featuring structural reforms, and duties to support the Commission when it deems that a State has an excessive deficit. The remaining obligations that signatory States must adhere to under the TSGC pertain to the duty to disclose future debt issuances and future significant national reforms to other contracting parties, as well as a very general duty to "work jointly towards an economic policy that fosters the proper functioning of the economic and monetary union and economic growth through enhanced convergence and competitiveness".[149]

The normative force of the obligations of the TSGC is, from the perspective of its internal dimension, high. Obligations are precise and clear, except for the very open and general coordination obligations in Article 9. From a formal perspective, since it is an international law agreement, non-compliance with its terms incurs State liability.[150] No formal dispute resolution mechanism is established in the Treaty for non-adherence to its obligations. However, one exception exists concerning non-compliance with Article 3 TSCG. If a signatory State fails to incorporate the golden rule into its national law, another signatory State can bring the matter before the CJEU, which will render a binding decision and can impose fines if the State continues to disregard the law enactment.[151] The latest assessment, from 2017, reported that all signatory States, except Spain, were adhering to the TSGC on this issue.[152]

Because of the lack of mechanisms for dispute resolution, the normative force of obligations for Member States, beyond the obligation of Article 3 TSCG, is low from an external perspective. Member States may face soft sanctions via retaliation

---

146 Peers 2012, pp. 405–407.

147 Rosas 2011, pp. 1318–1320.

148 Articles 4–7 TSCG.

149 Article 9 TSCG.

150 International Law Commission's Draft Articles on Responsibility of States for Internationally Wrongful Acts (2001), available at https://legal.un.org/ilc/texts/instruments/english/draft_articles/9_6_2001.pdf accessed 15 August 2025 and Chen 2015, pp. 497–508.

151 Article 8(1) and (2) TSGC.

152 European Commission (2017) The Fiscal Compact: Taking Stock available at https://ec.europa.eu/info/sites/default/files/c20171201_en.pdf accessed 15 August 2025.

by the contracting States, but there is no legal sanction for failure to comply with the TSCG's coordination obligations.

4.4.2 Obligations for the Member States Under the ESM Framework

The ESM assists Eurozone Member States experiencing financial distress. In some respects, it parallels the IMF's function as a stability instrument. The "shareholders" of this mechanism (Eurozone Member States) are represented in the Board of Governors by their respective finance ministers (exemplifying the *de facto* power of the Eurogroup within financial assistance procedures), and in the Board of Directors, as each country's governor appoints one director. Assistance is invariably conditional on the adoption of specific fiscal policy measures approved by the ESM.[153]

A contracting party (i.e., Eurozone Member States) facing financial difficulties must request assistance from the Board of Governors.[154] The Board of Governors will then solicit an assessment of the State's situation from the Commission and the ECB before deciding. If it offers stability support, the Board of Governors will task the Commission and the ECB with negotiating a MoU of policy conditions with the Member State.[155] Simultaneously, the ESM's Managing Director will prepare a draft facility agreement establishing the specific form of support (precautionary credit line, assistance for the re-capitalization of financial institutions, loans, and bond purchases in primary and secondary markets). After the Board of Governors approves the MoU and the Board of Directors approves the draft facility agreement, the ESM signs both documents. In the case of the MoU, the Commission represents the ESM in the signature, according to article 13(4) TESM, while for the facility agreement the signatory is the Managing Director. The ESM and the beneficiary Member State also sign the General Terms for ESM Financial Assistance Facility Agreements and the Standard Facility Specific Terms for ESM Financial Assistance.[156]

Additionally, the beneficiary Member State must prepare a MEAP whenever it seeks financial assistance from the ESM.[157] It falls to the Commission to ensure that such a program is entirely consistent with the MoU signed with the ESM.

---

[153] Articles 3 and 12(1) TESM.

[154] Article 13(1) TESM.

[155] Articles 5(6)(g) and 13(3) TESM.

[156] See ESM (2015) General Terms for ESM Financial Assistance Facility Agreements, available at https://www.esm.europa.eu/sites/default/files/general_terms_15122015_clean.pdf accessed 15 August 2025, and ESM (2015) Standard Facility Specific Terms for ESM Financial Assistance available at https://www.esm.europa.eu/sites/default/files/facility_specific_terms_15122015_clean.pdf accessed 15 August 2025.

[157] Article 7 of Regulation 472/2013 of the European Parliament and the Council.

According to the General Terms and the facility agreement, the assistance provided hinges on the beneficiary's compliance with the obligations stipulated in the MoU.[158] Thus, financial assistance from the ESM takes the form of a credit agreement governed by international law, as per the General Terms.[159] This approach contrasts with the IMF's structure, where financial assistance comprises a decision by the Executive Board of the Fund approving financial assistance measures and enabling the State to draw funds from the IMF in instalments.[160] There is no contractual link between providing assistance and fulfilling normative conditions such as default conditions. As Francisco Pereira Coutinho analogizes, the IMF MoU is akin to "a letter to Santa".[161] If a beneficiary State fails to meet the conditions, the IMF discontinues access to the Fund's credit line or resources, but no contractual liability ensues.[162] This scenario differs from that of the ESM system, where an agreement exists; failure to adhere to the obligations set therein can lead to contractual liability consequences for the defaulting party, such as compensation and assistance termination.

The MoU outlines the obligations for Member States. In the MoU signed between Cyprus and the ESM,[163] the conditions for assistance relate to the implementation of policy measures within specific timeframes. The beneficiary Member State must adopt measures touching on various policy areas, including welfare, pensions, tourism, housing, and public partnership programs. Numerous conditions concern the adoption of fiscal policy and structural policy measures that are precise and clear, with the intent being prescriptive ("measures will be adopted"). Consider, for example, the details of the health policy measures:

> To strengthen the sustainability of the funding structure and the efficiency of public health-care provision, the following measures will be adopted prior to the granting of the first disbursement of financial assistance:

[158] Article 3.2 of the General Terms for ESM Financial Assistance Facility Agreements, available at https://www.esm.europa.eu/sites/default/files/general_terms_15122015_clean.pdf accessed 15 August 2025. As for the facility agreement, see for example the conditions set in clause 2.1 of the Financial Assistance Facility Agreement between the ESM and the Kingdom of Spain, The Bank of Spain and Fondo de Reestructuracion Ordenada Bancaria (2012), available at https://www.esm.europa.eu/sites/default/files/migration_files/ffaspnmainagreementexecution130214.pdf accessed 15 August 2025.

[159] Article 16.1 of the General Terms for ESM Financial Assistance Facility Agreements, available at https://www.esm.europa.eu/sites/default/files/general_terms_15122015_clean.pdf accessed 15 August 2025.

[160] See IMF's Guidelines on Conditionality (2002), para 10, available at https://www.imf.org/External/np/pdr/cond/2002/eng/guid/092302.pdf accessed 15 August 2025 and Pereira Coutinho 2013, pp. 157–162.

[161] Pereira Coutinho 2013, p. 161.

[162] IMF's Guidelines on Conditionality (2002) para 9 available at https://www.imf.org/External/np/pdr/cond/2002/eng/guid/092302.pdf accessed 15 August 2025.

[163] Seen in European Commission (2013) The Economic Adjustment Program for Cyprus, pp. 66–76, available at https://ec.europa.eu/economy_finance/publications/occasional_paper/2013/pdf/ocp149_en.pdf accessed 15 August 2025.

f) abolish the category of beneficiaries class "B" and all exemptions for access to free public health care based on all non-income related categories except for persons suffering from certain chronic diseases depending on illness severity. Introduce as a first step towards a system of universal coverage a compulsory health care contribution for public servants and public servant pensioners of 1.5% of gross salaries and pensions. The measure will be reviewed by Q2-2014 with the program partners. For families with three or more dependent children, the participation in this health care scheme will be voluntary;
g) increase fees for medical services for non-beneficiaries by 30% to reflect the associated costs of medical services and create a co-payment formula with zero or low admission fees for visiting general practitioners, and increase fees for using higher levels of care for all patients irrespective of age;
h) introduce effective financial disincentives for using emergency care services in nonurgent situations;
i) introduce financial disincentives (co-payment) to minimize the provision of medically unnecessary laboratory test and pharmaceuticals; and
j) adopt a new decision by the Council of Ministers concerning a restructuring plan for public hospitals, improving quality and optimizing costs and redesigning the organizational structure of the hospital management, by putting into practice recommendations from the 2009 "Public Hospital Roadmap".[164]

The clauses in the ESM Facility Agreements and the ESM General Terms are also clear, precise, and unconditional, stipulating action and establishing causes for default and consequences for failing to comply with the MoU conditions,[165] as well as guarantee and indemnity clauses.[166] Consequently, the substantive normative force of assistance agreements is high.

Formally, these agreements also carry considerable legal weight. Not only do they set consequences for the creditor if the debtor fails to comply with the agreement, but the CJEU can also decide on matters related to their interpretation and application, providing a binding decision on the issue.[167] Thus, the debtor State may cease receiving assistance, lose access to credits, and be required to return received funds to the ESM.

The supervision of the financial assistance program through regular review missions conducted by EU institutions in the beneficiary Member State provides more strength to the conditions of the MoUs and MEAPs. Beneficiary Member States find themselves in a precarious position when subject to financial assistance, with their capacity to negotiate for different outcomes and more flexible application of measures being more limited than supervisory procedures.

---

[164] Ibid., 83–84.

[165] See Article 10 of the General Terms for ESM Financial Assistance Facility Agreements, available at https://www.esm.europa.eu/sites/default/files/general_terms_15122015_clean.pdf accessed 15 August 2025. See Forsthoff and Aerts 2020, pp. 996–1000.

[166] Article 14 of the General Terms for ESM Financial Assistance Facility Agreements, available at https://www.esm.europa.eu/sites/default/files/general_terms_15122015_clean.pdf accessed 15 August 2025.

[167] Ibid., Article 16.3 and Article 37 of TESM.

4.5 Conclusion: The Law and Power of EU Economic Governance

What is the legal strength of the rules and powers of EU economic governance, and to what extent are the Member States obliged to follow them when defining their economic policy?

According to EU primary law, Member States must comply with certain principles of economic and fiscal conduct, the most important of which involves running a sound budgetary policy, that is, avoiding deficits above the parameters set in the Treaties. The rules on excessive deficits are the strongest in terms of legal obligations and enforcement mechanisms. However, with the revisions of the SGP and the TSCG, compliance with the rules has become more flexible, making it harder to discern when an obligation contravenes the purpose of the rule. Furthermore, the other primary law rules on economic policy definition are principles, rendering them aspirational targets and objectives to be achieved on a best-effort basis, which lends them a low degree of legal strength.

The purpose of EU secondary law rules is to establish procedural structures for better coordination of national economic policies. Obligations for Member States pertain to compliance with monitoring and reporting procedures. The Council can issue individual (binding) decisions to Member States, initiating corrective procedures and imposing sanctions. Moreover, the Council can provide recommendations to Member States on courses of action to rectify deviations, imbalances, and excessive deficits.

The analysis in this work suggests that the legal strength of Council recommendations varies depending on the purpose of the procedure (preventive or corrective). In this sense, CSRs issued in the MSP, which encompass various recommendations with differing degrees of precision, and come with attached soft sanctions or warnings, have a low degree of legal strength. Recommendations in the EDP, and EIP have a distinct degree of normative force: obligations are more precise and unequivocal—typically consisting of numerical objectives to be met, with suggested means to achieve those targets—and are associated with stronger sanctions, such as financial penalties. The empirical assessment seems to corroborate this: while CSRs have low implementation rates, recommendations issued in corrective procedures like the EDP tend to be complied with or at least generate effects by prompting Member States to take actions to reverse the deficit.

This situation can be explained by considering the distinct purposes of the procedures and their interconnection. The MSP is the primary procedure for economic coordination: its aim is to organize and structure the fiscal and economic policies of Member States in alignment with EU rules and proposals. It also serves a preventive function of identifying and warning about possible deviations, but not necessarily of correcting them. The objective is not to impose but to guide, leaving room for Member States to implement policies. Orientations will vary depending on the economic and political context. Some flexibility in the coordination instrument is welcome to respect a degree of autonomy of Member States; hence, the varying degrees of precision in CSRs and the lack of robust sanctions within the MSP. It seems clear, then, that CSRs are non-binding instruments. However, this is not the case with corrective procedures, whose main objective is to rectify non-compliance with economic coordination rules—concerning deficit targets, medium-term fiscal plans and MIBs. In the EDP and EIP, there is a push for deviating Member States to adopt measures to reverse their situation: hence, greater precision and stronger enforcement mechanisms. These procedures are exceptional, whereas the MSP is standard and is enacted yearly. Therefore, EDP and EIP recommendations appear to be binding instruments.

Moreover, the analysis in this chapter also indicates that in corrective procedures, there might be a tension between the legal strength of the obligation—the targets and measures prescribed—and enforcement—the mechanisms to ensure compliance. In other words, it is challenging to determine the causal link between the obligation and the sanction when the obligation is less precise. In those cases, what degree of compliance is necessary to avoid triggering sanctions? In examples of recommendations issued under the EDP, some targets are precisely defined but include more imprecise policy goals. Sanctions apply when the addressed Member State does not act to correct the deviations from rules of fiscal discipline. The sanction's focus is primarily on the deviation itself, not on the corrective path chosen. That is: the emphasis is on correcting the target, not the means used to do so. In this sense, the obligation of corrective recommendations in the procedures of economic coordination is limited to achieving the targets for complying with the defined fiscal policy targets and does not necessarily include the measures to achieve said targets. Member States are bound to the objectives, not to the means. The question can be more complicated in the EIP, given that it is up to the Commission and Council to define what constitutes a MIB. Moreover, sanctions apply when there is a failure to comply with a recommendation, not to correct a deviation. In other words, the procedure is more flexible. Much depends on how EU institutions use quantitative indicators in the AMR to set quantitative targets and verify compliance by assessing whether those targets were achieved in line with EDP recommendations. The more precise the obligation, the easier it is to assess non-compliance, and the stronger the recommendation will be from a legal perspective.

It is crucial to stress that despite the normative force of these instruments, everything depends on a decision by the Council. Even if the switch to reverse qualified majority voting has strengthened the Commission's position, it is still the Council that controls the assessment of compliance with recommended action and the application of sanctions, holding the "bread and butter" regarding the ultimate efficacy of the coordination framework. This situation leaves the door open—as the sanction procedures involving Germany and France, and later Portugal and Spain[168] showed us—to a regulatory system with a reasonable degree of normativity but still subject

[168] Portugal and Spain were subject to the EDP and failed to correct their excessive deficits; the Council decided not to impose fines. See Council (2016) Excessive deficit procedure: Council agrees to zero fines and new deadlines for Portugal and Spain. Available at https://www.consilium.europa.eu/en/press/press-releases/2016/08/09/excessive-deficit-portugal-spain/ accessed 15 August 2025.

to extra-legal factors and dependent on the Member State's capacity for political bargaining for its practical application.[169] The risk is that it can lead, in a *de facto* politically asymmetric Union, to a situation where larger States are protected from these rules and standards but can enforce them on smaller States, against the political balance of status that should exist in the EU.[170]

In terms of assistance procedures, the legal strength of the powers of EU institutions and the legal acts enacted within them (MEAPs and MoUs) is high, both in relation to their prescriptive content and regarding the enforcement mechanisms that can be utilized for their judicial and administrative review.

In summary, the EU's capacity to normatively influence the outcome of national fiscal policy with its powers of economic policy definition and preventive supervision is limited. However, the Council and the Commission possess powers in supervisory corrective procedures that can significantly influence the definition of national fiscal policy. The issue with this arrangement is that the activation of enforcement mechanisms by EU authorities ultimately depends on a discretionary decision made at the Council level. This decision is not automatic, and it can be based on political rather than technical or normative criteria. In this sense, EU actions intended to force an effective change of national fiscal policy rely on the bargaining power of the Member States involved, which are based more on criteria of scale and opportunity rather than purely normative criteria. Despite all the rules that exist in the legal framework, the system is, in practice, "entirely discretionary".[171]

It is fair to say that while this last point casts a shadow over the effectiveness of the regulatory framework of EU economic governance, it also presents risks, as it can lead to discrepancies in the application of the rules and instances of discrimination between States.

The EU's capacity to influence and guide the definition of national policy is stronger from a normative perspective in procedures of economic policy assistance, where the use of MoUs generates strong and binding legal relations regarding the terms that the Member States must comply with to receive disbursements of financial support. At the same time, when a Member State requests financial assistance, it is already in a position with limited bargaining opportunities. In other words, the beneficiary Member State is politically vulnerable, subject to practical financial constraints that limit its capacity to avoid compliance with EU fiscal rules: in sum, its autonomy is already diminished.

Hence, and returning to the initial research question of this work, which is whether the constitutional setting of EU economic governance provides legal powers for EU institutions to guide, affect, and control the definition of national budget policy in a decisive manner, the following answers can be presented.

[169] See, for example, the study of Baerg and Hallerberg on the power of States to "edit" recommendations. Baerg and Hallerberg 2022, p. 73.

[170] A balance that is difficult to achieve and which is not properly identified in the literature. See Kukovec 2015, pp. 406–411.

[171] Leino and Saarenheimo 2019, p. 132.

The first answer is that the EU is not the ultimate decision-maker when it comes to national fiscal policy. According to the Treaties, the political authority to decide on fiscal policy rests with the Member States and their respective political institutions. The Member States are obligated to follow principles and rules regarding fiscal policy definition outlined in the EU Treaties, which were further reinforced by the TSCG and EU secondary rules. However, the constitutional model of economic governance established in the Treaties assigns the sole responsibility for fiscal policy definition and the generation of fiscal imbalances to the Member States. Even in situations of financial assistance, when states must comply with the conditions set by creditors, it is the national governments and parliaments that are responsible for passing and enacting fiscal policy measures. Fiscal policy at the EU level remains decentralized, and Brussels does not have a vote in national parliaments.

However, the second answer is that although Brussels does not possess a direct vote, it does have normative tools to influence and, in some cases, direct the definition of national fiscal policy by national government institutions. The EU's powers of economic governance allow the Council and the Commission to monitor economic developments in the Member States and intervene if deviations from targets and rules of economic governance outlined in EU law are identified. The intervention of EU authorities can result in two types of sanctions: reputational and financial. The acts issued in supervisory procedures in this area carry a high normative pressure. While these acts are formally recommendations, their purpose, drafting, intention, and the presence of sanctioning mechanisms for their administrative enforcement grant them a strong degree of legal force. Nevertheless, the ultimate force of these acts depends on a discretionary decision by the Council, which is free from any technical considerations. EU economic governance operates within a highly intergovernmental constitutional field, dependent on political consensus between national governments to be effective. Given these characteristics, it is difficult to agree with Professor Centeno's argument that economic governance is merely an "algorithmic procedure".

The third answer is that with a permanent structure for the provision of financial assistance, the EU's capacity to direct national budget policy has become very strong. Although financial assistance is exceptional and serves as an emergency measure, it is in this procedure where a strong connection exists between the form and substance of legally powerful instruments for developing national fiscal policy. Member States agree to comply with the conditions outlined in MoUs and MEAPs in exchange for financial support, and their margin of discretion to implement such measures is low.

In conclusion, EU powers of economic governance are extensive and can significantly affect national autonomy in defining fiscal policy. While these powers may be effective in managing economic responses to limit asymmetric shocks and maintain price stability, they create normative tensions within the EU's political setting, considering the limited role the EU should play in national fiscal affairs.

References

Abbot K et al. (2000) The Concept of Legalization. International Organizations 54:401–419

Alcidi C, Gros D (2017) How to strengthen the European Semester? CEPS Research Report 2017/15. Available at https://www.ceps.eu/ceps-publications/how-strengthen-european-semester/ accessed 15 August 2025

Alexander L (2019) Law and Politics: What Is Their Relation? University of San Diego School of Law Research Paper No. 19-412. Available at http://ssrn.com/abstract=3449352 accessed 15 August 2025

Al-Kadi R, Clauwaert S (2019) Socialising the European Semester? Measuring Member States' Implementation of Country-Specific Recommendations in the Social Policy Field. ETUI Working Paper 8. Available at: https://www.etui.org/Publications2/Working-Papers/Socialising-the-European-Semester accessed 15 August 2025

Amtenbrink F, Repasi R (2017) Compliance and Enforcement in Economic Policy Coordination in EMU. In: Jakab A, Kochenov D (eds) The Enforcement of EU Law and Values: Ensuring Member States' Compliance. Oxford University Press, pp. 145–181

Angerer J et al. (2020) Country-specific recommendations: An overview – September 2020. EGOV Briefing PE 624.404. Available at https://www.europarl.europa.eu/RegData/etudes/BRIE/2018/624404/IPOL_BRI(2018)624404_EN.pdf accessed 15 August 2025

Angerer J, Grigaitė K (2021) Country-Specific Recommendations for 2019, 2020 and 2021: a tabular comparison and an overview of implementation. EGOV Study 2. Available at https://www.europarl.europa.eu/thinktank/en/document/IPOL_STU(2021)651391 accessed 15 August 2025

Baerg N, Hallerberg M (2022) Council Checks of the Commission under the European Semester: Does Member State Power and Euroscepticism Still Matter? Journal of Common Market Studies 60:58–80.

Bardutzky S (2016) Constitutional Transformations at the Edge of a Bail-out: the Impact of the Economic Crisis on the Legal and Institutional Structures in Slovenia. Federalismi.it – Revista di Diritto Pubblico Italiano, Comparato, Europeo, 26/2016. Available at https://www.federalismi.it/nv14/articolo-documento.cfm?Artid=33069&content=&content_author= accessed 15 August 2025

Besson S (2005) The Morality of Conflict: Reasonable Disagreement and Law. Hart Publishing

Bobic A (2024) The Individual in the Economic and Monetary Union: A Study of Legal Accountability. Oxford University Press

Bockhorst D (2022) The Influence of the European Semester: Case Study Analysis and Lessons for its Post-Pandemic Transformation. Journal of Common Market Studies 60:101–117

Chalmers D (2012) The European Redistributive State and a European Law of Struggle. European Law Journal 18:667–693

Chamon M, Arriba-Sellier N (2022) FBF: On the Justiciability of Soft Law and Broadening the Discretion of EU Agencies. European Constitutional Law Review 18:286–314

Chen L (2015) An Introduction to Contemporary International Law: A Policy-Oriented Perspective. Oxford University Press

Cortês A (2010) Jurisprudência dos Princípios: Ensaio Sobre os Fundamentos da Decisão Jurisdicional. Universidade Católica Editora

Daly S (2021) The Rule of (Soft) Law. King's Law Journal 32:3–13

Dawson M (2011) New Governance and the Transformation of European Law. Cambridge University Press

Dermine P (2022a) The instruments of Eurozone fiscal surveillance through the lens of the soft law/hard law dichotomy – Looking for a new approach. Journal of Banking Regulation 23:7–18

Dermine P (2022b) The New Economic Governance of the Eurozone: A Rule of Law Analysis. Cambridge University Press

Deroose S et al. (2005) The Broad Economic Policy Guidelines: Past, Present and Future. Chatham House International Economics Programme Working Paper

Derrida J (1992) Force of Law: The Mystical Foundation of Authority. In: Cornell D et al. (eds) Deconstruction and the Possibility of Justice. Routledge, pp. 3–67
Dworkin R (1967) The Model of Rules. University of Chicago Law Review 35:25–29
Efstathiou K, Wolff G (2019) What Drives National Implementation of EU Policy Recommendations? Bruegel Working Paper 04. Available at https://bruegel.org/wp-content/uploads/2019/04/WP4-final-2.pdf accessed 15 August 2025
Eihmanis E (2023) Ten Years of the European Semester: From the Sovereign Debt Crisis to the COVID-19 Crisis. In: Adamski D et al. (eds) The Cambridge Handbook of European Monetary, Economic and Financial Integration. Cambridge University Press, pp. 290–304
Eliantonio M (2021) Judicial Review of Soft Law Before the European and National Courts: A Wind of Change Blowing From the Member States? In: Eliantonio M et al. (eds) EU Soft Law in the Member States: Theoretical Findings and Empirical Evidence. Hart Publishing, pp. 283–303
Eliantonio M et al. (2021) Introduction. In: Eliantonio M et al. (eds) EU Soft Law in the Member States: Theoretical Findings and Empirical Evidence. Hart Publishing, pp. 1–20
Fasone C (2015) Taking budgetary powers away from national parliaments? On parliamentary prerogatives in the Eurozone crisis. EUI Working Paper. Available at https://cadmus.eui.eu/handle/1814/36658 accessed 15 August 2025
Forsthoff U, Aerts J (2020) Financial Assistance to Euro Area Member States (EFSF and ESM). In: Amtenbrink F, Herrmann C (eds) The EU Law of Economic and Monetary Union. Oxford University Press, pp. 979–1024
Fromage D (2018) The European Parliament in the post-crisis era: an institution empowered on paper only? Journal of European Integration 40:281–294
Gentile G (2020) Ensuring Effective Judicial Review of EU Soft Law via the Action for Annulment before the EU Courts: a Plea for a Liberal-Constitutional Approach. European Constitutional Law Review 16:466–492
Gentile G (2021) To be or not to be (legally binding)? Judicial review of EU soft law after BT and Fédération Bancaire Française. Revista de Derecho Comunitario Europeo 70:981–1005
Hagg J (2018) What is Legal Validity? Lessons from Soft Law. In: Westermann P et al. (eds) Legal Validity and Soft Law. Springer International, pp. 19–45
Hodson D (2011) Governing the Euro Area in Good Times and Bad. Oxford University Press
Hodson D, Maher I (2001) The Open Method as a New Mode of Governance: The Case of Soft Economic Policy Co-ordination. Journal of Common Market Studies 39:719–746
Ilzetzki E (2021) Fiscal rules in the European Monetary Union. VoxEU, 10 June 2021. Available at https://cepr.org/voxeu/columns/fiscal-rules-european-monetary-union accessed 15 August 2025
Kelsen H (1949) General Theory of Law and the State. Harvard University Press
Kelsen H (1967) Pure Theory of Law. University of California Press
Kennedy D (1976) Form and Substance in Private Law Adjudication. Harvard Law Review 89:1685–1778
Kennedy D (1991) The Stakes of Law, or Hale and Foucault! Legal Studies Forum 15:327–366
Kukovec D (2015) Law and the Periphery. European Law Journal 21:406–428
Lamond G (2000) The Coerciveness of Law. Oxford Journal of Legal Studies 20:39–62
Leino P, Saarenheimo T (2016) On the limits of EU economic policy coordination. ADEMU Working Paper Series 36. Available at https://core.ac.uk/download/pdf/189878016.pdf accessed 15 August 2025
Leino P, Saarenheimo T (2019) Discretion, Economic Governance, and the (New) Political Commission. In: Mendes J (ed) EU Executive Discretion and the Limits of the Law. Oxford University Press, pp. 132–154
Lucas Pires M (2022) Unforgivable late admissions: the Court of Justice decides on bank resolution in BPC Lux 2 Sàrl (C-83/20). EU Law Live, 12 May 2022. Available at https://eulawlive.com/op-ed-unforgivable-late-admissions-the-court-of-justice-decides-on-bank-resolution-in-bpc-lux-2-sarl-c-83-20-by-martinho-lucas-pires/ accessed 15 August 2025

Luhmann N (1988) The Unity of the Legal System. In: Teubner G (ed) Autopoietic Law – A New Approach to Law and Society. De Gruyter, pp. 12–35
Maher I (2007) Economic Governance: Hybridity, Accountability and Control. Columbia Journal of European Law 13:682–688
Mahler I (2021) Revisiting Soft Law: Governance, Regulation and Networks. In: Eliantonio M et al. (eds) EU Soft Law in the Member States: Theoretical Findings and Empirical Evidence. Hart Publishing, pp. 21–38
Mariotto C (2022) The Implementation of Economic Rules: From the Stability and Growth Pact to the European Semester. Journal of Common Market Studies 60:40–57
McDougal M (1952) Law and Power. American Journal of International Law 46:102–114
McNeilly FS (1968) The Enforceability of Law. Noûs 168:47–64
Mendes J (2019) Executive Discretion in the EU and the Outer Boundaries of Law. In: Mendes J (ed) EU Executive Discretion and the Limits of Law. Oxford University Press, pp. 3–20
Nispen FK (2017) European Fiscal Governance: Better Safe than Sorry. EUI Working Paper SPS 2017/2. Available at https://cadmus.eui.eu/bitstream/handle/1814/46946/SPS_2017_02.pdf?sequence=1&isAllowed=y accessed 15 August 2025
Palmstorfer R (2014) The Reverse Majority Voting under the 'Six Pack': A Bad Turn for the Union? European Law Journal 20:186–203
Peers S (2012) The Stability Treaty: Permanent Austerity or Gesture Politics? European Constitutional Law Review 8:404–441
Pereira Coutinho F (2013) A natureza jurídica dos memorandos da Troika. Themis 24/25:147–179
Pereira Coutinho F (2016) Austerity on the loose in Portugal: European judicial restraint in times of crisis. Perspectives on Federalism 8:105–132 http://webarchive-2009-2021.on-federalism.eu/attachments/249_download.pdf accessed 15 August 2025
Peters A (2011) Soft Law as a New Mode of Governance. In Diedrichs U et al. (eds) The Dynamics of Change in EU Governance. Edward Elgar, pp. 21–51
Poiares Maduro M et al. (2017) A Crisis Between Crises: Placing the Portuguese Constitutional Jurisprudence of Crisis in Context. e-Pública: Revista Eletrónica de Direito Público 4:6–42. Available at http://www.scielo.mec.pt/pdf/epub/v4n1/v4n1a02.pdf accessed 15 August 2025
Rabello AM (2010) The 'Impossible Contract': From Roman Law to the Unidroit Principles Of International Commercial Contracts And The Principles Of European Contract Law. Fundamina 16:346–358
Raz J (1972) Legal Principles and the Limits of Law. Yale Law Journal 81:823–854
Raz J (1980) The Concept of a Legal System: an Introduction to the Theory of Legal Systems. Clarendon Press
Raz J (1983) The Authority of Law. Clarendon Press
Rosas A (2011) The Status in EU Law of International Agreements Concluded by EU Member States. Fordham International Law Journal 34:1304–1345
Schauer F (2015) The Force of Law. Harvard University Press
Schütze R (2016) EU Constitutional Law. Cambridge University Press
Senden L (2004) Soft Law in European Community Law. Hart Publishing
Snyder F (1993) The Effectiveness of European Community Law: Institutions, Processes, Tools and Techniques. Modern Law Review 56:19–54
Stefan O et al. (2019) EU Soft Law in the EU Legal Order: A Literature Review. Solar Working Paper 2019. Available at https://ssrn.com/abstract=3346629 accessed 15 August 2025
Terpan F (2015) Soft Law in the European Union — The Changing Nature of EU Law. European Law Journal 21:68–96
Thürer D (2009) International law as Progress and Prospect. Dike Verlag
Thygesen N et al. (2018) Reforming the EU fiscal framework: A proposal by the European Fiscal Board. VoxEU, 26 October 2018. Available at https://cepr.org/voxeu/columns/reforming-eu-fiscal-framework-proposal-european-fiscal-board accessed 15 August 2025
Tridimas T (2019) Indeterminacy and Legal Uncertainty. In: Mendes J (ed) EU Executive Discretion and the Limits of Law. Oxford University Press, pp. 40–63

Trubek DM, Cottrell P, Nance M (2005) 'Soft Law,' 'Hard Law,' and European Integration: Toward a Theory of Hybridity. University of Wisconsin Legal Research Paper No. 1002
Trubek DM, Trubek LG (2005) Hard and Soft Law in the Construction of Social Europe: the Role of the Open Method of Co-ordination. European Law Journal 11:347–363
Unger RM (1976) Law in Modern Society: Toward a Criticism of Social Theory. The Free Press
Variu M (2012) The Shaping of Infringement Procedures in European Union Law: The Rights and Safeguards of the Defendant Member State. Maastricht Journal of European and International Law 19:400–420
Violante T (2023) Judicial Accountability of Financial Assistance in the Case of Eurozone Debtor Countries. In: Dawson M (ed) Substantive Accountability in Europe's New Economic Governance. Cambridge University Press, pp. 240–266
Wellens KC, Borchardt GM (1989) Soft Law in European Community Law. European Law Review 14:267–321

Chapter 5
Federalism and the Concept of Federal Legality

Contents

Abstract This chapter examines the concept of federalism as a framework for analysing the distribution of political authority in complex constitutional systems, with a focus on the European Union's economic governance. It traces the historical and theoretical evolution of federalism from an international pact between sovereign units to a constitutive model of shared sovereignty, highlighting its conceptual ambiguities and dual nature—both cooperative and constitutive. The chapter identifies three core principles underpinning federal order: federal integrity (respect for the autonomy and equality of constituent units), federal loyalty (reciprocal commitment to the federal project), and federal adjudication (mechanisms to resolve conflicts of authority). Drawing on comparative insights from the United States and Germany, the chapter demonstrates how these principles structure the balance between self-rule and shared rule. Ultimately, the text advances the notion of federal legality—a dynamic equilibrium grounded in mutual respect, normative clarity, and institutional mechanisms that sustain the coexistence of distinct political authorities within a unified constitutional order.

Keywords Federalism · Sovereign pact · Federal order · Political authority · Federal principles

M. Lucas Pires, *The Federal Legality of EU Economic Governance*,
https://doi.org/10.1007/978-94-6265-747-2_5

5.1 The Convoluted Concept of Federalism

This book discusses the existence of several "symptoms" of a malady in the EU constitutional framework, regarding the legal setting of economic governance. For a better understanding and resolution of the problem, this malady should be named and identified,[1] meaning that such issues should be treated accordingly through analytical and critical discourse. The problem is to understand if the scope and extent of EU powers of economic governance is legally problematic. This has to do with the emergency of normative tensions associated with the exercise of ruling powers in a complex political setting: a setting with a centralized government that comprises different and relatively autonomous political units, each with its own space for ruling discretion.

To discuss this issue, then, it is necessary to adopt a research framework that allows for a comprehensive discussion of the central issues at stake, i.e., the power equilibrium in the definition of fiscal policy by the constituent units of a supranational setting. Power equilibrium refers to the normative justification (the legality and the legitimacy) of the actions of government institutions of the supranational setting against the constituent units. This question goes beyond matters of "pure" jurisdiction because the rules regarding areas of responsibility are, as discussed in the first part, inserted within an institutional system and subject to a political dynamic that complicates their interpretation. Therefore, adopting a theoretical and speculative research framework to discuss this problem can offer a platform for structuring the problems and their consequences in a clearer light and ultimately offer a more interesting avenue for discovering possible solutions.

The framework chosen to analyse this problem is federalism. Federalism is a concept with a significant history in political science. According to the Encyclopedia Britannica, federalism is the "mode of political organization that unites separate states or other polities within an overarching political system in a way that allows each to maintain its own integrity".[2] But federalism is not only the mode of organization but also the theory of how different political units should be organized under a broader political structure. In this sense, federalism is a research framework whose focus is precisely the degree of equilibrium of governmental power existent in a compound polity, that is, in a polity composed of several sub-polities that, despite the existence of central government institutions, enjoy a high degree of political autonomy.

However rich the symbolism and literary imagination of federalism is, its conceptual meaning (i.e., "the internal or intellectual phenomena that words are thought to label, as markers, or towards which words are thought to point"[3]) can be very confusing, making it challenging to comprehend its essence from a dogmatic standpoint. "When we read the usual definitions of federalism proposed by jurists," says

---

[1] "[I]f he had the language he wouldn't express itself with symptoms". Lerner 2019, p. 36.

[2] "Federalism" in Encyclopaedia Britannica (2023) available at https://www.britannica.com/topic/federalism accessed 15 August 2025.

[3] Boyd White 1990, pp. 28–29.

Olivier Béaud, "we are struck by their often vague, even contradictory character."[4] For all the doctrine and discussion about the topic, it is difficult to escape the feeling that the concept can be so loose, including within it many different and conflicting realities, that it ends up not representing anything *unique*, thus calling into question its utility and relevance from a philosophical and methodological perspective. This presents issues, as Patricia Popelier rightly points out:

> [T]heory depends on conceptual clarity. Insight into the essence of federalism and federal systems is crucial to understanding how states are formed and evolve, and how federalism relates to principles such as democracy and the rule of law. For legal theory, in particular, insight into this essence is vital for deriving normative requirements from the state structure. This is not a merely academic exercise: it has consequences [...].[5]

There are two interconnected reasons for the confusion surrounding the meaning of federalism. The first reason is empirical.[6] Many polities worldwide have adopted federalism as their mode of political organization, constituting themselves as self-proclaimed federations. An overview of several works on comparative federalism adequately illustrates the many versions of the federal model in place, with differences in structure (regarding, for example, political systems), "legal traditions or socio-political characteristics".[7] Some political communities identify themselves as federal and are considered the "archetype" of the phenomenon;[8] simultaneously, there are other political realities with significant federal characteristics in constitutional structure and dynamics.[9] Moreover, there are systems with political structures different from federalism—regionalism,[10] for example—but where the question of the division of government power through devolution or decentralization shares identical problems with power issues resulting from federal relations.

Instead of a single typical example of federalism that serves as the basic blueprint, what exists in practice are several versions or types of "[compound polities] with multiple levels of government, each with constitutionally grounded claims to some degree of organizational autonomy and direct legal authority over its citizens".[11] These are complex political communities where there is a strong division of governing powers between different territorial sub-units to the point that such sub-units are, to an extent, significantly autonomous from the "central" State. No federal structure is identical to another, despite sharing similar traits and dynamics.

The second challenge in using federalism as an analytical framework relates to the different conceptual meanings found in scientific literature. This difficulty arises from a tension between *the descriptive dimension of the concept* (the empirical reality

---

4 Beaud 2009, p. 12.

5 Popelier 2021, p. 12.

6 On the limitations of empirical methods of discussing federalism, see Tierney 2022, pp. 27–40.

7 Halberstam and Reimann 2014, pp. 4–5.

8 The United States of America ("US", "USA" or "United States"), Switzerland, and Germany. See Palermo and Kössler 2017, pp. 72–82.

9 Like the EU, for example (see Chap. 6 of this book).

10 Palermo and Kössler 2017, pp. 20–33.

11 Halberstam and Reimann 2014, p. 4.

of federalism, or more specifically, the generally accepted empirical experience of federalism, which pertains to the exercise of government power in federal States) and *the normative dimension* (the theoretical and philosophical principles of federalism). Depending on the cultural and political context, the federal experience and the federal principle can sometimes align, while at other times they may present diametrically opposed meanings. Daniel Halberstam aptly captures the situation when he writes:

> Federalism can be a charged and sometimes confusing word. A political rallying cry for decentralization in the United States, the F-word means more Brussels in Europe. Back when James Madison, Alexander Hamilton, and John Jay battled their opponents in pamphlets, both sides of the debate desperately sought the mantel of federalism to help their cause. And among academics, what is and what is not federalism has been embroiled in definitional squabbles that have been, at times, quite caustic and, more often, of questionable significance.[12]

Various definitions in the literature associate federalism with "legal arrangements between territorially distinct political communities",[13] or suggest that federalism implies the "coexistence within a compound polity of multiple levels of government each with constitutionally grounded claims to some degree of organizational autonomy and jurisdictional authority".[14] Others posit that federalism involves "the linking of individuals, groups, and polities in lasting but limited union in such a way as to provide for the energetic pursuit of common ends while maintaining the respective integrities of all parties",[15] or that "[f]ederalism is the theory or advocacy of federal principles for dividing powers between member units and common institutions".[16]

Despite their general accuracy, these definitions may lead to conceptual ambiguity. Taken to their extremes, they could potentially be applied to certain forms of international cooperation,[17] or to modes of State unification characterized by a high degree of regional political autonomy and decentralization or devolution of powers.[18] In other words, most definitions capture the *structural elements of federalism* but fail to clearly articulate *its essence and unique aspects*. The fact that these definitions originate from renowned authors in the field underscores the complexity of the theoretical task at hand.

---

[12] Halberstam 2012, p. 578.

[13] Schütze 2009, p. 15.

[14] Halberstam 2012, p. 580.

[15] Elazar 1987, p. 5.

[16] Follesdal 2018.

[17] What has been dubbed "world federalism": see Lloyd Junior 1949, pp. 16–28 and Marchetti 2006, 20 pp. 285–305. Jean L. Cohen argues for international organizations to evolve in the logic of federal models due to their pluralist political structures and forms of legitimation. See Cohen 2012, pp. 4–7.

[18] For example, Daniel J. Elazar describes the Portuguese State, which is a unitary State with decentralization of political (legislative and executive) powers to two territories (the archipelagos of Madeira and Azores, respectively), as having a federative element—Elazar 1987, pp. 55 and 79. For a critique of this approach, see Tierney 2022, p. 5.

This conceptual confusion can be traced back to the modern age's beginning when federalism signified an international pact between different sovereign political units, with political authority remaining with the participating States.[19] Thus, federalism was akin to a cooperative treaty. This internationalist meaning underwent an ingenious transformation during the political unification process of the North American colonies post-independence.[20] Advocates for greater integration among the States (known as "the federalists") proposed an innovative political setting that would govern both the States (e.g., their governments) and the peoples of those States directly. This entity, the United States of America's federation, would be autonomous and independent from the constituent States, exercising exclusive ruling competencies over specific policy areas. Moreover, the federal State's political structure would be elected not by the States and their governments, but by the "common people" of this "community of communities":[21] the peoples of all member States of the United States of America. As a result, the new political setting combined international elements, given that the States maintained their status as independent political communities and remained sovereign to a degree, with national elements through the creation of a new sovereign political entity to rule alongside the States over the people of the United States.[22] This arrangement was dubbed "federal", although the underlying political and legal structure was far more integrated than that of a classical federal setting. Consequently, federalism has become associated with the specific governmental organization structure of the United States of America since that time.

The transformation of federalism's meaning has prompted certain nineteenth-century European positivist doctrines of public law to equate federalism not with a *cooperative pact* between States (as it was prior to the establishment of the US Federation) but with a *constitutive reality*. They now define it as a mode of state organization in which the centre (the federal State) holds ultimate ruling authority over the periphery (the constituent States). This third shift in the tradition redefined a federal polity as a federal "State": a predominantly national entity with decentralized political organization features, where ultimate ruling power rested with the central government structures.[23] Thus, this last discussion concluded a trilogy of historical and conceptual perspectives, whereby federalism evolved to mean an international agreement for political integration, a form of decentralized State-building, or something dogmatically "exotic" (a *tertium genus*) that existed between the two—a political mutant defying clear and precise definitions.

[19] Schütze 2009, pp. 15–22. There were exceptions in political thinking against this view, such as Johanes Althusius: see Riley 1976, pp. 7–41.

[20] Halberstam 2018a, pp. 6–8; Schütze 2009, pp. 22–23.

[21] Cohen 2012, p. 87.

[22] Schütze 2020, pp. 8–19.

[23] Schütze 2009, pp. 30–35. See as an example of that view Jellinek 2000, pp. 454–456.

5.2 Federalism as a Type of Sovereign Pact

The challenge of identifying a distinct essence of federalism stems from this practical and theoretical confusion. The task is to ascertain whether federalism can be distilled into a more precise and structured political and legal philosophy with consequential implications from both a descriptive and normative standpoint. The complexities and contradictions risk turning the term into an empty catchphrase used merely for rhetorical purposes and lacking clear meaning. This is particularly relevant to, for example, EU federalism.[24]

Halberstam astutely points out that "for purposes of theoretical or empirical scholarship, it makes no sense to speak about the accuracy of one definition [of federalism] over another in the absence of a specific research project or theory regarding the causes, effects, or normative implications of the phenomenon being defined".[25] Heeding his advice, the aim of the present discussion is to critically analyse how political authority—that is, the basis and terms of the exercise of power in defining economic policy—is organized within a specific setting (e.g., the EU). Federalism is crucial as it concerns the distribution of ruling authority among independent and autonomous units within the same political setting. The federal framework offers a balance between self-rule and shared rule, political integration, and incorporation without the risk of assimilation and domination.[26]

As a legal phenomenon, federalism is a form of sovereign pact, that is, an exercise of sovereign power. Sovereign pacts (agreements made by sovereigns for the exercise of political authority) are crucial as they express not only self-limitation but self-limitation in the face of another: another collective, another member, another individual, or another institution.[27] They acknowledge a relation of power, its terms, and the conditions of existence. The agreement has a moral value in that it expresses both consent and promise, setting the terms for a new form of legitimate authority to exist. Simultaneously, the agreement acknowledges one's limitation in the face of the other, that is equal and has the same rights to existence and to partake in a common political enterprise. The contract—the pact, the agreement, the promise—is central to the formation of the community. Even Jean Bodin, who developed the concept of sovereignty, recognized the importance of contract when he argued that the sovereign could not be bound by its own commands, but had to comply with the promises and contracts he entered:

> From this conclusion we can derive another rule of state – namely, that a sovereign prince is bound by the contracts he has made, whether with his subject or with a foreigner. For since he is the guarantor to his subjects of the agreements and mutual obligations that they have

[24] As discussed in Chap. 6.

[25] Halberstam 2012, p. 582.

[26] I share many views on the conceptual framework of federalism with Larsen 2021, particularly in pp. 14–21.

[27] Loughlin 2003, pp. 68–71.

entered with one another, there is all the more reason why he must render justice for his own act.[28]

For the French legal philosopher, the sovereign is bound to contracts because of natural equity and his role as the supreme protector of order. Bodin even argued that the sovereign had less freedom than other legal subjects to avoid complying with contracts from a normative perspective. "That a prince who has contracted with his subjects is bound by his promise should thus be beyond all doubt".[29] Sovereign agreements—defined as the contracts, pacts, or covenants that establish the terms for the exercise of powers of political authority—are the means to set out the normative terms under which the legality of sovereign power can be assessed. They do not question the capacity of political communities; instead, they are expressions of their autonomy to decide how to organize and exercise government power. Agreements are acts of (self-determined and self-constituted) power, entered freely and rationally, providing sufficient legitimacy for the normative setting they vow to establish. The terms of the agreement necessarily represent the sovereign character of political communities and their autonomy. The existence of normative liability for failure to comply with the agreement does not question the supremacy of sovereignty, nor its absolute character, as it is a necessary consequence arising from the autonomy of political actors and individual subjects: that freedom implies responsibility. Being subject to an agreement does not question the sovereignty of the State; it just legally binds the way the State exercises its prerogatives.

Sovereign pacts can take various forms and carry different political implications. *Potentia*, or the capacity to exercise power, can be structured and organized between the members of a political community or various political communities for a multitude of purposes. Such possibilities can be broadly organized into two categories: constitutive and cooperative pacts.

Constitutive pacts establish the structure of authority within a political community. They represent the founding or re-founding of the political community as a self-determined autonomous entity. Constitutions of States are examples of sovereign constitutive pacts. These pacts do not establish the limits of *potestas*, as this is not possible;[30] instead, they are a product and representation of such *potestas*. They are an exercise of *potentia* that self-proclaims the existence of a national community, laying down the axiological values of the community, the organization of power, its government institutions, and forms of political participation within the community. Their specific political character and authority arise from the stature they provide to the political settlement as the charters of political ruling. Constitutions are pivotal instruments and symbols of a community's political and legal self-determination, defining

[28] Bodin 1992, p. 35.

[29] Ibid., p. 36.

[30] Hannah Arendt explains this persuasively when discussing the concept of revolution. For Arendt, a revolution, which is a space of a-legality and of political conflict, is the process of achieving a new beginning, a new foundation as a body politic. Revolution is only possible because of *potestas*, of the inherent, limitless and irresistible capacity of humanity to reset and reform the terms of its political engagement. See Arendt 1963, pp. 35–58.

the terms for the internal exercise of *potentia*—from the people to the people—and for the external exercise of *potentia*, establishing relations vis-à-vis the peoples of other communities.

Distinct from constitutive pacts are cooperative pacts, which establish and organize relations between different and independent ("sovereign") political communities. Like constitutive pacts, cooperative pacts are an act of *potentia*. However, the object of the latter is not to found or re-found a community, but to regulate the exercise of political authority in specific contexts *vis-à-vis* other entities (e.g., people, sovereigns, or other legal realities such as corporations). Treaties and conventions entered into by and between sovereign States, which form the fundamental legal acts of public international law, are examples of such pacts.[31]

What sets cooperative sovereign pacts apart from constitutive pacts is that the former lack the political character of the latter. The agreement does not represent the proclamation of the existence and autonomy of a single political community, but rather an effort of collaboration between different, pre-established communities or entities. Such collaboration can be more or less stringent, in institutional or legal terms, but does not entail setting up a new political community with its own *potentia*.[32]

What then, of the federal pact? Is it cooperative or constitutive? A federal polity is a compound polity, composed of several other polities that decide together to incorporate a new, permanent polity.[33] Such an agreement naturally involves a pooling of *potentia*, that is, the capacity to exercise sovereign powers vis-à-vis every other member of the polity and *vis-à-vis* external actors. In this sense, it is similar to cooperative pacts of sovereignty. However, the federal pact is not only cooperative but also constitutive because it establishes a new, unique political entity with *potestas*. A federation is more than just an entity for achieving objectives that could also be achieved through other forms of international cooperation, such as pooling of resources, benefits of self-defence, economies of scale for the provision of the well-being of all peoples of the federal polity, etc.[34] As Norman McLeod Rogers stated, there is a third purpose to federation: the achievement of "national stature", which can be translated to the achievement (with the founding) of *political singularity*.[35] A federation is a self-proclaimed act of a new community with political autonomy and identity, not just a form of sovereign collaboration. It is also constitutive in the sovereign sense.

Federalism holds a unique dual political character—both constitutive and cooperative—that underlines its originality, and the challenges associated with it from a philosophical and practical perspective. Consider the complex proposition of federalism: established political entities decide to create a new political entity—a new centre of

---

[31] Private parties are also subject to international law and can partake in international agreements. Rocha 2021, pp. 18–49.

[32] Chen 2015, p. 317.

[33] Carl Schmitt in Larsen 2021, p. 19.

[34] Halberstam 2012, pp. 583–592, and, critically, Tierney 2022, pp. 153–155.

[35] McLeod Rogers 1935, p. 340.

political authority with institutionalized government institutions[36] capable of ruling over their territories, without forfeiting their political autonomy or—vitally—their political existence. On one hand, we have the centre (the federation), comprising the people of each State, joined together as a *demoi*—a people of peoples.[37] On the other hand, we have the periphery, the federated or constitutive States, each composed of their different peoples, continuing to exist as distinct and independent political units. Thus, there are two types of federal bonds: those between the States and the federation (with the States acting as representatives of a singular political community) and those between the peoples of each State with the federation directly–as the common people of the federal compact.

Federalism, therefore, characterizes a sovereign pact that establishes a form of governmental organization that respects the coexistence and cooperation between different sets of political authority within the same territory. Each authority has its legitimate claim to self-determination as a unique political entity: the federation and the federated State; the people of the federation (the people of peoples) and the people of each federated State.

5.3 Principles of Federal Order

Achieving this delicate balance—on which the success of the federation hinges—requires the sovereign entities of the compound community to commit to normative principles of political equilibrium and respect.[38] First, the federation must respect the political singularity of the constituent units. Second, and reciprocally, the constituent units must respect the common cause of the federation, which involves respecting the diversity of every federal member and the unity of the federal project.[39] Finally, there needs to be a principle for assessing conflicts of authority between the two levels in a federation: the national and the federal.

Consequently, we can identify three principles of federal order in federal constitutional settings: the principle of federal integrity, the principle of federal loyalty, and the principle of federal adjudication. These principles are logically inherent to the idea of federalism and are essential for the sustainment of a federation. They serve as the fundamental axiological and normative criteria for assessing the structure and exercise of political authority. Understanding and categorizing these principles is

[36] Cohen 2012, p. 152.

[37] Schütze 2020, pp. 5–8.

[38] Michael Burgess uses the expressions "self-restraint" and "political empathy" to describe these properties of federalism. At the core, they are ideas of respect and balance: balance between the different political powers and respect for their unique and shared political character. See Burgess 2012, pp. 20–21.

[39] The complex "double-telos" of a federation: "the will to preserve the states as autonomous and the will to live together in a common union". Larsen 2021, p. 104. See also Beaud 2009, pp. 273–284; Diamond 1973, p. 130.

crucial for comprehending and discussing the implications of the federal bargain and the normative requirements of its practice.[40]

These three principles together form a triangle, where the first two principles – integrity and loyalty—are at the base, while the principle of adjudication lies at the apex. The dynamic of federal order heavily depends on how integrity and loyalty interact in the specific system. Systems generally favour one over the other, but this equilibrium can shift with context. Federal adjudication represents both the axiological basis for assessing the distribution of political authority in case of conflict, and the processes through which such conflict of authority is discussed and decided.

Each principle has different dimensions that require consideration. We will examine these dimensions in the following section using practical examples from the constitutions of two federal systems: the United States of America ("USA") and the Federal Republic of Germany ("Germany"). These two examples were chosen because they are unequivocal, "classic" types of federal systems: the USA being the founding system of "modern" federalism, and Germany being the largest federal State in Europe. Additionally, there are significant structural differences between these two federal systems regarding the specific implementation of the principles of federal order, which illustrates how these principles exist in all federal logic but adapt to the specific federal context in which they operate.

5.3.1 The Principle of Federal Integrity

The principle of federal integrity relates to the legal status and treatment of the federation's members in relation to one another (individually) and in relation to the federation (the collective of federated States).[41] After establishing the federation, each constituent State maintains its existence as an individual political entity, with its fundamental elements (territory, people, governing institutions, and constitutional norms). Neither the federation nor any other constituent State can question this existence or the elements on which it rests. This means they must not only respect but also protect the constitutive structures of each State against all threats, whether internal or external. Attacking the integrity of a State is, therefore, an attack on the federation, as the latter depends on the former. Furthermore, each constituent State enjoys the same legal status as the others within the federation. The federation is not a dominion of one State or people over others, but a plural community composed of several different communities in equal standing, and therefore, cannot be subjected to discriminatory actions by the States or the federation. There must be recognition from the federation of the equal status of States as sovereign entities and their peoples as part of the federation's common people.

---

[40] On the doctrine and principles of federalism, see Burgess 2012, pp. 20–21; Elazar 1987, pp. 154–197; Signe Larsen 2021, pp. 105–126; Tierney 2022, pp. 163–182; McLeod Rogers 1935, pp. 341–343.

[41] Tierney 2022, pp. 174–182; McLeod Rogers 1935, pp. 341–342.

Consequently, the essential practical outcome of the principle of federal integrity is the existence of States' legal status within the federation. In other words, States must have a set of rights that shield them against the actions of the federation and other federated States.

These rights of integrity can be divided into two categories. The first category concerns the right to respect the fundamental structures of the federated States. Federal interference can never jeopardize or significantly affect one of the fundamental elements of the State as an individual political entity. Such rights include the States' rights to respect their constitutional structures, territory, and its people in their cultural and political singularity. This also means rights to respect the State's core powers that have not been transferred to the federation. Although the federation is endowed with powers to act in certain policy areas, some powers remain with the constituent States. Therefore, federal integrity necessitates a division of powers between the federation and the constituent States.

The second category includes the right to equal standing and equal treatment of the federated States and their respective peoples within the federation.[42] States cannot generally be discriminated against by one another in positive or negative ways. They must enjoy the same rights and duties as others; the more significant the degree of differentiation between States, the larger the imbalance between forces and communities within the federation, which can lead to tensions.

In the American Constitution, the integrity of States is a crucial condition for the federation's functioning.[43] This is represented in section 4 of article IV (the "guarantee clause"), which assigns the federal government the duty to protect the republican form of government of the federated States, and to protect the States against all internal and external threats.[44] Additionally, the tenth amendment of the US Constitution states that the powers not delegated to the federation remain with the States, thus acknowledging the uniqueness and autonomy of States as sovereign entities.[45] The eleventh amendment grants sovereign immunity to States in private actions taking place in federal courts.[46]

In Germany, the integrity and autonomy of the federated States (the *Länder*) are established in its Basic Law.[47] The territory of the *Länder* is protected in article 29 of the German Constitution ("GC"), which states that altering the territory of the Federal Republic requires approval from the affected States. Article 30 acknowledges the sovereignty of the federated States and, therefore, their political autonomy as self-determined, singular entities.[48] Article 91 sets the terms for the duty of the federation (and other *Land*) to act when the "existence or free democratic basic order of the Federation or of a *Land*" is at risk. Finally, article 79(3) GC on the rules

---

[42] McLeod Rogers 1935, pp. 342–343.

[43] Alexander 1986, p. 15.

[44] Williams 2018, pp. 625–634.

[45] Halberstam 2004, pp. 791–800.

[46] Alexander 1986, pp. 4–6; Halberstam 2004, pp. 799–800.

[47] On the status of States in German federalism, see Renzsch 1989, pp. 17–32.

[48] The degree of autonomy may be different from that in the US. See Günlicks 2003, pp. 390–391.

for amending the Basic Law establishes the inadmissibility of any constitutional amendment "affecting the division of the Federation into *Länder*", thus guaranteeing both the existence of the States and the federation as autonomous entities.[49]

The US and Germany offer different examples of the division of powers between the federation and the constituent states. The US is traditionally considered an example of dual federalism, while Germany is an example of cooperative federalism. The difference between the two types of systems concerns the degree of interaction between government institutions at the two levels of political authority. In dual federalism, the two spheres of political authority (federal power and national power) act separately, while in cooperative federalism, the two spheres collaborate in the exercise of federal political authority.[50] It is crucial to note that no system is entirely dual or fully cooperative, and the degree of interaction between the federation and the federated States in the exercise of political authority can change based on circumstances.[51]

Setting categorizations aside, both the US Constitution and the German Basic Law have explicit provisions detailing how power is divided. The constitutions of both federations establish the spheres of policy action for the federation—with the German Constitution providing more detail than its American counterpart, as it also outlines the spheres of exclusive competence of the *Länder*. In the US, Section 8 of Article I establishes the powers of Congress, with the last paragraph presenting the "necessary and proper clause", an open clause meant to be used strictly.[52] The Tenth Amendment further stipulates that the Constitution delegates powers to the federation. Therefore, beyond the scope of enumerated powers, the States remain sovereign and retain the ability to act. In the German Basic Law, Articles 70–74 outline the division of legislative competence in the federation by establishing the areas of exclusive powers of the federal government, while Articles 83–86 organize executive powers, with the *Länder* given the competence to execute federal laws.[53]

As for the integrity of equality, it is not explicitly stated in the US Constitution, but it is unequivocally identified and accepted in US constitutional practice.[54] As expressed by the US Supreme Court, "equality of constitutional right and power is the condition of all the States of the Union, old and new".[55] Such equality implies that "the States in the Union are coequal sovereigns under the Constitution".[56] This principle also holds true in German constitutional law. The principle of equality of States is not explicitly written in the Constitution; however, it is an integral part of

---

49 Leonardy 1999.

50 Schütze 2009, pp. 75–107; Günlicks 2019, pp. 1283–1285.

51 See Schütze 2009, p. 76.

52 Maxeiner 2014, pp. 492–521.

53 Günlicks 2003, pp. 81–89; Adam and Möllers 2014, pp. 492–521.

54 See the Supreme Court cases of Pollard's Lessee v. Hagan, 44 U.S. (3 How.) 212, 228–29 (1845); Knight v. United States Land Ass'n, 142 U.S. 161, 183 (1891); Shively v. Bowlby, 152 U.S. 1, 13 (1894) and PPL Montana, LLC v. Montana 565 U.S. 576 (2012).

55 Escanaba Co. v. City of Chicago, 107 U.S. 678, 689 (1883).

56 PPL Montana, LLC v. Montana 565 U.S. 576 (2012) 591.

constitutional practice and has been recognized by constitutional doctrine. According to Marcus C. Pleyer:

> This legal principle, which stipulates that the states are to be treated equally in the case of their essential equality and, vice versa, that they are entitled to unequal treatment in the case of essential inequality, can be extracted from various sources in the constitution: it follows from the rule of law as well as from the principle of federal loyalty, and ultimately, [...] it also results from a synopsis of the member-state-related norms of the Basic Law.[57]

Like their American counterparts, German States enjoy the same rights under the Basic Law, including rights of political participation and the power to exercise their autonomy within the scope of powers designated to them under the federal compact.

5.3.2 *The Principle of Federal Loyalty*

While the federation relies on the integrity of the States, this is only one side of the story. Federalism is transformative in the sense that when constituent States join the federal compact, they accept substantial changes to their political status: they become part of a new community and enter a novel form of political existence. By way of the federal compact, these States are incorporated into a wider structure—the federation –and are obligated to comply with the common goals and rules set during the federation's establishment. In essence, federated States must respect the federation's principles, objectives, and powers that are shared by all other Member States. To oppose the federation is to oppose its members, the other States, and their peoples.

The other component of the integrity axis is loyalty, which pertains to the integrity of the federation itself. The formation of a federation serves a purpose and for it to succeed, the constituent States must demonstrate loyalty to the federal project. Furthermore, loyalty implies that the constituent States must comply and cooperate with the federation, recognizing, respecting, and upholding its fundamental values and principles, while submitting to its political authority as laid out in the federal compact. A failure to abide by federal values and rules infringes upon the federal compact and if done persistently, can jeopardize the federation's existence. Consequently, the federation must retain the authority to enforce compliance with common rules among the States. States must uphold duties of respect, obedience, and collaboration with the federation and its governing bodies for the achievement of the latter's goals. Hence, while States possess integrity rights, they are also subject to duties of loyalty.

What exactly are these duties of loyalty? They involve respecting the fundamental elements of the federation, its values, and its rules—essentially, a duty of political reciprocity.[58] They embody the "commitment to membership in a community with

[57] Pleyer 2005, p. 336. See also Lutz 2014, pp. 222–224.

[58] Tierney 2022, p. 239.

others—presumably despite the occasional disagreement with fellow members".[59] Essentially, federated States must abide by the federal compact, and are duty-bound to apply and uphold it within their respective territories, within their legal frameworks, and concerning the other constituent units. As per the principle of loyalty, "each level or unit of government must always act to ensure the proper functioning of the system of governance as a whole".[60] In this regard, constituent States cannot take measures that infringe upon federal values or rules—they must respect federal authority.

Two examples of loyalty within the US constitution are Section 10 of Article I and Para Two of Article VI. The former outlines the powers prohibited to the States, such as those pertaining to international relations and the ability to issue currency, while the latter defines the relationship between federal law and national law, where the former holds supremacy over the latter—also known as the "supremacy clause".[61] As per the supremacy clause, the federal constitution "shall be the supreme Law of the Land; and the Judges in every State shall be bound thereby, anything in the Constitution or Laws of any state to the Contrary notwithstanding."

In the German Basic Law, the commitment to loyalty is evident in the previously mentioned eternity clause of Article 79(3) and the internal emergency provision of Article 91. Additionally, the German Constitutional Court developed the doctrine of "federal comity", which stipulates that the Federation and the *Länder* must be loyal to federalism and thus must conduct their affairs in a way that does not jeopardize the character of the sovereign pact in which they coexist.[62] In the words of the Court, matters must be conducted in a manner "friendly to the idea of federation".[63] The supremacy of federal law is set forth in Article 31 of the German Basic Law, immediately following the norm that acknowledges the sovereign powers of the *Länder*.

5.3.3 The Principle of Federal Adjudication

From a normative perspective, integrity and loyalty are the two main principles of the federal bargain, as they address the central issue of federal order: the balance between the rights of the States as individual communities and their rights as part of a federal collective, or a super-community. On the other hand, federal adjudication is a principle of federal practice relating to how this balance is effectively achieved in terms of the exercise of political authority.

---

[59] Young 2014, p. 1146.

[60] Halberstam 2018a, p. 3.

[61] Halberstam 2001, pp. 220–227.

[62] Kommers and Miller 2012, pp. 90–94.

[63] Leonardy 1999.

A federation is established to fulfil a set of purposes and must possess the powers to pursue them adequately, both internally and externally.[64] Simultaneously, the federation must respect the reserved space of autonomy of the constituent States and, in certain cases, compete with the States in exercising governmental power. The overlap between these two spheres of power can generate conflicts of authority that must be resolved. Therefore, federal adjudication concerns the method of deciding who ultimately has political authority over a specific subject or policy–the federation or the constituent States. This involves two aspects: firstly, directional principles serving as criteria for assessing the exercise of power in light of the federal compact; and secondly, institutional mechanisms to decide on the application of these principles and establish in practice the scope of political authority of one level versus the other. Both issues need to be considered separately.

5.3.3.1 Criteria for Reviewing Federal Adjudication

When establishing a federation, the federal constitution delineates the spheres of political authority. Policy areas can be reserved for the States (exclusive national competences) or reserved for the federation (exclusive federal competences). Within these policy fields, neither party can interfere with the other. However, this division of powers is not rigid, leading to situations where the federation and the States can act concurrently and where the scope of federal authority may be ambiguous. Federal balance is not static; it shifts according to context and necessity. "A means must be available for the alteration of constitutional arrangements in conformity with changing relationships of the purposes which the federation is designed to serve".[65] It might be necessary to pursue a particular policy, to exercise a specific degree of power that, although not explicit, is implied.

In practice, the federation often has a dimensional advantage (bringing benefits of economies-of-scale and combating possible forms of policy parochialism) over the States when acting. However, even if such action might be more efficiently and effectively pursued at the federal level than at the national one, there is a risk of the centre encroaching on the legitimate sphere of *potentia* of the federate State. Therefore, normative guidelines must be in place to assess the suitability and appropriateness of the federation's action. The principles of integrity and loyalty are the obvious starting points and fundamental boundaries. The federation cannot override the constituent States acting legitimately under their competences, and the latter must respect the federation's authority when it is legitimately acting within its competences. However, there is a substantial grey area between these two boundaries that requires some form of normative guidance to understand to what extent the federation can act and, consequently, to what extent the constituent States must respect federal authority.

---

[64] On the complexity of external powers of the federation, see Cyr 2017.

[65] McLeod Rogers 1935, p. 343.

The defining normative principle for the organization of the exercise of federal power is subsidiarity.[66] Subsidiarity is based on the idea that governmental actions should ideally be taken by a body closer to the subjects affected by the decision.[67] Hence, to address local issues, local bodies; to solve national issues, national bodies; and to resolve federal issues, federal bodies. Only when the respective governmental body is incapable, by itself, of addressing the issue, or the issue is better handled by the other level of authority, does subsidiarity allow for the "centre" (i.e., national vis-à-vis local, federal vis-à-vis national) to intervene and act.[68]

The principle of subsidiarity allows for the consideration of the federal merits of action when it is unclear who should act or not. It requires an assessment of the measure, its purpose, and its execution to understand if it skews the federal balance excessively to one side or the other, thus putting the federal equilibrium at risk of fragmentation or assimilation. The extension of the action of the higher level of authority must always respect the legitimacy of the initial level of decision-making and not excessively surpass it. In other words, it must be adequate, necessary, balanced, and appropriate—in short, proportional[69]—to the purpose and means it aims to achieve and implement, in line with the federal compact.

Subsidiarity is often complemented by another principle of federal structure, pre-emption.[70] Under pre-emption, when the federation establishes its authority over a regulatory space, the federated States lose the ability to regulate that policy area again. Once the ability to regulate a specific subject is "captured" by the centre, it remains with the centre. Subsequently, the federation may opt to devolve powers to the peripheries when it deems that national and local governments are better positioned to act regarding specific policies. However, such a "release" of governmental power is at the discretion of the federation.

In terms of the principle of power organization, the idea of subsidiarity is not explicitly mentioned in the US Constitution. Nevertheless, it is inherent in US federal politics, guiding and influencing, even if only "implicitly", the exercise of federal powers.[71] Pre-emption is also an established principle of American federal law,[72] along with the doctrine of implied powers.[73] The German Constitution adopts the principles of subsidiarity and pre-emption in articles 72(1) and (2) of its Basic Law, while the principle of implied powers has limited expression in constitutional practice.[74]

---

[66] Halberstam 2012, pp. 585–586; Bermann 1994, p. 337. For a critical perspective, see Golemboski 2015, pp. 535–541.

[67] Golemboski 2015, p. 528.

[68] Halberstam 2012, p. 586.

[69] Schlink 2012, pp. 722–725, and regarding its application in federal systems, see Mills 2010, pp. 384–386.

[70] Nelson 2000, pp. 225–226.

[71] Bermann 1994, pp. 403–407; Mills 2010, pp. 431–436.

[72] Nelson 2000, p. 225.

[73] Gardbaum 1994, pp. 781–783.

[74] Günlicks 2003, p. 56.

5.3.3.2 Mechanisms for Adjudicating Federal Authority

The issue of mechanisms for adjudicating federal authority raises two questions. The first question is about the deciding authority: *which* level of authority should be responsible for deciding on the adjudication of federal conflict? The second question concerns the method of adjudicating federal authority: *how* should one assess if federal authority is being exercised within the boundaries of the federal compact?

"A successful federal system must remain flexible enough to allow for effective governance and yet be stable enough to prevent radical centripetal or centrifugal shifts of power that undermine the principle of shared rule".[75] What is fundamentally at stake in federal conflicts is the extent, suitability, and legitimacy of the federation's actions. As the federation comprises the States and their peoples and is, therefore, a collective project, it seems appropriate that federal conflicts should be discussed at the federal (collective) level, where the representatives of different federal interests are represented. The federation consists of the States, which were existing political entities at the time of its founding, with their sovereignty established before the federal compact. The compact represents the sovereign contract agreed upon by the States, with the powers conferred on the federation and their extension. No individual State has the legitimate authority (nor can it claim to have) to review the terms of the compact by itself with an external effect that impacts others. Such a decision, since it pertains to the exercise of collective authority, must be evaluated by the collective through federal adjudicatory means and institutions, such as federal courts. These institutions can review the actions of States, peoples, and institutions in light of federal constitutional law, thus acting as "umpires" of the federal bargain.[76]

On the other hand, a counterargument could be made that federated States have legitimate authority to protect their community from overbearing actions by the federation and could therefore resist federal intervention by, for instance, refusing to apply a federal law that they consider a violation of their constitutional prerogatives or ultra vires (contrary to the federal compact). They could also resist a debatable central "bias" of federal courts to rule in favour of the federation.[77] However, such a counterargument must consider that the federated States are part of the federation which they willingly joined, accepting a reduction of their autonomies and submitting in certain areas to this new form of political authority. If it is true that they have a right to resist when their fundamental elements are unduly and illegally (according to the federal pact) interfered with by the federation, they cannot use such unilateral resistance to reject legitimate claims of federal action. Doing so would constitute an abuse of integrity and a violation of loyalty. A solution for a collective problem should be found in collective, common forums, and "ought to be established under the

[75] Halberstam 2018b, p. 143.

[76] Lenaerts 1990, p. 263.

[77] Halberstam 2018b, pp. 147–150.

general rather than under the local Governments".[78] Consequently, federal adjudication is subject to two institutional modes of conflict-solving: one that is deliberative (or political *strictu sensu*) and another that is judicial.

Deliberative adjudication takes place during the decision-making process, prior to the enactment of legal action. It enables both levels of a federation's authority, the national and the federal, to legitimately participate in enacting federal acts. The two centres of the legitimacy of political authority must be included in the federal political process and have an equal standing and say in the definition of federal policy and action. If this is the case, federal conflict can be channelled, discussed, and resolved through deliberative means, accommodating different interests, perspectives, and preferences while allowing for negotiation between the various actors. Participation and engagement in deliberative political processes at the federal level can mitigate the risk of federal power abuses and national resistance, with the final legal act issued by the federation representing a form of compromise among the collective interests at stake. Conversely, if the capacity of the two centres of legitimacy to participate in the federal political process leans more towards one side than the other, it will lead either to a limited and weak federation (if the balance tilts towards the States) or to a dominant federation (if the balance tilts towards the federal level), with the federal order being affected one way or the other.

In the US political system, the federal people (i.e., the American people) are represented in the House of Representatives (proportional to the population of each State)[79] and elect the executive body of government, the President.[80] The Senate, the second legislative chamber with concurrent powers with the House of Representatives, once represented the States (as members were appointed by the States' legislatures).[81] However, that role has been questioned since Senators (two per State) have been directly elected since the beginning of the twentieth century. Yet, in principle, the US political system allows for this balance of representation and participation between the peoples in their various capacities, as "We the People": the federal people and the federated people.[82]

Contrarily, in the German federal political system, the people of the federation are represented in the federal parliament, with the executive government being appointed based on election results.[83] The States are represented at the federal level in a second legislative chamber—the *Bundesrat*—by delegations appointed by the local governments.[84] The *Bundesrat* plays a crucial role in passing legislation that falls under the provisions of concurrent powers and those where the *Länder* is competent to execute the law, thereby protecting the interests of the federated States.[85] In this way, the

[78] Madison 2009, p. 83.

[79] Article I, section 2 of the Constitution of the United States of America.

[80] Article II, section 1 of the Constitution of the United States of America.

[81] Article I, section 3 of the Constitution of the United States of America.

[82] Schütze 2020, pp. 9–11.

[83] Article 38(1) and article 62 of the Constitution of the Federal Republic of Germany.

[84] Article 50 and article 51(1) of the Constitution of the Federal Republic of Germany.

[85] Günlicks 2003, pp. 343–354.

States and the federal people have political prerogatives that establish a necessary power balance at the federal level.

Judicial modes of adjudication are exercised by courts when reviewing legal acts of the federation or when assessing cases concerning the exercise of federal prerogatives. Federal supreme courts (the highest courts at the federal level) are tasked with ultimate authority to consider conflicts of federal competence. These courts are the constitutional courts of the federation, having competence and procedural legitimacy to assess the terms of the federal compact and its extension.

Both the US and German federations have federal courts (the Supreme Court and the Federal Constitutional Court, respectively) in place. Both play a vital function in adjudicating federal disputes within their respective jurisdictions and thus in maintaining the balance of federal order.[86] Article 93 of the German Basic Law expressly assigns to the Constitutional Court the power of adjudicating disputes between the federation and the *Länder*, as well as disputes between the latter. Similarly, in the US Constitution, Section 2 of Article III outlines the powers of the Supreme Court.

5.4 Conclusion: The Idea of Federal Legality

At its core, federalism is the theory of federation: a pact that forms a new type of political authority, defining the terms of its exercise within a territory composed of other equivalent and independent sovereigns. This pact is complex, as it necessitates the co-existence of different spheres of political authority, each with legitimate claims of self-determination, even if incorporated into a collective project of political existence.

The federal dynamic is flexible, adapting to each obstacle it encounters, sometimes leaning more towards the States, sometimes more towards the federation. It is a challenging dynamic, but feasible based on mutual respect, where the integrity of constituent units is upheld, and the loyalty to the federal project is never in question. What distinguishes federalism is its transformative nature. It involves the creation of a new community, inherently plural and diverse, capable of forging political and cultural bonds of belonging to an idea of permanent union—a promise of existence as a collective for the future.

The political principles of federalism—integrity, loyalty, and adjudication—are foundational elements of any federal system. Though they may manifest differently in varying federal settings, they are always present as they are essential for striking a balance between two levels of political authority with equivalent legitimate claims of self-determination within a single territory. Together, they form the essential normative criteria to assess the authority of federal action within the scope of the specific federal compact, and to understand the political dynamics in a specific federation, along with the challenges it faces. Understanding these principles enables a more comprehensive discussion of any federal system.

---

[86] Benz 2017, pp. 193–222; Somin 2017, pp. 440–481.

References

Adam J, Möllers C (2014) Unification of Laws in the Federal System of Germany. In: Halberstam D, Reimann M (eds) Federalism and Legal Unification: A Comparative Empirical Investigation of Twenty Systems. Springer International, pp. 492–521

Alexander J (1986) State Sovereignty in the Federal System: Constitutional Protections Under the Tenth and Eleventh Amendments. Publius 16:1–16

Arendt H (1963) On Revolution. Penguin Books

Beaud O (2009) Théorie de La Féderation. Presses Universitaires de France

Benz A (2017) The Federal Constitutional Court of Germany: Guardian of Unitarism and Federalism. In: Aroney N, Kincaid J (eds) Courts in Federal Countries: Federalists or Unitarists? University of Toronto Press, pp. 193–222

Bermann G (1994) Taking Subsidiarity Seriously: Federalism in the European Community and the United States. Columbia Law Review 94:331–456

Bodin J (1992) On Sovereignty: Four chapters from the Six Books of the Commonwealth. Cambridge University Press

Boyd White J (1990) Justice as Translation: An Essay in Cultural and Legal Criticism. The University of Chicago Press

Burgess M (2012) In Search of the Federal Spirit: New Comparative Empirical and Theoretical Perspectives. Oxford University Press

Chen L (2015) An Introduction to Contemporary International Law: A Policy-Oriented Perspective. Oxford University Press

Cohen J (2012) Globalization and Sovereignty: Rethinking Legality, Legitimacy, and Constitutionalism. Cambridge University Press

Cyr H (2017) Treaty Powers of Federated States and International Law. Thinking About Federalism 17. Available at https://www.juspoliticum.com/articles/Treaty-Powers-of-Federated-States-and-International-Law accessed 15 August 2025

Diamond M (1973) The Ends of Federalism. Publius 3:129–152

Elazar D (1987) Exploring Federalism. Alabama University Press

Follesdal A (2018) Federalism. In: Zalta E (ed) The Stanford Encyclopedia of Philosophy. Stanford. Available at https://plato.stanford.edu/entries/federalism/ accessed 15 August 2025

Gardbaum S (1994) Nature of Preemption. Cornell Law Review 79:767–815

Golemboski D (2015) Federalism and the Catholic Principle of Subsidiarity. Publius 45:526–551

Günlicks A (2003) The Länder and German Federalism. Manchester University Press

Günlicks A (2019) German Federalism and Recent Reform Efforts. German Law Journal 6:1283–1295

Halberstam D (2001) Comparative Federalism and the Issue of Commandeering. In: Nikolaidis K, Howse R (eds) The Federal Vision: Legitimacy and Levels of Governance in the US and the EU. Oxford University Press, pp. 213–251

Halberstam D (2004) Of Power and Responsibility: The Political Morality of Federal System. Virginia Law Review 90:731–834

Halberstam D (2012) Federalism: Theory, Policy, Law. In: Rosenfeld M, Sajó A (eds) The Oxford Handbook of Comparative Constitutional Law. Oxford University Press, pp. 576–608

Halberstam D (2018a) A People for Certain Purposes: On the History and Philosophy of Federalism(s) in the United States and Europe. Public Law and Legal Theory Research Paper Series 619. Available at https://papers.ssrn.com/sol3/papers.cfm?abstract_id=3241597 accessed 15 August 2025

Halberstam D (2018b) Comparative Federalism and the Role of the Judiciary. In: Caldeira G et al (eds) The Oxford Handbook of Law and Politics. Oxford University Press, pp. 142–164

Halberstam D, Reimann M (2014) Federalism and Legal Unification: Comparing Methods, Results, and Explanations Across 20 Systems. In: Halberstam D, Reimann M (eds) Federalism and Legal Unification: A Comparative Empirical Investigation of Twenty Systems. Springer International, pp. 3–67

Jellinek G (2000) Teoría General del Estado, 1911. Fondo de Cultura Económica

Kommers D, Miller R (2012) The Constitutional Jurisprudence of the Federal Republic of Germany. Duke University Press

Larsen S (2021) The Constitutional Theory of the Federation and the European Union. Oxford University Press

Lenaerts K (1990) Constitutionalism and the Many Faces of Federalism. The American Journal of Comparative Law 38:205–263

Leonardy U (1999) The institutional structures of German federalism. Working papers/Friedrich-Ebert-Stiftung, London Office. Available at https://library.fes.de/fulltext/bueros/london/00538008.htm#E10E18 accessed 15 August 2025

Lerner B (2019) The Topeka School. Granta

Loughlin M (2003) The Ten Tenets of Sovereignty. In: Walker N (ed) Sovereignty in Transition. Hart Publishing, pp. 55–86

Lloyd Junior W (1949) The United Nations and World Federalism. The Antioch Review 9:16–28

Lutz C (2014) Vielfalt im Bundesstaat: Eine verfassungsrechtliche Standortbestimmung der Gesetzgebung der Länder im Bundesstaat des Grundgesetzes. Lit Verlag

Madison J (2009) The Conformity of the Plan to Republican Principles – Federalist no. 39. In: Genovese M (ed) The Federalist Papers. Palgrave Macmillan

Marchetti R (2006) Global Governance or World Federalism? A Cosmopolitan Dispute on Institutional Models. Global Society 20:287–305

Maxeiner J (2014) United States Federalism: Harmony Without Unity. In: Halberstam D, Reimann M (eds) Federalism and Legal Unification: A Comparative Empirical Investigation of Twenty Systems. Springer International, pp. 491–521

McLeod Rogers N (1935) The Political Principles of Federalism. The Canadian Journal of Economics and Political Science 1:337–347

Mills A (2010) Federalism in the European Union and the United States: Subsidiarity, Private Law, and the Conflict of Laws. University of Pennsylvania Journal of International Law 32:369–455

Nelson C (2000) Preemption. Virginia Law Review 86:225–305

Palermo F, Kössler K (2017) Comparative Federalism: Constitutional Arrangements and Case Law. Hart Publishing

Pleyer M (2005) Föderative Gleichheit. Duncker & Humblot

Popelier P (2021) Dynamic Federalism: A New Theory for Cohesion and Regional Autonomy. Routledge

Renzsch W (1989) German Federalism in Historical Perspective: Federalism as a Substitute for a National State. Publius 19:17–33

Riley P (1976) Three 17th Century German Theorists of Federalism: Althusius, Hugo and Leibniz. Publius 6:7–41

Rocha A (2021) Private Actors as Participants in International Law: A Critical Analysis of Membership under the Law of the Sea. Hart Publishing

Schlink B (2012) Proportionality (I). In: Rosenfeld M, Sajó A (eds) The Oxford Handbook of Comparative Constitutional Law. Oxford University Press, pp. 718–737

Schütze R (2009) From Dual to Cooperative Federalism: The Changing Structure of European Law. Oxford University Press

Schütze R (2020) Models of Demoicracy: Some Preliminary Thoughts. EUI Working Papers 2020/08. Available at https://papers.ssrn.com/sol3/papers.cfm?abstract_id=3658493 accessed 15 August 2025

Somin I (2017) The Supreme Court of the United States: Promoting Centralization More Than State Autonomy. In: Aroney N, Kincaid J (eds) Courts in Federal Countries: Federalists or Unitarists? University of Toronto Press, pp. 440–481
Tierney S (2022) The Federal Contract: A Constitutional Theory of Federalism. Oxford University Press
Williams R (2018) The Guarantee Clause. Harvard Law Review 132:602–687
Young E (2014) Exit, Voice, and Loyalty as Federalism Strategies: Lessons from the Same-Sex Marriage Debate. University of Colorado Law Review 85:1133–1153

Chapter 6
Federal Legality in the EU Constitutional Order

Contents

Abstract This chapter examines the relationship between federalism and the EU, tracing the historical and political association between the two and assessing the EU's unique sovereign character. It argues that the EU embodies elements of both cooperative and constitutive federalism, combining Member States' continued autonomy with a shared supranational project. The analysis outlines how the EU's legal and institutional framework reflects the three core principles of federal order—integrity, loyalty, and adjudication—through provisions such as the principles of conferral, subsidiarity, and respect for national identity, as well as the supremacy of EU law and the protection of EU fundamental values. Drawing on these principles, the chapter explores the dynamic balance of political authority between the national and supranational levels, highlighting the EU's flexibility, political nature, and reliance on consensus. It concludes that federalism provides a suitable analytical framework for understanding the EU's constitutional structure, its evolving balance of power, and its distinctive model of shared governance.

Keywords Federalism · European Union · Sovereignty · Constitutional order · Federal principles

M. Lucas Pires, *The Federal Legality of EU Economic Governance*,
https://doi.org/10.1007/978-94-6265-747-2_6

6.1 Federalism and the EU

Federalism and the EU have long been strongly associated with an association that predates the creation of the EEC in 1957.[1] The terms "federation" and "federalism" were frequently referred to in the preparatory works of the Coal and Steel Community, as well as the projects for the Treaty establishing the European Defense Community and the European Political Community.[2] When proposing the plan for the creation of the EEC, what is now considered the founding expression of the telos of European integration, Robert Schuman stated that the "[t]he pooling of coal and steel production" was "a first step in the federation of Europe", and that the CSC would "lead to the realization of the first concrete foundation of a European federation indispensable to the preservation of peace".[3] Altiero Spinelli advocated for a federal Europe, first with the Ventotene manifesto[4] (published during the Second World War) and then in his plan that led to the approval, in 1984, of the Draft Treaty on a European Union by the European Parliament.[5] In his speech at the University of Zurich, Winston Churchill also argued for the European States to form a "kind of United States of Europe" following the Second World War.[6]

This association of federalism with the EU persists and forms part of the ongoing political discussion surrounding the EU. In these discussions, federalism signifies a political evolution where EU Member States confer additional tasks and competences to the EU and its institutions, leading to increased political integration.[7] Such a movement incites both criticism and support, sparking passionate political debates. For example, Margaret Thatcher famously criticized the EU's "founding fathers" in her Bruges address for aiming to model the EU upon the US political model and contended that European integration could not be an end in itself.[8] On the opposite side, Joschka Fischer argued for enhanced political integration to promote the establishment of a European Federation (with a capital "F").[9]

Moreover, the association of federalism with the EU extends beyond political discourse as a tool for political construction. Academic literature from the fields of

---

[1] Sidjanski 2000, pp. 7–42; Burgess 2000, pp. 62–76.

[2] See for example article 8(2) of the Treaty establishing the European Defence Community (1952) establishing that the structure of its governing institutions would remain in place until a new "federal or confederal" organization replaces them. Available at https://www.cvce.eu/en/obj/treaty_instituting_the_european_defence_community_paris_27_may_1952-en-2af9ea94-7798-4434-867a-36c4a256d0af.html accessed 15 August 2025. See also Deschamps 2016.

[3] Schuman 1950.

[4] Spinelli and Rossi 1944, pp. 9–30.

[5] Bieber 2008, pp. 18–23.

[6] Churchill 1946.

[7] In this sense, EU federalism means something different than US federalism, generally associated with the protection of the rights of Member States. See Halberstam 2012, pp. 577–579.

[8] Thatcher 1988.

[9] Fischer 2000.

political science, international relations, and law, dedicated to the study of European Integration, has also adopted federalism as an analytical model for assessing the EU. Some studies even draw explicit comparisons between the political structure of the EU and that of other federations. From the European perspective, such analytical arguments were advanced by Mauro Cappelletti, Monica Seccombe, and Joseph Weiler in their project "Integration through Law".[10] From the American side, significant contributions came from Eric Stein and Peter Hay.[11] Scholars devoted to federal theory have used the EU as an example of a federation in the making.[12] This argument continues today, with several authors from the fields of constitutional law, international law, federalism, and EU law regularly contributing to the argument that the EU, both structurally and dynamically, is an exemplar of a federation.[13]

Despite this connection, the association between federalism and the EU requires deeper exploration and analysis.

Federalism is a complex model of political organization whose normative underpinning, from the perspective of its sovereign character, is both cooperative and constitutive. The EU represents a unique type of political setting, the sovereign character of which has proved controversial and subject to different interpretations in literature. In fact, if one were asked to pinpoint the most controversial, complex, and frequently discussed topic in EU legal studies—the issue that has arguably claimed the most significant share of attention in academic literature and beyond—the answer would likely be the question concerning the sovereign character of the EU legal order: the question about what type of legal order the EU *represents*.

It is undisputed that the EU is a legal entity of public law, incorporated by agreements among States. The question is: is it a cooperative type of entity, or a constitutive type of entity? The multitude of answers generated in this discussion can generally be grouped into two positions. The first position asserts that the EU legal order is an international legal order constituted through treaties negotiated between sovereign, independent States wishing to establish a framework for institutionally enhanced policy coordination.[14] The second position contends that the EU legal order is "exceptional" because it represents a unique form of political integration among sovereign states, unlike international law, following the interpretation of the Treaties made by the CJEU in 1963 in the *Van Gend en Loos* case. In that decision, the CJEU famously stated that the "[European Economic] Community constitutes a new legal order of international law".[15] The question for proponents of the second position is how to qualify this "new" type of legal order: if it is something that is not international

[10] See Cappelletti et al.'s series of five volumes on Integration Through Law: Europe and the American Federal Experience (Cappelletti et al. 1985–1988).

[11] Stein 1981, pp. 1–27; Hay 1966, especially pp. 79–204.

[12] McKay 1996, 1999; Burgess 2000.

[13] Some important contributions are Lenaerts 1990, pp. 205–263; Weiler 2011, pp. 54–70; Schütze 2009a; Larsen 2021; Kovačević 2017; Bellamy and Castiglione 2005, pp. 293–310.

[14] See, for all, de Witte 2011, pp. 53–56. A different view, not so complete and persuasive, comes from Hartley 1999, pp. 131–136.

[15] CJEU, Van Gend en Loos v. Nederlandse Administratie der Belastingen, 1963, Case C-26/62.

law and, therefore, for lack of a better term, is "supranational"—which, in a sense, is no different from recognizing it as merely a "special" form of international law, albeit more advanced than other systems—a system that "already possesses certain characteristics of a constitution".[16] In academic studies, it is fair to say that, by and large, the second position is the mainstream view.

The truth is that the EU is a political setting with a more developed institutional structure than an international organization. It exercises direct political authority over the citizens of its Member States and holds competence in a range of policy areas that covers almost every sovereign policy area. While there are different degrees of legislative and executive intensity, the EU can enact binding rules over many areas, holding more legal power than any other international organization. There are "signs of an ambition that extends beyond the simple market" to a form of deeper political integration.[17]

Simultaneously, the EU's governance relies more on the agreement between Member States' heads of governments than on the will of its people(s), and the effectiveness of its law depends on the work of national public administrations and courts. Moreover, from a social perspective, opinions on the EU remain mixed: it is a project that is supported and cherished, generating both claims of belonging and rejection (as the Brexit referendum epitomized), yet not in the same way as a State. It is not that the EU "lacks a will-based imagination of the political",[18] but rather that its claim to social loyalty is more utilitarian, more technocratic, and rational than "national". It is this "plasticity" of the EU that makes it difficult to discern a substantive dynamic and to provide a clear answer about the character of its legal order, which is not quite international, yet at the same time, not quite constitutive or constitutional.

What distinguishes an international order from a constitutional one? Both emerge from pacts and both concern the organization of *potestas* through institutional structures. Their essential difference lies in their normative purpose. An international legal order is premised on establishing cooperation between the States, at the governmental level, with limited political integration and assimilation, especially in constructing a common identity or a fully-fledged community. In an international order, politics operates at the structural and technical level but is limited in terms of aggregation and community-building. It is cooperative but not constitutive: internationalism does not foster a strong call for political belonging but remains fixed at a limited discursive and aspirational level of politics, an order of interaction between diverse peoples and societies of peoples (States).[19] Cooperation is limited to achieving a functional and often limited objective (e.g., peace, trade, health, among others). In this sense, international organizations are more akin to platforms, functioning as specialized forums and frameworks, each with its own institutional and legal structures to solve

---

[16] Craig 2001, p. 135.

[17] Lucas Pires 1998, p. 39. See also Habermas 2012, pp. 1–12.

[18] Haltern 2003, pp. 18–19.

[19] Ibid, p. 25. See also Allot 1999, p. 37; Klabbers 2002, pp. 18–34.

specific common problems without any concept of self-determination and national singularity. There is no *potentia*, just *potestas*.

On the other hand, a constitutional order is a distinct kind of political entity: it symbolizes the order of a singular, self-determined community established for ongoing existence as a political unit. In other words, a constitutional order represents a collective—of people—bound by a cultural connection that underpins its founding and transformation into a unique entity in the world, wishing to shape its global existence as a distinctive collective. Such a connection may be multifaceted in several ways, but it is premised on forming a permanent centre for political existence under a shared governmental structure within a defined territory. The aim is not to create a platform, forum, or organization, but a complete entity of self-government for a fully formed community, capable of making the necessary decisions for the polity's survival and development.[20]

The EU is not a State, neither in form nor in substance; it neither presents itself as such, nor is it perceived and accepted as one. It does not represent a nation and has difficulty in asserting itself within a speech of nationhood.[21] At the same time, participation and integration in the EU form an integral part of the political framework of its Member States, and the question *of* and *for* Europe (i.e., more EU authority, less EU authority, different EU authority) is a critical political issue in national legal orders.[22] In fact, the Member States are part of a political collective that forms an integral component of their ongoing political existence. Moreover, a process of popular participation, a sophisticated institutional governance framework, and an authoritative legal system make the EU "extraordinary" from the perspective of international law.

More than an international organization or a State without form (which is what the phrase "constitutionalism without a constitution" implies),[23] the EU's body politic has a significant degree of uniqueness, of *political singularity*. Such singularity does not entirely conform to any conceptual or philosophical template. The EU's sovereign character owes much to the will of its Member States (and their respective internal dynamics), evidenced repeatedly in the way they advance EU law and the EU political-legal order through legislation, Treaty amendment, and political commitment to the successful interpretation and implementation of the Treaties. The EU's sovereign character also owes much to the actions of the joint governmental institutions (Parliament, Commission, CJEU, and ECB) in the way they interpret and safeguard the legal framework, according to the powers granted to them by the Treaties. Ultimately, the EU demonstrates elements of both cooperative and constitutive approaches, something that acknowledges and requires the Member States to continue existing as distinct political communities, but within a broader singular political project.

[20] Grimm 2016, pp. 359–364.

[21] See Habermas 2003, pp. 86–100; Delanty 2005, pp. 405–421.

[22] On the transformative side of EU law in Portuguese constitutional law see Moura Ramos 2001, pp. 131–139; Pereira Coutinho and Piçarra 2019, pp. 591–603.

[23] Cohen 2007, p. 127.

It is this unique political character of the EU (neither entirely national nor international) that helps explain the suitability of federalism for discussing and understanding its political character and structure. The association between the EU and the political theory of federalism can be justified for four reasons.

First, the EU is a compound polity, a political entity composed of several other sovereign entities. It is the product of an agreement by such entities to form a new political collective capable of exercising powers of authority, through legal and institutional means, over a range of policy areas. The substantive character of the agreement goes beyond mere cooperation, considering the degree of political integration to which the Member States have committed themselves in virtually all policy fields. EU Treaties are based on a constitutive logic, not of a State, but of a governmental apparatus that exercises state-like authority on a supranational basis. The existential purpose of the EU, in this regard, and considering the values and policy objectives it pursues, extends beyond international cooperation, towards developing a specific form of existence and achieving common good.

Second, the authority of the EU is more akin to national-constitutional than international. The EU exercises power over the national governments of the constituent States and their citizens. The Treaty of Rome already established the direct applicability of regulations, while in the aforementioned case of *Van Gend en Loos*, the CJEU declared that provisions of the Treaty, as long as they were clear and unconditional, could have direct effect and be relied upon by private parties in court.[24] Furthermore, EU law is also supreme to national law in areas where competence to act has been granted to its legislative bodies.[25] The Member States, either in government or through national executive and judicial bodies, have accepted this state of affairs: constitutional conflict arises only at the level of the most fundamental issues, primarily concerning the integrity (that is: fundamental aspects of constitutional structure) of these States. Finally, the authority of EU law is derived from its system, as the CJEU also acknowledged in *Van Gend en Loos*. Thus, there are two levels of political authority: the EU (supranational) level, and the Member-States (national) level, organized according to the terms of the agreement entered into by the Member States. This is a clear federal characteristic.

Third, while the supranational level holds the powers to directly affect the legal order at the national level, it is the latter that partakes in the decision-making processes of the former, either as singular entities represented through national governments or as citizens of the compound polity (as *European citizens*, represented in the European Parliament). Thus, the EU can be described as a "demoicracy", a democracy composed of several demos, where individuals maintain a "dual" political relationship as members of a broader community and as members of their national communities.[26] There is a level of political commitment that is distinct—deeper and more integrated—than participation in international forums and cooperation.

24 Robin-Olivier 2014, pp. 168–169.

25 Avbelj 2011, pp. 744–754.

26 Schütze 2020, pp. 26–35; Brink 2021, pp. 928–932.

Indeed, the EU bestows a new existential and enhanced political status upon its Member States and citizens: one of its objectives is to foster collective consciousness and introduce a new political form of (post-)national magnitude. This political stature comprises values, rights, and duties to which States and citizens are subjected, and the effectiveness of such rights and duties is safeguarded and enforced by an institutional framework. It may not be a full-fledged "national" body, but rather a strong supranational "coat" that drapes over the Member States. In this sense, the transformative aspect of political identity brought about by EU membership modifies its members' political and legal stature, even if it does not embody a comprehensive notion of nationality.

Nationality is a cultural tie to a form of collective self-existence and thus entails a political, emotional ("erotic"), and physical (territorial or familial) connection between the collective and its members. As Joseph H. Weiler posits, there is no "eros" in EU citizenship, implying there is no effective bond to the EU as there is with a nation; instead, what exists is a rejection of a totalitarian idea of nationality that dominates and subjugates all others into one.[27] However, there is a political connection and status founded on an identifiable axiological basis of mutual respect, support, liberty, and non-discrimination. Therefore, a rational bond can be discussed, desired, displayed, and defended. In essence, it is a status that is also identitarian and can induce feelings of belonging. It represents a different form of political connection compared to nationality. Still, it also has its strengths and capacity to build bonds, creating a robust political community, albeit one predominantly governed through technocratic principles and a political logic of over-compromise and consensus. It is fascinating to observe how the "imaginary community" of the EU[28] generates its cultural bonds through economic forms of interaction, rooted in EU freedoms, while simultaneously cultivating a sense of community—of values, rules, objectives, and principles.

The counter-argument to characterizing the EU as a federation hinges on its lack of features of a "complete" federal polity. This argument is predicated on the absence of powers and institutions observed in other "traditional" forms of federalism, for instance, in the field of defence and security policy or the existence of an influential parliamentary chamber.[29] However, given that no two federations are alike, it seems challenging to pinpoint a "correct" or "standard" model of federal polity to use as a unique paradigm—a point referenced in the previous chapter. Furthermore, most federations were the products of historical developments where the balance between the two spheres of political authority continuously evolved, with one sphere traditionally expanding more than the other (usually, the federal level). This process was driven by political practice and jurisprudential interpretation. In this context, federalism is dynamic, a process that is always in motion.[30] Hence, the absence of certain political features and powers does not impede considering the EU a federation;

[27] Weiler 1997, pp. 495–519.

[28] Anderson 2016.

[29] See Moravisck 2001, pp. 163–164.

[30] Popelier 2021, pp. 46–49.

rather, the EU can be, much like some federal States were in their early stages, a "polity for specific purposes only", still formulating and organizing its form of a federal compact.[31] In the EU, the precise delineation of the federal balance embedded in the system deviates from other federations.

In conclusion, federalism is not only suitable and appropriate as an analytical framework to explore how political authority functions, in theory and practice, in the EU. It also facilitates an organized philosophical discourse for normative analyses and debates regarding the EU's existence, purpose, potential, and limits.

6.2 The Political Principles of EU Federalism

The political principles of federalism signify the fundamental tenets of the constitution and the exercise of political authority in the federal settlement. These principles act as the fundamental criteria upon which federal order is predicated and aid in understanding how the federal balance between the two levels of political authority (the federal and the national) is established. These principles are the principle of federal integrity, the principle of federal loyalty, and the principle of federal adjudication.

These three principles of federal order are present in the EU settlement. The following section will delve into each of these three principles and how they manifest in the EU legal context, and what their content entails.

6.2.1 EU Principles of Federal Integrity

Federal integrity refers to the acknowledgement of the uniqueness of each constituent unit as integral parts of the federation. This principle enforces duties of respect towards the legitimate autonomy and sovereign character of the constituent States, which the federation and its governing institutions are obliged to uphold.

The EU principle of federal integrity is set in article 4(1) and (2) TEU, which reads:

1. In accordance with Article 5, competences not conferred upon the Union in the Treaties remain with the Member States.
2. The Union shall respect the equality of Member States before the Treaties as well as their national identities, inherent in their fundamental structures, political and constitutional, inclusive of regional and local self-government. It shall respect their essential State functions, including ensuring the territorial integrity of the State, maintaining law and order and safeguarding national security. In particular, national security remains the sole responsibility of each Member State.

---

[31] Halberstam 2018, p. 30.

This provision enumerates four sub-principles of integrity: the principle of conferral, equality of States, respect for national identities, and respect for essential State functions.

6.2.1.1 Principle of Conferral

The principle of conferral implies that the EU has only the competences explicitly granted to it in the Treaties by the Member States. This principle is understood in two ways. Firstly, the EU can act only within the policy areas and the legal forms, terms, and procedures specified in the Treaties. Secondly, beyond these areas, Member States retain autonomy. Compliance with the EU's action is mandatory within the confines of the Treaties, but outside these, Member States have the right to reject the EU's interference in their internal affairs. Therefore, the Treaties limit the autonomy of both the EU and the Member States in exercising their respective political authority.

As discussed in the first part of this work, the EU's political authority is organized according to types of competences. Each type identifies *who* can exercise political authority and *to what normative degree* such institution can act regarding a particular policy area. There are three types (and a half[32]) of competence: exclusive (only the EU can act in those areas), shared (both the EU and the Member States can act, with the EU being able to legislate to some degree, depending on the terms set in the specific legal basis of the Treaty), and cooperative (the Member States are the primary actors and the EU has powers to define general orientations and to set structures for supporting better coordination among the Member States, or, in the case of article 6 TFEU, to support and complement Member States' actions). If the EU acts outside this range, its action is incompetent and, therefore, subject to be declared invalid by the CJEU.

The Treaties establish two "flexibility clauses" in articles 114 and 352 of the TFEU. These rules allow the EU to have a wider margin of action when pursuing two objectives: (better) functioning of the internal market, in article 114, and attainment of the Union's objectives when the Treaties did not establish any necessary power, in article 352. Although both norms seem to provide broad powers to the EU, they are subject to interpretative and procedural guidelines (regarding article 114, set out in the case-law of the CJEU,[33] and regarding article 352, set out in its own text and also in the CJEU's case-law[34]) that limit their scope of action.

Whenever the EU acts, it is assumed that it has implied powers (limited by the scope of action according to the Treaties) at internal and external levels. At the internal level, implied powers mean that EU institutions can take all acts necessary to satisfy the competence's purpose—for example, in coordinating competences, the

[32] The "half" part refers to the substantive differences between cooperative competences set out in article 5 and cooperative and complementary competences set out in article 6 TFEU. See Chap. 3 of this work.

[33] See, critically, Davis 2017, pp. 74–89.

[34] See Kellerbauer and Klamert 2019, pp. 2072–2079.

EU can establish legal duties for the Member States to share information with each other on matters of social policy.[35] At the external level, implied powers mean that the EU can negotiate international agreements whenever it has the competence to decide on the matter at the internal level.[36]

6.2.1.2 Equality of Member States

In federal systems, the principle of State equality under the integrity lens means all States are equally sovereign concerning federal law and power, possessing identical rights and obligations. It grants the right to fair and non-discriminatory treatment by the federation's governing institutions.

The normative meaning of Article 4(2) follows such rationale.[37] In this sense, EU institutions must not treat the Member States in analogous situations differently. The CJEU also often connects the principle of equality of States and the general principle of non-discrimination of citizens.[38] In this sense, for the Court, discrimination of different States is mostly considered as discrimination between the different peoples of the EU.[39] The CJEU acknowledges that all Member States and peoples have the same standing in the face of EU law, thus acknowledging the importance of the principle of equality established in the Treaties: not only in article 4(2) TEU, but also in the norms of EU citizenship—article 18(1) TFEU—and articles 21–23 of the Charter of Fundamental Rights of the European Union.

It is important to note that the EU's federal balance is fragmented in the sense that there are differences among States regarding the degree of legal integration. For example, not all EU Member States participate in the EMU nor does the Charter bind all Member States. Such legal imbalance leads to a necessary differentiation regarding the EU's powers over some or the other Member States, given their obligations under EU law.[40] However, such differentiation cannot affect the legal status of Member States as essential components of the EU legal order, that is, as subjects to general rights and principles and worth of the same degree of legal respect by EU institutions.

---

[35] CJEU, Federal Republic of Germany and others v. Commission, 1987, Joined cases 281, 283, 284, 285 and 287/85, paras 28–30.

[36] CJEU, Commission v. Council, 1971, Case C-22/70 and article 3(2) TFEU.

[37] Rossi 2017, pp. 23–25. See also Wouters 2001, pp. 315–346.

[38] See for example CJEU, Italian Republic v. Commission of the European Economic Community, 1963, Case C-13/63, and CJEU, The Queen v. Minister of Agriculture, Fisheries and Food, 1995, Case C-44/94.

[39] See, for example, the assessment of the CJEU in CJEU, Portugal and Spain v. Council, 1992, Joined Cases C-63/90 and C-67/90, paras 36–37 and 44.

[40] See, in general on differentiation, Wouters 2001; Schimmelfennig and Winzen 2020.

6.2.1.3 Respect for National Identities

The third sub-principle of federal integrity, respect for national identities, has been the subject of extensive development and debate in EU law over the past decade, both in legal literature and case law at the EU and national constitutional court levels.[41] This is largely due to various constitutional conflicts around applying EU rules in sensitive areas, such as fundamental rights,[42] budgetary issues,[43] and monetary integration.[44]

Essentially, respect for national identities is about how EU institutions should treat the Member States and their legal orders within the EU constitutional framework. The principle mandates that EU institutions, in their actions, should avoid harming the fundamental characteristics of the Member States as self-determined communities. These characteristics may or may not be defined in national constitutional law. This principle must be balanced against EU law's supremacy, considering how an EU law measure impacts a fundamental provision of national law and whether it is a valid claim to reject the application of EU law in a specific situation.[45]

However, what precisely constitutes an element of national identity is somewhat vague. Identifying basic elements, such as language, symbols, political form of government, and political decentralization, is feasible. But beyond this, it becomes a complex task because different political orders might regard different aspects as fundamental due to their unique cultural and historical traditions. The Court of Justice of the European Union (CJEU) has avoided a one-size-fits-all definition of what constitutes an element of national identity. Instead, it leaves it to the discretion of national courts and institutions to determine what elements of their national identity should be respected by EU law.[46] This approach allows the CJEU to assess the value of a claim of national identity in terms of EU law and verify its validity. The CJEU can then understand if the claim is valid (i.e., if the claim refers in effect to a fundamental element of basic national political order that is being genuinely affected by EU law) and if such claim is in line with EU fundamental values.[47]

This principle is not absolute; it needs to be read in conjunction with the principle of federal loyalty and respect for EU values. Thus, a claim for respect for national identity can only be legally upheld if it aligns with the major values of EU law. It is not a "get out of jail card" to sidestep principles collectively agreed upon within the federal pact. Otherwise, the federal bond would be meaningless against Member

[41] See Cloots 2015; see also Faraguna 2017, pp. 1617–1640; Millet 2014, pp. 253–276.

[42] For example, CJEU, Ilonka Sayn-Wittgenstein v. Landeshauptmann von Wien, 2010, Case C-208/09.

[43] CJEU, Hungary v. Parliament and Council, 2022, Case C-156/21.

[44] In CJEU, Heinrich Weiss and Others, 2018, Case-493/17 para 14, one of the arguments of the parties in the national proceedings was that the measures of the ECB undermined German constitutional identity.

[45] Brink 2022, pp. 104–106.

[46] See CJEU, Ilonka Sayn-Wittgenstein v. Landeshauptmann von Wien, 2010, Case C-208/09, paras 86–87.

[47] Faraguna 2017, pp. 1636–1638; Millet 2014, pp. 264–266.

States' understanding of what is fundamental to them, and the effectiveness of EU law would be significantly compromised.

6.2.1.4 Respect for National State Functions

Respect for national state functions relates to EU interference in the exercise of Member States' self-governance. The principle requires the EU to avoid affecting, through its actions, the exercise of fundamental powers of the Member States' government. The effect on state functions must be serious and severe, involving a limitation of political functions that effectively prevents them from being suitably and autonomously exercised by the State's ruling bodies.[48]

What is considered "a fundamental state function" for the purposes of this norm? It refers to the essential roles a State must fulfil as an independent and self-determined political entity. These roles include, for example, legislation enactment, public affairs administration, justice adjudication, public order maintenance (a function explicitly reserved to the Member States in the Treaties), military affairs management, national electoral procedures, and international relations.

6.2.2 EU Principles of Federal Loyalty

Federal loyalty concerns the integrity of the federal compact: the primary duties and principles that the Member States must comply with for the sake of the stability and success of the federation (in other words, the "glue" to keep the federal construction together).[49] The federal institutions of government guarantee the implementation of these principles, which can use administrative and judicial mechanisms to deter (and, in the event of a violation, sanction) Member States from non-complying with federal constitutional rules. Furthermore, individual citizens can also, within the judicial mechanisms of preliminary ruling and state liability, enforce EU law against national institutions.

In the EU's federal framework, the principles of loyalty are the principle of respect for EU law, set out in Article 4(3) TEU, the principle of respect for EU values, established in articles 2 TEU and 7 TEU, and the principle of equality of States, set out in Article 4(2) TEU.

6.2.2.1 Respect for EU Law

According to article 4(3) TEU, Member States must comply with the obligations set out in the Treaty and other acts of EU law. Furthermore, they cannot take "any

[48] See Klamert 2019, p. 45.

[49] Sharpston 2012, pp. v–viii.

measure which could jeopardize the attainment of the Union's objectives". Failure to comply with EU law can lead to the institutions launching an action for infringement, which can end with applying financial penalties by the CJEU until compliance is restored. The Commission is responsible for supervising the application of EU law and initiating proceedings with the CJEU, according to articles 17(1) TEU and 258 and 260 TFEU.

Therefore, article 4(3) establishes the principle of respect for EU law in a general sense, whereby the Member States explicitly declare their bond to the EU legal order and its obligations. The principle includes the duty of sincere cooperation, according to which the EU institutions and the Member States shall collaborate and support each other in executing the Treaties.[50] Sincere cooperation is an obligation of mutual respect that shall exist, according to article 4(3), between the EU and the Member States.

In addition, Article 4(3) has another dimension related to the character of the supremacy of EU law over national law. As per the CJEU's understanding—accepted to a large extent by the Member States—national law cannot override EU law when the EU is competent to act.[51] Member States' authorities (legislators, public administration, and courts) must apply, implement and adjudicate EU law and disregard national law whenever the latter conflicts with EU legislation (primary or secondary).[52]

6.2.2.2 Respect for EU Fundamental Values

The EU is a polity based on the existence of diverse peoples with diverse cultures and traditions that respect one another and their shared history as part of the same territory. The purpose of the EU is to establish a closer union among these peoples: to do so involves taking down political and social barriers through non-discrimination and equality. Additionally, the EU is a form of collective action that requires mutual support between States and collaboration to establish a closer union that is balanced and equal, where no State (no people) deserves more than the other. The EU is, therefore, a liberal polity that respects the freedom of individuals inherent to their dignity: that is its constitutional identity.[53] At the same time, the EU exists to serve the interests of the citizens of the Member States and their citizens, who must be able to participate in the EU political process. Furthermore, given the EU's powers and capacity to impact on the lives of its citizens, such action must be politically legitimized by its citizens. Additionally, the action of the EU must comply with constitutional tenets of transparency, non-arbitrariness, publicity, and other values inherent in the broader and complex term identified simply as the rule of law.

---

[50] Klamert 2014, pp. 23–25.

[51] See on supremacy Schütze 2016, pp. 118–134.

[52] CJEU, Amministrazione delle Finanze dello Stato v. Simmenthal SpA, 1978, Case C-106/77, paras 13–26.

[53] See CJEU, Hungary v. Parliament and Council, 2022, Case C-156/21, paras 124–127.

The EU Member States acknowledge the axiological basis of their political connection in the Treaties.[54] Therefore, the political bond that forms the EU federation is based on a series of values. The values set in article 2 TEU are human dignity, freedom, democracy, equality (specifically, non-discrimination and equality between men and women), the rule of law, tolerance, pluralism, and solidarity.

Some of these values find expression in other parts of the Treaties. For example, article 18 TFEU prohibits any discrimination based on nationality, and article 19 (1) TFEU provides EU powers for taking measures to fight discrimination based on a series of categories. Article 9 TEU further states that the EU respects the equality of its citizens. The principle of democracy and its dimensions (i.e., duties of institutional transparency, clarity, and proximity) is expressed in the provisions of articles 9–12 TEU. One dimension of the rule of law is set in article 19(1) TEU on the norms regarding the CJEU. A further definition of the rule of law is set in article 2(a) of Regulation 2020/2092 of the European Parliament and the Council (the "conditionality Regulation").[55] Finally, there is the Charter of Fundamental Rights, where several of the values find rights that express them—and Member States have a duty to respect the rights of the Charter whenever they apply or implement EU law.[56]

The values are part of EU law; therefore, compliance with them is subject to judicial review by the CJEU. In its jurisprudence, the Court has directly referred to the values or applied a norm expressing them. Two examples include the review of a measure based on Article 19 TEU and Article 47 of the Charter, which pertain to adequate judicial protection, one of the dimensions of the rule of law principle, in the cases *Associação Sindical de Juízes* and *Commission v. Poland*.[57] However, there are non-judicial mechanisms to sanction non-compatibility with EU values.

A political mechanism is set in article 7 TEU and consists of a deliberative procedure at the level of the Council. If the Council finds a severe and persistent infringement of EU values by one of the Member States, it can decide to apply political sanctions by suspending some rights provided by the Treaties to the Member State in question.[58] The procedure has never been applied due to failure to reach unanimity (the necessary decision-making rule) in declaring a breach of EU values as severe and persistent.[59]

An administrative sanctioning mechanism is provided by the conditionality regulation previously mentioned, which aims to protect the Union budget. Article 5 of the Regulation grants powers for the Commission to suspend the transfer of financial benefits and other rights related to the execution of funds from the Union budget whenever it finds that a Member State is not complying with the rule of law principle.

---

[54] Kochenov 2017, pp. 9–10.

[55] Regulation (EU, Euratom) 2020/2092 of the European Parliament and the Council of 16 December 2020 on a general regime of conditionality for the protection of the Union budget.

[56] On the charter, see de Búrca 2013, pp. 168–184.

[57] CJEU, Associação Sindical dos Juízes Portugueses v. Tribunal de Contas, 2018, Case C-64/16 and CJEU, Commission v. Republic of Poland, 2021, Case C-791/19.

[58] Besselink 2017, pp. 128–133.

[59] Ibid., 141–144.

6.2.2.3 Equality of States and Differentiated Integration

The principle of State equality also underscores loyalty in EU law, considering the roles Member States play in shaping EU law formally and materially, and the implications of their actions on other States.

A unique attribute of the EU's federal bargain lies in the substantial degree of political autonomy that constituent States possess, especially when compared with other federations like the US and Germany. This points to an intergovernmental rationale that guides significant governance decisions. National governments, the Member States, hold the authority to approve amendments to the Treaties, both formally and within the confines of national constitutional law and international law agreements. Thus, the power to decide on substantial constitutional transformations of the EU and amendments to fundamental provisions rests with the Member States. Unanimity is required for such changes, which complicates the amendment process in terms of both scope and timeline. The simplified revision procedure also requires unanimity, but this is restricted to a single part of the Treaty.

Member States can influence the constitutional status quo of EU membership in two ways. The first involves differentiated integration, permitted within the Treaties via the procedure of enhanced cooperation as set forth in articles 326–334 TFEU.[60] The objective of this procedure is to enable Member States to pursue deeper integration, developing a more comprehensive legal framework pertaining to specific policy areas covered by the Treaties, excluding domains where the EU holds exclusive competence. Given that enhanced cooperation can cause distortions in the Treaty framework by creating new rights and obligations for participating Member States, this procedure must respect the rights and status of non-participating States. As stipulated in Article 327 TFEU, this includes the right to equality. This obligation extends not only to participating Member States and their proposal, but also to the Commission and the Council, tasked with approving and ensuring that enhanced cooperation aligns with the Treaties.

Additionally, Member States can influence the constitutional status quo of EU membership through international agreements.[61] Although EU law partially limits the competence of Member States to act as sovereign entities in the international arena, they retain autonomy in determining their international relations, both bilaterally with third States and multilaterally with other EU States, outside the EU's jurisdiction. This autonomy allows for the establishment of cooperation legal frameworks outside the scope of the Treaties. The risk here is that some Member States may exploit these frameworks to pursue objectives mirroring those of EU integration, bypassing the Treaty and its norms, setting rules for a select few, and thereby generating de facto legal discrimination between participating and non-participating States. In such scenarios, Member States would be in violation of the principle of equality, negatively impacting loyalty to the federal order.

---

[60] See de Witte 2019, pp. 6–7; Fabbrini 2012, pp. 5–10.

[61] de Witte 2019, pp. 7–10.

6.2.3 EU Principles of Federal Adjudication

The third and final subset of the principles of federal order comprises the principles of federal adjudication. These principles address disputes over political authority between the federal and national government levels. Federal adjudication not only involves the principles for resolving such disputes, but also the political and judicial mechanisms available for implementing these principles and making decisions on federal disputes. This ultimately establishes the balance of political authority within the federation concerning specific policy issues.

In the EU legal order, the principles of federal adjudication consist of subsidiarity, proportionality, and pre-emption, as set forth in articles 5(3) and (4) TEU, and 2 TFEU. The political and judicial methods for resolving federal disputes are integrated into the operations of EU deliberative and judicial government institutions.

6.2.3.1 Subsidiarity, Proportionality, and Pre-emption

The principle of subsidiarity is a core constitutional principle of the EU legal order.[62] As stated in article 5(3), first paragraph TEU, the EU can only act in policy areas that are not exclusively under its competence if its action is necessary for achieving an objective in a way that is considered better than if the action was to be pursued by the Member States. This principle must be paired with the principle of proportionality, which posits that EU action should not exceed what is necessary to achieve the objectives of the Treaty. Control over the application of the principles of subsidiarity is both political and judicial, implemented respectively by national parliaments before EU action is enacted and by the CJEU after the EU action has been undertaken. As for the principle of the pre-emption, it is set out in article 2(2) TFEU, which establishes limitations to the action of Member States once the EU exercises its powers under the category of shared competences.[63]

6.2.3.2 Mechanisms for the Resolution of Federal Disputes

In the EU federal compact, the CJEU is the judicial entity with the competence to ultimately assess the validity of EU acts in terms of the founding Treaties and whether a State has violated its obligations under EU constitutional law. In this context, the CJEU is, according to the Treaties, the final judicial arbitrator of federal legality, interpreting and defining the terms of the federal compact when adjudicating cases brought to it via one of the various judicial mechanisms established in the Treaties.

Usually, matters related to Member State compliance with EU law are addressed through an action for infringement (initiated by the Commission or by a Member

---

[62] On subsidiarity, see Schütze 2009b, pp. 525–531; Fabbrini 2018, pp. 221–242.

[63] On the principle of pre-emption in the EU, see Schütze 2016, pp. 134–145; Soares 1996, pp. 203–245.

State).[64] Conversely, issues regarding the legality of EU action are handled through the action for annulment (initiated by a Member State or an EU institution and, in rare cases, by an individual party).[65] The mechanism of a preliminary ruling, wherein national courts ask the CJEU for clarification on the interpretation and validity of EU law, has also facilitated control over federal legality within the EU legal order.[66] The CJEU, when responding to a question from a national court, typically clarifies the meaning of the EU law provision in question and asserts the incompatibility of national law provisions that conflict with that meaning, thereby reaffirming EU law authority and concurrently limiting Member States' autonomy. In some cases, the Court may rule that an EU law provision, brought to its attention through a preliminary reference, is invalid in light of the Treaties.[67]

Despite the Court's role in adjudicating federal legality, a long history of judicial conflict exists between the constitutional courts of the Member States and the CJEU over who is the ultimate arbitrator of federal legality. Some of the most renowned instances of federal judicial conflict originated from the Czech constitutional court in *Landtova*,[68] the German Constitutional Court's decision in *Weiss*,[69] and the Polish Constitutional Court's verdict on the relationship between EU law and Polish constitutional law.[70] In these rulings, the national constitutional courts assessed the validity of EU legal acts (and of EU Treaties) in relation to their national constitutions. The rationale behind this is that Member States partake in EU integration to the extent that their national constitutions permit. Consequently, EU action cannot exceed the bounds of the Treaties without encroaching illegitimately upon the constitutional autonomy and integrity of Member States. National constitutional courts thus believe that, according to their respective constitutions, they have a legitimate right to evaluate the legality of EU norms against their basic laws and, in turn, control the exercise of political authority by the EU.

Such conflicts—demonstrations of "constitutional pluralism", as it has been referred to within a section of EU law doctrine[71]—are common in federal systems. Given the absence of absolute political supremacy between the federation and federal states, it is expected that the national level might reject the application of federal law if it deems it illegal against its fundamental rules. Similarly, it is logical and rationally appropriate for such an action, when taken by national courts, to be considered illegal under the federal agreement that entrusts the adjudication of federal disputes

---

64 Article 258 TFEU.

65 Article 263 TFEU.

66 Article 267 TFEU. On preliminary ruling, see Moura Ramos 1994, pp. 221–234; Tridimas 2015, pp. 403–431.

67 Such as in CJEU, Digital Rights Ireland Ltd v. Minister for Communications, Marine and Natural Resources and Others and Kärntner Landesregierung and Others, 2014, Joined Cases C-293/12 and C-594/12.

68 Czech Constitutional Court's judgement (Pl. ÚS 5/12).

69 Judgement of 5 May 2020 2 BvR 859/15, 2 BvR 980/16, 2 BvR 2006/15, 2 BvR 1651/15).

70 Judgement of the Polish Constitutional Court K 3/21.

71 See, for the doctrine of constitutional pluralism, Walker 2002, pp. 317–359; Pierdominici 2017, pp. 121–153. See, also, its critique in Cruz 2018, pp. 27–52.

to a federal court. Hence, the judicial conflict, in practical and realistic terms, is a zero-sum game between two entities acting legitimately within the context of their respective constitutional laws. Ultimately, the resolution will involve an exercise of coercion wherein the larger entity will attempt to enforce its perspective (and it is entitled to do so under federal law), and the federated entity will attempt to resist this coercion (as it is also entitled to do so under its national law). The entity with greater coercive capacity or resistance will prevail. However, the final decision is one of force, not of law.

Despite the frequent discussions about constitutional dialogue through courts in federal procedures and how this dialogue of judicial and legal reasoning helps mitigate constitutional conflict, the problem in these "hard" cases[72] remains fundamentally political. It relates to the organization and definitions of political authority within the federation, the essence of the federal agreement. Courts are constrained to the law, its interpretation, definition, and application. They must remain loyal to their respective constitutions, which are essentially legal expressions of a political agreement, continuously subject to contextual and practical tensions regarding its purpose, meaning, and applicability. Therefore, their capacity to provide resolutions is limited. To avoid conflicts of force, the resolution of such constitutional conflicts depends more on the deliberative mode of entanglement, i.e., how national and federal government institutions agree to and consent to shifts in the power balance between one sphere and the other. This consensus can be facilitated through judicial dialectics.

However, even though politics are an integral part of judicial reasoning (since all positive law is, essentially, a political creation), judicial discourse is merely one method of constructing normative meaning. It could be argued that it may not be the most effective, given that the primary purpose of the judicial function is to adjudicate disputes through methodological forms of legal reasoning.[73] It is not to openly debate political problems regarding their practical urgency or potential ramifications. Moreover, it is not the judiciary's role to determine the best practical option—only the one that is most legally acceptable in light of the law. Political decisions, driven by opportunity, debate, risk, deliberation, and choice, are more effective and legitimate when made by institutions designed for such considerations. Therefore, constitutional conflicts concerning the fundamental tenets of the federal agreement, i.e., the extent of political authority granted respectively to the national and federal side, should (and ultimately are resolved) by deliberative political bodies.

It should be understood, however, that these issues are *federal* matters, and thus, they have collective significance since they affect the political structure that all constituent members share. Therefore, it falls to the federal deliberative bodies of government (where Member States and their peoples, united *as the peoples* of the federation, are represented) to manage and resolve these tensions of political authority. At the EU level, this responsibility is handled by the three deliberative government bodies: the Parliament, the Council, and the European Council.

---

[72] To use the expression of Dworkin 1978, p. 8.

[73] See Waldron 2006, pp. 1369–1379.

It should be noted, however, that within the EU federal compact, the intergovernmental bodies of the Council and the European Council play a more pivotal role in resolving federal conflicts than the Parliament. The reasons are varied but are related to the powers granted to the former institutions under EU constitutional law concerning fundamental decision-making procedures (such as legislation, budget negotiation, treaty amendment, use of the flexibility clause, and enhanced cooperation). The intent of such choice is apparent in that these are the political bodies composed of members of national governments and demonstrates how the former does not wish to relinquish control over the trajectory of European integration. While it is true that the Parliament also participates in these procedures and can play a crucial role through its vote, the Parliament (along with the Commission) functions more as a federal counterbalance to the national (or intergovernmental) force that continues to shape the Treaties, as several recent examples (including the management of the financial crisis, the migration crisis, the pandemic, and the rule of law situation) demonstrate.

6.3 Conclusion: The Federal Order of the EU

The history and dynamics of each federation invariably shape the organization and distribution of political authority between its two tiers of government. This distribution is perpetually in flux, contingent on context, and subject to forms of political discussion via judicial, administrative, or deliberative means. Nevertheless, the federal pendulum's swing must occur within a constitutional framework that provides normative boundaries, ensuring that the balance struck maintains the guarantee of the federal order. The essence of the federal order will always be safeguarded if both spheres respect their mutual integrity and the federation's collective objective.

In the EU constitutional framework, we can identify explicit articulations of the foundational political principles of federalism: integrity, loyalty, and adjudication. There is a federal order with unique features concerning where the federal balance is struck. Despite arguments about the increasing "federalization" of the EU since Maastricht, with competencies and powers extended over nearly every policy area and the enhanced status of the European Parliament, the pendulum seems to lean more towards the national side. Though clear principles of loyalty exist within the EU framework, the principles of integrity are expressly set out and appear first in the Treaty, specifically in the initial clauses of Article 4 TEU. This deference to national integrity is evident, especially when compared with American and German federalism models. The acknowledgment of respect for national identity, constitutional structures, and functions, along with how Treaty provisions concerning principles of federal structure—such as conferral, subsidiarity, and pre-emption—are arranged, underscore the importance of respect for national integrity within the EU constitutional framework. Moreover, the significant roles of the two intergovernmental bodies of the EU government, the European Council and the Council, in fundamental decision-making procedures and the critical role of national institutions in the application, implementation, and adjudication of EU law, underscore the national side's influence in the federal settlement. Finally, Member States retain considerable autonomy, particularly regarding international and military relations, fiscal policy, and social policy definition, beyond the scope of the Treaties.

How does this influence manifest in terms of the dynamic of federal government? The federal government in the EU, due to the weight of the intergovernmental logic and ethos, often becomes either excessively technocratic, overly legalistic, and rigid (usually critiques directed at the Commission or the Agencies), or overly "realistic" politically, with a focus on effectiveness, compromise, and pragmatism, or, to use a term that has an almost "fetishistic" resonance in EU politics and practice, excessively reliant on "consensus".[74]

Another significant impact of the federal framework on the dynamic of government is the flexibility of action. The EU constitutional framework remains impressively open to transformations either through Treaty-enabled modes (such as enhanced cooperation) or through the actions of EU institutions (and Member States), often validated ex-post by the judicial review of the CJEU (based on functional and teleological interpretation modes of EU law). The adaptability of EU law also demonstrates how the federal balance dramatically shifts in legal terms, usually leaning towards the federal side of the pendulum.

In sum, what is apparent in the EU federal dynamic is the pivotal role that politics still play in its definition. Politics is conducted through procedures but also beyond them, made through judicial decisions but also executive actions. Politics is a form of conflict and discussion outside the realm of force, arrived at by agreement, consent, and compromise, based on reasons that encompass legal considerations, other forms of normativity, and other rational and opportunistic justifications. To claim that the EU is apolitical is incorrect; if there is one characteristic the EU embodies, it is a political structure designed for debate, discussion, and resolution of choices concerning the common good of a complex community amidst differing and divergent interests. Moreover, the model of the organization of this political construction is distinctly federal, guided by principles of respect for the different participants and for their respective spheres of potential: of sovereign independent States and a sovereign political body representing a common will, a shared project, and a joint destiny.

References

Allot P (1999) The Concept of International Law. European Journal of International Law 10:31–50

Anderson B (2016) Imagined Communities: Reflections on the Origin and Spread of Nationalism. Verso

Avbelj M (2011) Supremacy or Primacy of EU Law – (Why) Does it Matter? European Law Journal 17:744–763

[74] Heisenberg 2005, pp. 65–67.

Bellamy R, Castiglione D (2005) Building the Union: The Nature of Sovereignty in the Political Architecture of the EU. In: Karmis D, Norman W (eds) Theories of Federalism: A Reader. Palgrave, pp. 293–310

Besselink L (2017) The Bite, the Bark, and the Howl: Article 7 TEU and the Rule of Law Initiatives. In: Jakbo A, Kochenov D (eds) The Enforcement of EU Law and Values: Ensuring Member States' Compliance. Oxford University Press, pp. 128–144

Bieber R (2008) The Spinelli Draft Treaty: a Remnant of Better Times or Inspiration For a Constitutional Settlement? PE 410.673 European Parliament, pp. 18-23. Available at https://www.europarl.europa.eu/document/activities/cont/200903/20090316ATT51977/20090316ATT51977EN.pdf accessed 15 August 2025

Brink M (2021) The European Union's democratic legislature. International Journal of Constitutional Law 19: 914–942

Brink M (2022) When Can Religious Employers Discriminate? The Scope of the Religious Ethos Exemption in EU Law. European Law Open 1: 89-112 available at https://www.cambridge.org/core/journals/european-law-open/article/when-can-religious-employers-discriminate-the-scope-of-the-religious-ethos-exemption-in-eu-law/1380E2E1692B0DAF1BAA0F327E809A43 accessed 15 August 2025

Burgess M (2000) Federalism and European Union: The Building of Europe, 1950–2000. Oxford University Press

Cappelletti M, Seccombe M, Weiler J (1985–1988) Integration through Law: Europe and the American Federal Experience. De Gruyter

Churchill W (1946) Address given at the University of Zurich. Available at https://www.cvce.eu/en/obj/address_given_by_winston_churchill_zurich_19_september_1946-en-7dc5a4cc-4453-4c2a-b130-b534b7d76ebd.html accessed 15 August 2025

Cloots E (2015) National Identity in EU Law. Oxford University Press

Cohen A (2007) Constitutionalism without Constitution: Transnational Elites between Political Mobilization and Legal Expertise in the Making of a Constitution for Europe (1940s–1960s). Law & Social Inquiry 32:109–135

Craig P (2001) Constitutions, Constitutionalism, and the European Union. European Law Journal, 7: 125–150

Cruz J (2018) What's Left of the Law of Integration? Decay and Resistance in European Union Law. Oxford University Press

Davis G (2017) The Competence to Create an Internal Market: Conceptual Poverty and Unbalanced Interests. In: Garben S, Govaere I (eds) The Division of Competences between the EU and the Member States: Reflections on the Past, the Present and the Future. Hart Publishing, pp. 74–89

de Búrca G (2013) After the EU Charter of Fundamental Rights: The Court of Justice as a Human Rights Adjudicator? Maastricht Journal of European and Comparative Law 20:168-184

de Witte B (2011) The European Union as an international legal experiment. In: de Búrca G, Weiler J (eds) The Worlds of European Constitutionalism. Cambridge University Press, pp. 19-56

de Witte B (2019) The Law as Tool and Constraint of Differentiated Integration. EUI Working Paper 2019/47. Available at https://cadmus.eui.eu/bitstream/handle/1814/63604/RSCAS_2019_47.pdf?sequence=1& accessed 15 August 2025

Delanty G (2005) The Idea of a Cosmopolitan Europe: On the Cultural Significance of Europeanization. Revue Internationale de Sociologie 15:405-42

Deschamps É (2016) The European Political Community. CVCE, 8 July 2016

Dworkin R (1978) Taking Rights Seriously. Duckworth

Fabbrini F (2012) The Enhanced Cooperation Procedure: A Study in Multispeed Integration. Centro Studi Sul Federalismo Research Paper. Available at http://webararchive-2001-2021.csfederalismo.it/attachments/article/835/CSF-RP_Fabbrini_ENHANCED%20COOPERATION_October2012.pdf accessed 15 August 2025

Fabbrini F (2018) The Principle of Subsidiarity. In: Schutze R, Tridimas T (eds) Oxford Principles of European Union Law, Volume I: The European Union Legal Order. Oxford University Press, pp. 221–242

Faraguna P (2017) Constitutional Identity in the EU — A Shield or a Sword? German Law Journal 18:1617–1640

Fischer J (2000) Speech on the ultimate objective of European Integration. Available at https://www.cvce.eu/en/obj/speech_by_joschka_fischer_on_the_ultimate_objective_of_european_integration_berlin_12_may_2000-en-4cd02fa7-d9d0-4cd2-91c9-2746a3297773.html accessed 15 august 2025

Grimm D (2016) Constitutionalism: Past, Present and Future. Oxford University Press

Habermas J (2003) Making Sense of the EU: Toward a Cosmopolitan Europe. Journal of Democracy 14:86–100

Habermas J (2012) The Crisis of the European Union: A Response. Polity Press

Halberstam D (2012) Federalism: Theory, Policy, Law. In: Rosenfeld M, Sajó A (eds) The Oxford Handbook of Comparative Constitutional Law. Oxford University Press, pp. 576–608

Halberstam D (2018) A People for Certain Purposes: On the History and Philosophy of Federalism (s) in the United States and Europe. Public Law and Legal Theory Research Paper Series 619. Available at https://papers.ssrn.com/sol3/papers.cfm?abstract_id=3241597 accessed 15 August 2025

Haltern H (2003) Pathos and patina: The failure and promise of constitutionalism in the European imagination. European Law Journal 9:14–44

Hartley TC (1999) Constitutional Problems of the European Union. Hart Publishing

Hay P (1966) Federalism and Supranational Organizations: Patterns for New Legal Structures. University of Illinois Press

Heisenberg D (2005) The institution of 'consensus' in the European Union: Formal versus informal decision-making in the Council. European Journal of Political Research 44:65–90

Kellerbauer M, Klamert M (2019) Article 352. In: Kellerbauer M et al (eds) The EU Treaties and the Charter of Fundamental Rights: A Commentary. Oxford University Press, pp. 2072–2079

Klabbers J (2002) An Introduction to International Institutional Law. Cambridge University Press

Klamert M (2014) The Principle of Loyalty in EU Law. Oxford University Press

Klamert M (2019) In: Kellerbauer M et al (eds) The EU Treaties and the Charter of Fundamental Rights: a Commentary. Oxford University Press, pp. 36–60

Kochenov D (2017) The Acquis and Its Principles: The Enforcement of the 'Law' versus the Enforcement of 'Values' in the EU. In: Jakbo A, Kochenov D (eds) The Enforcement of EU Law and Values: Ensuring Member States' Compliance. Oxford University Press, pp. 9–27

Kovačević B (2017) Europe's Hidden Federalism: Federal Experiences of European Integration. Routledge

Larsen S (2021) The Constitutional Theory of the Federation and the European Union. Oxford University Press

Lenaerts K (1990) Constitutionalism and the Many Faces of Federalism. American Journal of Comparative Law 38:205–263

McKay D (1996) Rush to Union: Understanding the European Federal Bargain. Oxford University Press

McKay D (1999) Federalism and European Union: A Political Economy Perspective. Oxford University Press

Millet FX (2014) The Respect for National Constitutional Identity in the European Legal Space: An Approach to Federalism as Constitutionalism. In: Azoulai L (ed) The Question of Competence in the European Union. Oxford University Press, pp. 253–276

Moravisck A (2001) Federalism in the European Union: Rhetoric and Reality. In: Nikolaidis K, Howse R (eds) The Federal Vision: Legitimacy and Levels of Governance in the US and the EU. Oxford University Press, pp. 161–187

Pereira Coutinho F, Piçarra N (2019) Portugal: The Impact of European Integration and the Economic Crisis on the Identity of the Constitution. In: Albi A, Bardutsky S (eds) National Constitutions in European and Global Governance: Democracy, Rights, the Rule of Law. T.M.C. Asser Press, pp. 591–639

Pierdominici L (2017) The Theory of EU Constitutional Pluralism: A Crisis in a Crisis? Perspectives on Federalism 9:121–153. Available at http://archive.sciendo.com/POF/pof.2017.9.issue-2/pof-2017-0012/pof-2017-0012.pdf accessed 15 August 2025

Pires F (1998) Amesterdão: do Mercado à Sociedade Europeia. Principia

Popelier P (2021) Dynamic Federalism: A New Theory for Cohesion and Regional Autonomy. Routledge

Ramos RM (1994) Das Comunidades à União Europeia: estudos de Direito Comunitário. Coimbra Editora

Ramos RM (2001) The Adaptation of the Portuguese Constitutional Order to Community Law. In: Kellermann A (ed) EU Enlargement: The Constitutional Impact at EU and at National Level. T.M.C. Asser Press, pp. 131–140

Robin-Olivier S (2014) The evolution of direct effect in the EU: Stocktaking, problems, projections. International Journal of Constitutional Law 12:165–188

Rossi LS (2017) The Principle of Equality Among Member States of the European Union. In: Rossi LS, Casolari F (eds) The Principle of Equality in EU Law. Springer International, pp. 3–42

Schimmelfennig F, Winzen T (2020) Differentiated EU Integration: Maps and Modes. EUI Working Paper RSCAS 2020/24. Available at https://cadmus.eui.eu/server/api/core/bitstreams/a9a1c74f-207e-56a7-affa-bb0501f110fa/content accessed 15 August 2025

Schuman R (1950) Declaration on the proposed creation of the European Coal and Steel Community

Schütze R (2009a) From Dual to Cooperative Federalism: The Changing Structure of European Law. Oxford University Press

Schütze R (2009b) Subsidiarity after Lisbon: Reinforcing the safeguards of federalism? Cambridge Law Journal 68:525–536

Schütze R (2016) EU Constitutional Law. Cambridge University Press

Schütze R (2020) Models of Demoicracy: Some Preliminary Thoughts. EUI Working Papers 2020/08. Available at https://papers.ssrn.com/sol3/papers.cfm?abstract_id=3658493 accessed 15 August 2025

Sharpston E (2012) Preface. In: Cloots E et al (eds) Federalism in the European Union, pp. i-viii

Sidjanski D (2000) The Federal Future of Europe: From the European Community to the European Union. Michigan University Press

Soares AG (1996) Repartição de Competências e Preempção no Direito Comunitário. Edições Cosmos

Spinelli A, Rossi E (1944) Problemi della Federazione Europea. Edizioni del Movimento Italiano Per La Federazione Europea

Stein E (1981) Lawyers, Judges and the Making of a Transnational Constitution. American Journal of International Law 75:1–27

Thatcher M (1988) Speech to the College of Europe – The Bruges Speech. https://www.margaretthatcher.org/document%2F107332 accessed 16 September 2025

Tridimas T (2015) The ECJ and the National Courts: Dialogue, Cooperation, and Instability. In: Chalmers D, Arnull A (eds) The Oxford Handbook of European Union Law. Oxford University Press, pp. 403–431

Waldron J (2006) The Core of the Case Against Judicial Review. The Yale Law Journal 115:1346–1406

Walker N (2002) The Idea of Constitutional Pluralism. The Modern Law Review 65:317–359

Weiler J (1997) To Be an European Citizen: Eros and Civilization. Journal of European Public Policy 4:495–519

Weiler J (2011) Federalism Without Constitutionalism: Europe's Sonderweg. In: Nicolaidis K, Howse R (eds) The Federal Vision. Oxford University Press, pp. 54–70

Wouters J (2001) Constitutional Limits of Differentiation: The Principle of Equality. In: de Witte B et al (eds) The Many Faces of Differentiation of EU Law. Intersentia, pp. 315–346

Chapter 7
EU Economic Governance and Federal Legality

Contents

Abstract This chapter examines the relationship between federalism and fiscal authority in the European Union, focusing on how the allocation of fiscal powers affects political autonomy and the constitutional balance of federal systems. It outlines the principles of fiscal federalism, including taxation, spending, redistribution, and liability, and explores the tensions between state autonomy and federal coordination. The analysis then turns to the EU, showing how the Maastricht model and subsequent euro-crisis reforms redefined the EU's fiscal federalism through enhanced supervision, conditional financial assistance, and new sanctioning procedures. While these reforms increased EU oversight and influence, Member States remain the ultimate decision-makers, particularly in sanctioning and financial liability. The chapter concludes that EU economic governance illustrates both the necessity and risks of federal intervention in fiscal matters: it safeguards stability but also challenges the principles of federal integrity, loyalty, and adjudication, thereby testing the federal legality of the EU's constitutional order.

Keywords Fiscal federalism · European Union · Economic governance · Federal balance · Fiscal authority

M. Lucas Pires, *The Federal Legality of EU Economic Governance*,
https://doi.org/10.1007/978-94-6265-747-2_7

7.1 Federalism and the Problem of Fiscal Authority

Of all the policy areas, fiscal policy is one of the most sensitive from the perspective of federal authority.

The exercise of fiscal authority is a fundamental characteristic of a political unit. It is through its exercise that a political unit raises funds to support its action and provide services to its constituents. The level of political autonomy of a political unit is inherently linked to its level of fiscal autonomy. As eloquently termed by James Madison, the "power of the purse",[1] enables the government (broadly defined to include both the parliamentary and executive branches) to make decisions, serving as a precondition for a state's self-governance capacity. Restrictions on fiscal powers in law lead to limitations on government capacity and, inevitably, to constraints on the political unit's autonomy and its people's self-governance.[2]

Within a federation, the constituent units have political autonomy and, consequently, they also possess fiscal autonomy and liability (i.e., they should be responsible for their fiscal policy choices). The federation also has political autonomy, and, therefore, fiscal autonomy. The federation's actions and resource allocation can be conducted with or without the intermediation of state powers, forces, and budgets. Moreover, the federation typically manages currency matters and thus is concerned with price stability and can produce regulations to address inter-state issues.[3]

As discussed in Chap. 1 of this book, fiscal policy involves decisions about the collection and expenditure of financial resources by a political community. In federal (economic) theory, this issue is referred to as "fiscal federalism", which pertains to the distribution of fiscal authority within a compound polity.[4] Fiscal authority, in this context, encompasses the power to tax, the power to spend, and the power to redistribute or allocate resources.[5] The challenge of fiscal federalism involves devising normative solutions to handle the economic and financial consequences of coexistence in a complex polity.[6] Such problems generally stem from the economic, political, and social interdependence that exists between the federation's constituent units and their inability to independently manage collective issues, such as spillover effects of individual action on the collective and the existence of discrepancies between the federal units.

In a federation, constituent units are subject to the actions of other units with whom they share common values, a common market (i.e., standard rules on trade and movement of production factors such as workers, capital, and goods[7]), and a common currency. The coexistence of distinct, reasonably autonomous units can lead

---

1 Madison 2009, p. 146.

2 Rodden et al. 2003, p. 4.

3 Broadway and Shah 2009, pp. 9–11.

4 Oates 1999, p. 1121; Rodden 2004, pp. 18–20.

5 Musgrave 1959, p. 5.

6 Ibid., p. 11; Shah 2007, pp. 9–21.

7 See Balassa 1961, pp. 1–2.

to competing and divergent actions and cause distortions between States.[8] Variations in taxation, regulatory standards, social assistance, and economic growth may result in inequality between states if not properly addressed. These divergences can also trigger asymmetric economic shocks that could strain the federation's fiscal stability, affecting national and local debts and currency prices. There is also the question of fiscal liability: whether the federation is responsible for bailing out federated states and assuming their debts (and the legal terms under which such assumption works), or if each State is left to bear its debts alone, dealing with the costs of default. All things considered, fiscal federalism raises questions about federal intervention in the fiscal capacities of the constituent units.[9]

The fiscal purpose of the federation is, economically speaking, to ensure a fair and efficient balance among the constituent units, thereby aiding them in reconciling and responding to the collective obligations of mutual commercial openness.[10] Two governance traits must be present to guarantee equity and efficiency. The first is the existence of a central redistributive capacity for allocating collective resources to local political units, reducing disparity costs between them, and helping to prevent the onset of asymmetric economic shocks.[11] The second is the establishment of normative frameworks (either federal or local, or both) that facilitate economic stabilization.[12] These aspects of fiscal authority (redistribution, allocation, and coordination) inherently imply constraints on national fiscal autonomy (for example, limits on running a budget deficit, or debt ceilings). They also entail the federation exercising some degree of fiscal authority (and, consequently, government power) over the constituent units and their citizens.

It becomes evident, from the perspective of federal principles, that the exercise of fiscal authority has the strong potential of generating issues concerning the legitimacy of the action of the federal government. In fact, there is a challenging relationship between integrity and loyalty regarding fiscal competence. On one hand, autonomy in fiscal matters is an integral element of sovereign autonomy, making its protection crucial to constituent states' capacity to govern their people. On the other hand, federated states must act as constituent units of a political collective in which individual action may generate adverse implications for other members of the federation. Recognizing these issues, each federate State should understand the essential role that federal intervention plays in ensuring economic and political balance. The question, therefore, concerns the extent to which the federation should be allowed to interfere in the definition of national fiscal policy—or, put differently, how limited the fiscal powers of the constituent states should be due to federal (collective) considerations. The issue is not about the normative limitation of local powers *per se*—such a normative limitation is a precondition for joining a federation. The problem lies in

---

[8] Broadway and Shah 2009, pp. 498–516.

[9] Yilmaz and Zahir 2020, pp. 30–40.

[10] Broadway and Shah 2009, pp. 16–17 and 29.

[11] Spahn 2007, pp. 75–78.

[12] Hagen 2007, pp. 107–129.

determining the extent of such limitations and the federation's capacity to control a state's fiscal autonomy.

7.2 Fiscal Federalism in the EU

What is the EU's model of fiscal federalism, or, put differently, how is fiscal authority allocated in the EU's federal compact?

The Maastricht model established that fiscal authority remained with the Member States, except for Treaty rules prohibiting budget deficits of more than 3% and debts of over 60% GDP. However, the power to impose sanctions for failure to comply with such rules was allocated with the Member States, which reinforced, in practice, their constitutional position in this field. It was clear from this model (and the saga of France and Germany versus the Commission proved it) that Member States held both "the knife and the cheese" regarding fiscal authority in the EU federal compact.

During the euro crisis of 2009–2013, with the failure of the Maastricht rule-based model to deter national governments from running high deficits, Member States decided to strengthen the fiscal authority of the EU. They did so by developing the economic governance framework, without breaking with the policy premises first established in the Maastricht Treaty: EU fiscal authority would continue to be limited to coordination of economic policies, to powers of economic orientation and fiscal supervision, and the Member States would continue to be solely responsible for their own fiscal policy definition.

Nevertheless, the constitutional reform enacted during the euro crisis brought about two critical changes to this scenario. The first was a restructuring of preventive and corrective supervision of national fiscal policy developments in terms of rules and procedures; the second was the introduction of an institutional and permanent framework for providing financial assistance. Regarding the former, supervision procedures became more organized, transparent, and stringent. The Member States now had to regularly share economic outlooks and fiscal plans with EU institutions, becoming subject to continuous fiscal assessments. In addition, new procedures for enhanced supervision of Member States subject to financial difficulties were introduced.

After the reform, EU institutions continued not to have formal powers to command Member States to define their fiscal policies and can only provide guidance through non-binding instruments. However, new sanctioning procedures (such as the EIP) were introduced to encourage compliance with the supervisory procedures and, in this way, promote more compliance with the EU's fiscal policy targets. As for financial assistance procedures, Member States established an international facility, the ESM, to assist Member States in financial distress. Member States also agreed on the creation of an EU facility for assisting Member States in need that remains (formally, at least) in force. In both cases, assistance is provided only if the beneficiary states comply with enacting substantial policy reforms proposed by EU institutions.

Much has been said and written about the restructuring of the economic governance framework during the euro crisis.[13] The question that remains is to understand how the fiscal federalism paradigm in the EU changed post-euro crisis: whether there was any shift in the balance of fiscal authority that existed prior to the crisis or not.

At first glance, things seem to remain the same as before the crisis: the fiscal authority of the EU is limited to economic coordination. However, the way such coordination occurs has significantly changed. Nowadays, national budgetary discussions and proceedings are more exposed to EU normative and political pressure. EU supervision also extends beyond the budget, covering a country's broad fiscal and economic setting. With the European Semester, there is also a system for public communication of reports, budgets, and information available to the public, national governments, and market agents, thus increasing the level of public and private scrutiny of national fiscal policy. In other words, the EU has a greater presence in fiscal policy definition.

The establishment of a normative framework of financial assistance also provided the EU with a new element of fiscal authority. First, the EU has the institutional and normative capacity to react to economic shocks by providing financing to Member States. Secondly, by linking financial assistance to compliance with economic policy conditions, the EU can decisively interfere with and direct the definition of national fiscal preferences through binding instruments. Thirdly, the experience of the financial assistance programs provided during the euro crisis to Greece, Portugal, Ireland, and Cyprus was challenging and had significant social and political effects. The negative allure and experiences of fiscal assistance can generate an extra layer of deterrence for national governments, making them more fiscally prudent to avoid non-compliance with EU fiscal rules. Suffice to say that this new form of awe adds, in substance, more power to the EU's sphere of fiscal authority.

Nevertheless, the decisive element of the constitutional framework of EU economic governance remains unchanged: the control that the Member States continue to exercise in preventive and corrective supervision and the new area of financial assistance. In other words, the effectiveness of economic governance continues to depend, ultimately, on the decisions of Member States in the Council. If the Member States disagree with the application of sanctions, there will be no penalties for failures to comply with the rules. Although the Commission has a much more influential role nowadays in the procedures of supervision of Member States' fiscal policies, with the receiving and collection of fiscal and economic data, and in the negotiation, implementation, and supervision of programs of financial assistance, in the end, it is still up to the Member States to decide on the application of sanctions for non-compliance with rules of economic governance. Therefore, Member States still hold the most crucial set of keys in the constitutional sphere of EU fiscal authority.

Lastly, and supplementing this point, the fact that the forms of financial assistance are subject to conditionality implies that fiscal liability remains with the Member States and not with the EU, due to the no-bailout clause and its interpretation by the

[13] See Tuori and Tuori 2014, pp. 85–116; Craig 2016, pp. 19–40; Menendéz 2012, pp. 41–98.

CJEU in *Pringle*. The responsibility of repaying the funds provided by the EU with interest lies with the Member States.

Therefore, as stated in the first part of this work, there is a significant and seemingly unresolvable tension between the normative framework and the normative practice in the legal framework of EU fiscal federalism. This can be termed the "squaring of the circle" of the constitutional setting of the EU powers of economic governance. From a legal perspective, fiscal authority predominantly resides with the Member States. However, the EU possesses an array of administrative tools and powers to monitor and guide (and indeed exert pressure on) the definition of national fiscal policy. Simultaneously, the EU body with the final say in managing budgets is the Council, where the Member States are represented. The EU Parliament does not hold any significant power in economic governance.[14] The political process of EU fiscal federalism is therefore dominated by the executive and the inter-governmental political bodies of the EU, where national political preferences and compromise play a crucial role, often to the detriment of collective needs.

7.3 Powers of Economic Governance and Principles of Federal Balance

Assessing how EU powers of economic governance align with the principles of federal balance involves asking three questions. First, do the powers of economic governance of the EU impact the political autonomy of Member States and their rights to resist EU interference in their domestic autonomy as outlined in the Treaties? Second, does the EU framework of economic governance in any way affect the loyalty that Member States owe to the EU political project (meaning, the loyalty they owe to one another as equal sovereign units)? Third, how do the principles governing the exercise of EU (federal) power and the institutional mechanisms available in the Treaties (deliberative and judicial) for resolving conflicts of federal authority apply to economic governance?

EU economic governance involves three sets of powers: definition (proposing general and individual orientations of fiscal policy to the Member States), supervision (preventive and corrective monitoring of fiscal and economic developments in the EU and the individual Member States), and assistance (provision of financial support to the Member States facing financial distress). To answer the question of the constitutionality of EU economic governance with the principles of federal balance, it is therefore crucial to analyse the relationship of the three powers with each of the three principles. By examining each principle individually, it is possible to fully understand the many ways the powers of economic governance affect (or not) that specific dimension of the federal balance, or, in the case of the principle

[14] Fromage 2017, pp. 159–175. The picture has not improved much: see Fromage and Markakis 2022, pp. 385–401.

of federal adjudication, how the normative and institutional tools for safeguarding balance apply in the field of economic governance.

7.3.1 *Economic Governance and the Principle of Federal Integrity*

Federal integrity concerns the rights of the Member States to be protected against undue and abusive federal intervention. Abusive federal intervention refers to any federal action that disproportionately affects the autonomy of Member States to the point of impacting their sovereignty's limits as self-governed political units. Included within these rights is also a right to equal treatment of the federation's members.

The EU's four principles of federal integrity are established in Articles 4(1) and (2) of the TEU. The first principle is the principle of conferral, the general principle ruling EU competences. The second principle is the principle of equality (of treatment) of Member States. The third principle is the principle of respect for national constitutional identity (or the principle of respect for fundamental structures of the State). The fourth and last principle is the principle of respect for national fundamental political functions.

7.3.1.1 Federal Integrity and Powers of Economic Policy Definition

According to the principle of conferral—that is, how competences were allocated to the Union—the EU holds the competence to aid in coordinating the economic policies of Member States. Thus, as discussed in Chap. 2, the EU cannot stipulate with binding authority what national fiscal policy should be; it can only generate policy orientations and guidelines (both general and individual) that are non-binding. Binding acts must be confined to rules on the method and structure of economic governance (as per articles 121 and 136 TFEU, as used in the past) but cannot impose a new obligation on the Member States to adopt specific fiscal policy measures. Moreover, if a Member State does not adhere to the general orientations, the only penalty available is a warning.[15] In this sense, powers of definition respect the principle of conferral balance: the definition of fiscal policy is a national competence limited by binding Treaty rules.

EU powers of economic policy definition also respect the principle of equality of States. All Member States are subject to the orientations and guidelines issued by EU institutions under Article 121 TFEU. Moreover, to this day, there have been no instances of discrimination against Member States by EU institutions in the definition of the policy guidelines and norms issued under the legal basis of Article 136(1) TFEU (except for the acts issued regarding the EFSM) have all had a collective destination (although article 136 allows only for measures taken concerning the Eurozone).

---

[15] Article 121(4) TFEU.

As for the principle of respect for national constitutional identity, there is also no problem in terms of integrity. The definition of economic policy by EU institutions is limited to issuing non-binding guidelines and orientations that the Member States can disregard (as long as they do not substantiate a violation of Treaty rules on economic structures and excessive deficits). The same can be said of the principle of respect for fundamental State functions: it is the Member States that control the definition of fiscal policy and must collaborate to determine the optimal path for each State to individually follow in order to achieve collective economic objectives.

In summary, EU powers of economic policy definition, both in theory (their normative framework) and practice (their application), respect the principle of federal integrity in all its dimensions. The principle of conferral sets the scope of the Union's competence in this regard, where the competence for fiscal policy definition remains with the Member States, and the EU's competence is limited to the production of non-binding orientations. Federal integrity is therefore safeguarded if the clause of article 136 TFEU is not utilized outside the scope of coordination and as a flexibility clause in economic policy definition.

7.3.1.2 Federal Integrity and Powers of Economic Policy Supervision

The Treaties confer on the EU powers to monitor Member States' fiscal policy developments for two purposes. The first is established in the MSP to support a "closer coordination" of economic policies.[16] Therefore, according to the principle of conferral, economic governance requires EU institutions—the Commission and the Council, respectively—to have powers to oversee national economic developments. Moreover, the Treaty also permits EU institutions, in corrective procedures, to impose sanctions on the Member States. Consequently, in regard to these two supervisory procedures, there is no conflict with the principle of conferral.

The EIP is problematic concerning its compatibility with the principle of conferral. In its preventive part, the EIP could serve as an additional layer of the MSP, covering a specific range of elements to monitor and analyse according to the general economic orientations. In this sense, it could be respectful of conferral. The issue, however, lies in its corrective part, as it is the only supervisory procedure establishing a sanction mechanism that is not based on the Treaty. The only (serious) sanctions to be applied to the Member States in procedures of economic policy supervision concern failures to comply with the EDP rules. The Treaty does not state that the Member States should monitor economic "balances", nor does it define what a macroeconomic imbalance is (a definition that, as observed earlier, is broad and problematic because it can cover all types of elements affecting the economy of a State).

Moreover, the EIP establishes penalties for failure to comply with recommendations. Therefore, constraining Member States' fiscal policy autonomy to an extent that exceeds the scope of the Treaties (and beyond the mere concept of "coordination", therefore outside of the scope of the legal basis of article 136 TFEU) is not

[16] Article 121(3) TFEU.

in line with the principle of conferral, adding a layer that can impact the sphere of sovereign autonomy that Member States possess according to the EU's federal principles. This idea is an abstract consideration because no EIP has been initiated yet. However, the normative basis is problematic from a federal perspective of integrity.

Regarding the principle of equality, there is an issue with the application of rules by EU institutions. The Commission, which is responsible for monitoring and evaluating the developments of national fiscal policy, was criticized in 2015 by the European Court of Auditors for inconsistent application of the EDP's rules.[17] It was also the Commission that did not escalate the procedure of infringement when France continually failed to follow recommendations to rectify its deficit. Infamously, former President of the Commission Jean-Claude Juncker declared that an EDP on France was not initiated because "It is France."[18] The Commission was not as forgiving with other Member States: for instance, Portugal and Spain had a sanctions procedure initiated against them after failing to comply with EDP rules, two years after their respective assistance programs had ended. The Council ultimately decided to cancel the fine due to Portugal and Spain's commitment to economic adjustment.[19] Other Member States, such as Belgium, took (according to the Commission) inadequate actions to rectify excessive deficits, yet no procedural sanction was applied.[20] There are other instances (concerning Italy, for example) where there is a lack of congruence between the official actions of EU institutions and the rules of the system.[21] Such inconsistent application of the rules and the procedures (without clear reasoning) challenges the EU's adherence to the principle of equality of States.

Furthermore, even if the Commission does pursue an EDP and escalates to apply sanctions, it is uncertain to what extent the Council will decide to enforce penalties when certain States are involved. The case of France and Germany in 2000 highlighted the significance of power structures in European integration as the application of EDP rules is neither transparent nor automatic. In this respect, integrity as equality of treatment of States seems imbalanced or at risk of becoming imbalanced in the EDP.

The risks of inconsistent and discriminatory application of supervisory procedures also exist in the MSP and the EIP, given their institutional similarities with

---

[17] European Court of Auditors (2015) Financial Assistance Provided to Countries in Difficulties, pp. 8, 28–42, and p. 73, available at https://www.eca.europa.eu/Lists/ECADocuments/SR15_18/SR_CRISIS_SUPPORT_EN.pdf accessed 15 August 2025.

[18] Guarascio 2016.

[19] See, for Portugal, Council Implementing Decision (EU) 2017/2350 of 9 August 2016 on imposing a fine on Portugal for failure to take effective action to address an excessive deficit [2017] OJ L336/24 and for Spain Council Implementing Decision (EU) 2017/2351 of 9 August 2016 on imposing a fine on Spain for failure to take effective action to address an excessive deficit [2017] OJ L336/27.

[20] Regarding Belgium, see Council Decision of 21 June 2013 establishing that no effective action has been taken by Belgium in response to the Recommendation of 2 December 2009 [2013] OJ L190/84 and the history of the EDP with Belgium in https://economy-finance.ec.europa.eu/economic-and-fiscal-governance/stability-and-growth-pact/corrective-arm-excessive-deficit-procedure/closed-excessive-deficit-procedures/belgium_en accessed 15 August 2025.

[21] See Dermine 2022, pp. 188–192.

the EDP (Commission as the monitoring entity and Commission and Council as corrective enforcers). In the case of the EIP, financial penalties can also be imposed for infringement of Council recommendations. In this regard, integrity as equality could be jeopardized within the procedures of economic policy supervision, both preventive and corrective.

The principles of respect for constitutional identity and fundamental state functions can be influenced depending on the interpretation of the EDP, whether it is a qualitative or a quantitative reading of the rule. If EDP evaluation is focused on reaching specific quantitative criteria such as deficit reduction, structural deficit reduction, or debt reduction, then the EDP does not inherently put the principles of fundamental identity and function at risk: Member States have the autonomy to decide which policies to adopt to meet such quantitative targets. If the evaluation is qualitative, respect for national constitutional identity and functions can be affected, for instance, if the Commission requests the supervised Member State to adopt specific policy measures in certain areas (like labour market liberalizations or spending decisions in national security or other important policy areas). It is unlikely that the Commission and the Council would issue such authoritative recommendations or qualitative-only-based assessments; usually, recommendations in the corrective arm are drafted as orientations with no commanding language and involve both qualitative and quantitative assessments. Also, in practice, procedures typically conclude once quantitative compliance with (at least) the budget deficit rule occurs. Therefore, integrity in its dimension of respect for national fundamental structures and functions does not seem to be threatened by powers of economic governance.

One thing that could influence the principle of national state functions is its impact on national budgetary procedures or administrative entities. EU institutions can wield influence in the drafting and negotiation of national budgets. Member States can be subject in the EDP and the ESP to regular on-site monitoring and review missions by the Commission to see if corrective measures are being adopted. Such presence of EU institutions serves a supervisory function—to check if the government of the Member State is acting according to EU rules and agreements—but there is the risk that it can also have a substantial effect in guiding and influencing choices of budget execution and development while sidelining democratic procedures. Given the situation in which supervised States are in, with the risk of incurring sanctions (EDP) or requesting financial assistance (ESP) and their autonomy to act limited, there is a possibility that EU institutions can have a decisive say in government action. That would be, however, against the principle of national integrity, as it would constitute an abusive position over the State's autonomy.

In this sense, there are some problems regarding the principle of integrity and powers of economic policy supervision. A corrective supervisory mechanism like the EIP seems to be a step too far considering the Treaties and the sanction mechanisms established therein, thus affecting the principle of conferral by granting more powers to the EU than it should have in this competence field. As for equality, the history of the EDP shows an inconsistent application that discriminates among the

Member States. Finally, concerning constitutional structures and functions, supervision presents risks of undue power interference with national budgetary procedures and government execution of budgetary programs through informal methods.

7.3.1.3 Federal Integrity and Powers of Economic Policy Assistance

Economic policy assistance is, from a legal perspective, the most stringent procedure of economic governance, wherein supervised states must comply with conditions set in the MoU in exchange for the disbursement of funds. Consequently, it is the procedure of economic governance where the principle of integrity is most at risk due to the vulnerable position that assisted Member States find themselves in, which restricts their government's autonomy and capacity for action, subjects them to EU powers, and empowers EU institutions to direct the design and implementation of national fiscal policies.

The primary issue affecting integrity is the form of limitation on national autonomy. It is a given that a Member State's government has limited options for action within financial assistance procedures. That EU institutions can indirectly command or decisively influence the design of national fiscal policy (thus possessing *de facto* competences that exceed the principle of conferral but direct the Member State in the adoption of policies concerning revenues and expenses) is also not debatable. Central to the issue of federal integrity is how legitimate such a reduction of national autonomy is from a perspective of sovereign respect. It is, therefore, essential to understand how much autonomy (legal and factual) the assisted State has in requesting assistance and defining the conditions attached to the assistance. Additionally, it is crucial to comprehend the role EU institutions have in the design and enforcement of such conditions—i.e., the capacity of the EU to constrain national action. Lastly, the form of assistance (i.e., via the EFSM or the ESM) provided influences the balance between the EU and its Member States.

There are two procedures for requesting financial assistance: an internal, EU-based one (the EFSM) and an (apparently) external one (the ESM) that is, however, governed by EU law to a certain extent. In the former, a Member State in financial distress must request assistance from the Commission and the Economic and Financial Committee by submitting a draft economic and financial adjustment program outlining its needs (the Member State must first discuss its needs with the Commission and the ECB).[22] The Council must approve such a draft through a decision that establishes the general economic policy conditions. Only after this happens can the Commission conclude a MoU with the beneficiary Member State, establishing conditions that the Council can unilaterally alter during the duration of the program.[23]

In the case of the ESM, the initiative for entering the procedure is also national: the Member State in financial distress must inform the President of the Eurogroup, the President of the ECB, and the Commissioner responsible for monetary affairs,

[22] Article 3(1) of Council Regulation (EU) No 407/2010.

[23] Ibid., Article 3(7).

before having to draft a MEAP to submit to the Council.[24] However, it should be noted that the Council may decide to recommend a request for financial assistance if the distressed Member State is under the ESP. The MEAP is a declaration indicating the risks for the Eurozone caused by the Member State's situation and the measures proposed to correct the situation and restore the State's capacity to finance itself in markets.[25] The MEAP, however, is made "in agreement with the Commission, acting in liaison with the ECB and, where appropriate, with the IMF".[26] Therefore, the MEAP is already a negotiated project between the distressed Member State and EU institutions. After the Council accepts the MEAP, the Commission and the beneficiary Member State can sign the MoU, which must align with the MEAP.

The initiative of requesting financial assistance belongs to the Member States, but the terms of financial assistance must be previously discussed (EFSM) or agreed upon (ESM) with the Commission and the ECB. Furthermore, in the EFSM, assistance must be approved by the Council; in the ESM, it is approved by the Council (MEAP) and the Board of Governors of the ESM (MoU). Regarding the autonomy of negotiating the conditions of financial assistance, Member States do not seem to have much latitude. In the case of the EFSM, the general economic policy conditions are not negotiated (at least on paper) but decided by the Council, which can alter them by decision following a recommendation from the Commission. In the case of the ESM, the MEAP must be agreed upon with the Commission and then approved by the Council; the MoU is then negotiated with the Commission (the only time the term "negotiation" appears in relation to financial assistance is in the ESM Treaty), but the conditions must be approved by the ESM Board of Governors (the members of which are the members of the Eurogroup).

Therefore, although Member States take the initiative in requesting financial assistance—meaning that the EU cannot unilaterally impose financial assistance upon them—their autonomy in defining the economic conditions is considerably limited. While this may invariably hold true in practice, given the challenging economic circumstances that financially distressed Member States face, it appears that, in legal terms (considering EU and ESM Treaty rules), Member States do not enjoy autonomy in determining the conditions of economic assistance.

Limitations on the exercise of sovereign powers are deemed legitimate if consent and agreement exist, and if such consent can be freely given, that is, devoid of coercive fear. However, this is not the case in procedures of EU economic policy assistance, wherein even in the request phase, the State is not entirely free, but rather subject to the political and normative pressures exerted by EU institutions. In this context, the assisted State risks becoming subservient to the interests and demands of the EU and other Member States, implying that the integrity of the State as an autonomous political unit is significantly restrained and suppressed during this period. The federal

[24] Article 5 and article 7(1) of Regulation (EU) No 472/2013 of the European Parliament and of the Council.

[25] Ibid., Article 7(1).

[26] Ibid.

balance becomes perilously threatened in these circumstances, prone to executive dominance by EU institutions.

Such a degree of subordination to the power of EU institutions in law and practice entails other risks from the perspective of federal integrity. Economic policy conditions of MoUs often encompass policy measures related to core sectors in which the EU does not have the authority to direct, such as the structure and size of pension systems, social security, health care, and organization of local autonomies, among others. Moreover, the implementation of MoUs is monitored by EU institutions, which can impact national policymaking by withholding the disbursement of funds until economic conditions are met. In this manner, MoUs can challenge the principle of conferral and respect for national constitutional structures and functions. Equality of treatment depends on how EU institutions determine the conditions applied between different Member States.

There are ways to preserve the federal balance in these areas. One method is to attribute the ownership of the policy measures enacted to comply with economic conditionality to national policy-making authorities. In this way, national governments and other political institutions can still present alternatives to creditors regarding the program's implementation without being directed by the creditors to make decisions. The more cooperative the financial assistance—in other words, the greater the flexibility national governments have in defining, executing, and implementing economic policies—the more the integrity is safeguarded.

Nonetheless, it is with the procedures of economic assistance that the highest risk for the principle of federal integrity in all its dimensions arises, given the potential for the EU federation to control and dominate the assisted State through legal and practical mechanisms, and to use such procedures to impose measures contrary to national interests. Furthermore, it remains uncertain whether the available political modes of resolving the federal conflict can effectively protect the federal balance in this context; in fact, they might even exacerbate the situation, as we will explore further below.

7.3.2 Economic Governance and the Principle of Federal Loyalty

Federal loyalty pertains to the duties of respect owed by the constituent States to the federation and the federal cause. These duties of respect involve, in a positive sense, duties of cooperation and compliance with federal law, participation in the federation's political process, and cooperation with the federation to achieve federal goals. Conversely, these duties include an obligation of non-interference with federal action if such action aligns with the terms of the federal compact.

The EU's federal principles of loyalty, established in article 4(3) TEU and the case law of the CJEU concerning the principle of supremacy, consist of respect for EU law and EU structures. According to the principle of loyalty, Member States must respect the EU and cooperate with its institutions to fulfil the Treaties' goals. Moreover, Member States must adopt measures to ensure the execution of EU law (primary and secondary) and refrain from interfering with the pursuit of EU goals and with the actions of EU institutions. Furthermore, the principle dictates that a Member State should not undertake actions that negatively affect the federal balance and violate the principle of equality of States.

Evaluating the compatibility of economic governance powers with the principle of loyalty proves challenging due to the constitutional nature and aims of such powers. The EU holds a coordinating competence concerning fiscal policy, which implies that political authority resides with the Member States. This normative choice permeates not only the power setting (for instance, the "soft", non-binding nature of the powers and their scope) but also the institutional structure of governance. The two principal actors in EU economic governance are the EU's executive body (the Commission) and the inter-governmentally composed Council. The former exercises the technical power of administering economic governance powers, while the latter wields the political power of making and confirming ultimate decisions. In this regard, the national governments of Member States control the political process and the decisions concerning EU economic governance competences.

Loyalty, in this context, pertains to respect for duties of coordination, which primarily involve two aspects: firstly, compliance with the rules of economic governance (rules of economic policy definition, supervision, and assistance); and secondly, participation in the exercise, deliberation, and decision of economic policy coordinating procedures. Consequently, although the rules of economic governance are more flexible and less stringent than in other policy areas where the EU has the power to extensively regulate, Member States are still obligated to participate in decision-making procedures and cannot jeopardize the achievement of EU objectives within this policy area.

The subsequent analysis explores loyalty from the perspective of rules and powers of economic governance, compliance with such rules and procedures, and participation in their definition, deliberation, and decision.

7.3.2.1 Federal Loyalty and Rules and Powers of Economic Policy Definition

EU rules of economic policy definition are laid out in articles 120 and 126 TFEU. Member States are obliged to enact their economic policies to accomplish the goals of the EU within the framework of the BEPGs, while adhering to open market and free competition rules and observing the principles of stable prices, sound public finances, and a sustainable balance of payments. Moreover, Member States should avoid running deficits over 3% GDP and public debts exceeding 60% GDP. As discussed in Chap. 4, these rules (and the corresponding system for their interpretation and application) do not possess strong normative value, which renders Member States' duty of respect somewhat flexible. Hence, it is not possible to consider non-compliance as a breach of loyalty.

Furthermore, EU powers of economic policy definition do not strictly bind Member States. By implementing the economic guidelines, Member States merely have a best-effort obligation to follow or achieve the proposed framework of economic policy recommendations. Unsurprisingly, compliance with BEPGs is low,[27] and the only available sanction (public warning) is infrequently utilized.

Participation in the guideline definition process is part of the broader duty of Member States to coordinate their economic policies at the EU level. In this regard, loyalty is assessed by observing how participation in the procedures of economic definition unfolds. The competence for economic policy definition rests with the Commission (initiative) and the two inter-governmentally composed political institutions: the Council and the European Council.[28] Therefore, according to the Treaties, it falls upon the Member States to approve and issue the BEPGs. However, in practice, no BEPGs have been enacted since 2015, indicating that it has been seven years since the EU Member States last issued common economic guidelines and orientations. On one hand, such omission signifies a failure of the Member State to comply with the procedures, which is ultimately inconsistent with the principle of loyalty. On the other hand, it also demonstrates how the BEPGs are not effective instruments for stimulating economic convergence among the Member States, to the point of not being followed or issued.

In this sense, there appears to be an issue with federal loyalty due to Member States' inaction in following EU norms and economic policy orientations and formulating BEPGs. At the same time, the provisions of economic policy definition lack substantial normativity due to their soft and flexible character, which further weakens the strength of loyalty duties. Nevertheless, the failure to elaborate BEPGs constitutes a failure to comply with the duty to coordinate economic policies at the EU level, as stipulated in Article 5(1) TFEU and Article 119 TFEU.

7.3.2.2 Federal Loyalty and Rules and Powers of Economic Policy Supervision

Economic policy supervision consists of two sets of rules and procedures: preventive and corrective. The preventive rules of economic policy supervision consist of binding norms that require Member States to disclose and communicate to the Commission and the Council their current and prospective economic policy measures, including their annual budgetary plans. In terms of powers, the EU—through the Council—issues the CSRs addressed to the Member States on their economic policy.

Loyalty as compliance in these procedures—the MSP and the ABF—must be assessed in two ways: first, by considering the level of cooperation of Member States with EU institutions in disclosing and sharing national economic policy information during the European Semester; and second, by examining national compliance with

[27] Hodson 2011, pp. 81–87; Meyer 2004, pp. 814–831.

[28] Article 121(2) TFEU.

CSRs. In terms of the former, there is active compliance by the Member States, while in the case of the latter, the situation is different, as discussed in Chap. 3. However, CSRs are non-binding instruments, and from a normative perspective, their obligation is not clear and precise, thus rendering compliance (and loyalty) legally flexible.

As for loyalty as participation, there is no issue concerning preventive procedures of economic supervision: the Council regularly deliberates and decides on CSRs. The situation is somewhat different regarding rules and procedures of corrective economic policy supervision. Member States must rectify any deviation from economic targets and rules in the Treaty (EDP) or secondary legislation (EIP). Failure to take corrective measures can lead to the application of sanctions. The powers of EU institutions involve identifying deviations and recommending corrective measures, which the Member States are free to enact or not. EU institutions can also apply binding decisions in identifying deviations and applying sanctions; the latter being a competence of the Council.

Loyalty as compliance must be evaluated in a dual sense: firstly, by looking at the correction of deviations and imbalances; and secondly, at the Member State's follow-up actions for correcting such deviations and imbalances.[29] In the first sense, Member States tend to correct excessive deficits, and therefore they end up complying with the normative objective of corrective supervision. In the first sense, Member States tend to correct excessive deficits, and hence they end up complying with the normative objective of corrective supervision. In the second sense, the situation is less clear: Member States take measures to correct deficits, but these measures are not necessarily identical to those recommended by EU institutions. However, since the objective of correction is (from a normative perspective) the most precise and clear objective, it can be said that Member States respect EU law rules and goals, at least in relation to deficit reduction. A different situation pertains to debt reduction, as more than half of the Eurozone Member States' debt exceeds the maximum target of 60%.[30]

Moreover, Member States regularly discuss and decide on recommendations and identification of deviations under the Commission's proposal, thus abiding by the principle of loyalty. However, Member States have not agreed on applying sanctions to Member States for failure to correct an excessive deficit, contradicting the Commission's recommendation, and when an excessive deficit occurred. This can be viewed as a loyalty issue, since by not applying the Treaty's rules, Member States in the Council effectively decided not to comply with EU law.

At the same time, it is EU law—and the Treaty—that gives the Council the autonomy to exclusively decide and base its discretionary criteria on the application of a sanction for non-compliance with excessive deficit rules (as the CJEU stated in the case of *Commission v. Council*, regarding the EDP to Germany and France). Such feature of the legal system is a deviation from the normative allocation of political authority to the national level in the field of economic governance. Therefore, the

[29] To this day, no EIPs have been applied to Eurozone countries.

[30] See the data of the European Commission (2025) available at https://ec.europa.eu/eurostat/web/products-euro-indicators/w/2-21072025-ap accessed 15 August 2025.

legal framework of corrective supervision ends up establishing the principle that the Member States should not run an excessive deficit (binding rule), but ultimately, from an operational perspective, what constitutes an excessive deficit (that has not been corrected) is a matter of a political decision of the Council, which means that it is a decision of the Member States).

In conclusion, and similar to powers of economic policy definition, assessing the compatibility of economic policy supervision with EU principles of federal loyalty is complex due to the less stringent character of normative obligations in this area and the political basis on which decisions are taken. Member States are failing to comply with the coordination of economic policies when deciding not to impose sanctions on fellow Member States that have violated the rules on economic conduct, infringing, if not the rules, at least the spirit of fiscal rules of economic governance set in the Treaties.

7.3.2.3 Federal Loyalty and Powers of Economic Policy Assistance

Economic policy assistance is the area of coordination that holds more normative power from a legal perspective. Given the complex financial situation of Member States requesting assistance and Member States under assistance programs, there is a strong incentive to observe all rules and procedures and cooperate with EU institutions. The level of national autonomy here is, as previously discussed, low.

Economic policy assistance is also an area where the participation of Member States has a dual role, being made both as members of an EU political body (the Council) and as members of an international body (the ESM). These characteristics affect compliance with the principle of loyalty differently than other economic governance procedures.

In terms of loyalty as compliance with EU law, the level of adherence of Member States to MoUs and the implementation of conditions and prosecution of the objectives is generally high.[31] This is because Member States must comply with the conditions in MoUs to receive funds from the facilities provided by the EFSM or the ESM, and such conditionality makes loyalty to the rules of the MoUs necessary. Compliance with MoU conditions occurs through enacting economic and social policy measures plus achieving numerical targets regarding budget deficits and public debt. While the original MoU is never fully enacted (generally, the program undergoes modifications during its implementation to respond to internal and external developments),

[31] As per the opinion of the Commission. For Portugal, see European Commission (2014) The Economic Adjustment Program for Portugal 2011–2014, pp. 75–84, available at https://ec.europa.eu/economy_finance/publications/occasional_paper/2014/pdf/ocp202_en.pdf accessed 15 August 2025; for Ireland see European Commission (2013) Economic Adjustment Program for Ireland: Autumn 2013 Review, pp. 45–59, available at https://ec.europa.eu/economy_finance/publications/occasional_paper/2013/pdf/ocp167_en.pdf accessed 15 August 2025; for Cyprus, see European Commission (2014) The Economic Adjustment Program for Cyprus: Fifth Review - Summer 2014, pp. 49–62, available at https://ec.europa.eu/economy_finance/publications/occasional_paper/2014/pdf/ocp209_en.pdf accessed 15 August 2025.

it is observed to the point of the assisted Member State arriving at an economic and financial situation that is considered satisfactory, having achieved critical economic targets of fiscal and public debt consolidation.

Assessing loyalty as participation involves observing how the Member States engage in the political process of enacting, approving, and following assistance programs. Here, the tables turn, for the duty of participating in these procedures is more on the assisting Member States than with the assisted ones. Although it is the Commission that negotiates and agrees on the MEAPs and MoUs in the EFSM and the ESM frameworks, it is the Council—representing the Member States, already represented in the ESM's board of governors—that has the power to define the conditions of the MoU and the disbursement of funds, as well as to change the MoUs' conditions unilaterally (in the case of the EFSM). Therefore, the Member States actively participate in the decision-making procedures.

There is a key subtlety here that impacts loyalty. It relates to how assistance programs empower or strengthen power dynamics between the assisted Member State, the EU, and other Member States. Without a doubt, when asking for financial assistance, beneficiary States are aware that the ultimate providers of the funds will be other Member States, either via the EU budget or the ESM financing. The creditor-debtor relationship was more evident during the euro crisis due to the legally hybrid EFSF being set up as a private fund with the Member States as shareholders.[32] During the financial crisis, a division emerged between creditors and debtors, with the former (and a segment of their public opinion) advocating for rule compliance and commenting on the latter's measures and compliances.[33] This relationship was not new: it mirrored political differences and existing debt relationships that had established these power traits among the Member States.[34] In this regard, economic power imbalances among Member States can lead to complicated situations where creditor States utilize the institutional and legal framework of financial assistance to impose policy choices on assisted States. In doing so, creditor States appear to be effectively dominating the national political process, thereby contravening the principle of federal equality of States. As discussed in Chap. 3, financial assistance under the ESM is also a form of EU law application that the States—particularly when approving MEAPs in the Council—must respect. Federal balance is at risk if assistance is not seen as solidarity for a Union member in need, but rather as an imposed punishment for previous non-compliance, hence creating a sense of economic dominium (and discrepancy of powers) between some Member States and others.

Therefore, the greatest threat to the principle of loyalty pertains to how financial assistance mechanisms can be used not to accomplish collective goals, like EU's financial and economic stability and limitation of spillover effects for its Member States, but rather to act as a tool for economic policy centralization, leading to

---

[32] See Kilpatrick 2015, pp. 334–335.

[33] Brunnermeier et al 2016, pp. 1–9; Landesmann 2015, pp. 60–87.

[34] Pérez 2019, pp. 989–1014; Matthijs and McNamara 2015, pp. 229–245; Dyson 2014, pp. 591–633.

political repression of State autonomy. This threatens the integrity of States and also poses a threat to federal loyalty, as it constitutes an abuse of the EU's constitutional setup to limit a State's political autonomy. Loyalty and integrity are intrinsically linked, as the former (loyalty to the federation) requires recognizing and protecting the political integrity of Member States. The experiences of the financial crisis and the ongoing rhetoric and confrontational discourse post-crisis between northern and southern States suggest that this is a scenario that cannot be disregarded.

Lastly, there is the issue of the ESM and the establishment of inter-State forums for enhanced cooperation and integration outside the proper scope of the EU Treaties. The CJEU validated the ESM Treaty in *Pringle*, thus confirming its compatibility with EU law and the powers of Member States to establish normative instruments outside the scope of the Treaties when the EU lacks the competence to rule on the matter. This argument seems legally robust. The ESM Treaty's history indicates that it was the second-best option for policy action: it was established as an international law instrument due to the failure to agree on amending the Treaties to incorporate an EU stability mechanism.[35] This "escape" is more due to practical reasons than a desire to evade EU law, and thus it was not considered (rightly, in my opinion) a deceiving of the EU legal order. Furthermore, EU institutions play crucial roles in the ESM, and the CJEU has already declared its authority to review the actions of the institutions within the ESM framework. It could also be argued that the ESM Treaty is, in fact, an example of loyalty to EU values and objectives in a teleological sense; that is, its aim is to promote EU integration and support the monetary union, thereby aiding in achieving sustainable economic growth and financial stability. Thus, from the perspective of federal loyalty, the ESM Treaty's setting is not problematic.

7.3.3 Economic Governance and the Principle of Federal Adjudication

The principle of federal adjudication is the last constitutional principle of federal balance used to assess the EU's powers of economic governance. Federal adjudication involves the normative principles directing federal action and the institutional mechanisms that resolve authority disputes between constituent States and the federation.

There are two guiding principles of federal action, namely the principle of subsidiarity and the principle of proportionality, as laid out in Article 5(1) TEU. The exercise of EU competences must conform to these two principles, implying that outside the scope of exclusive competences, the EU can only act when its action is more apt to achieve a result than Member States' action. Furthermore, EU action must not exceed the objectives of the Treaties.

---

[35] Peers 2012, pp. 406–407.

There are also two institutional mechanisms for resolving conflicts. The first is the deliberative mode—where federal conflict is channelled through deliberations of executive or parliamentary bodies. This mode prioritizes political reasoning, including discussions and bargaining based on technical and opportune criteria. It is through this mode that the interests of the different political spheres of the federation (federal government, national governments, national peoples, and the federal people) participate in the governance and resolution of federal issues. The second mode is the judicial mode, where the CJEU resolves federal conflicts by interpreting and defining the meaning of federal rules. This mode is conflictual and based on legal reasoning, considering legal norms and their interpretation.

7.3.3.1 Federal Adjudication and Powers of Economic Policy Definition

Powers of economic policy definition involve the enactment of BEPGs. Since BEPGs are non-binding, they do not constitute any decisive federal action: the EU's action in this respect does not go beyond the Treaties' objective (coordination of economic policies). Thus, it does not pose any threat to federal adjudication concerning subsidiarity and proportionality.

Regarding conflict resolution modes, economic policy definition powers are exercised by inter-governmentally composed institutions, namely the Council and the European Council, with assistance from the executive body, the Commission. The interests represented are those of national governments and the EU executive government, not the interests of national or federal peoples (at least directly). While judicial mechanisms for resolving federal conflicts exist, it is difficult to envisage a situation where a BEPG would lead to a judicial conflict, given its non-binding and guiding nature. Thus, powers of economic policy are constitutionally neutral concerning the principle of federal adjudication.

7.3.3.2 Federal Adjudication and Powers of Economic Policy Supervision

Preventive powers of economic policy supervision relate to requesting Member States' information on defining economic and budgetary targets and policies in the MSP and the ABF procedures. It also encompasses powers to issue CSRs, formally non-binding legal acts that, in substance, set criteria for the orientation of national economic policy. These powers, in form and substance, as soft law acts that recommend adopting certain behaviours, do not violate the principle of subsidiarity. Moreover, requesting national information to centralize data and make it transparent for all Union members in the economic policy area is within the normative telos of coordination competences. Such powers do not infringe unfairly and disproportionately on the autonomy of Member States. Plus, the powers do not exceed the objective of economic cooperation and compliance with economic rules and paradigms set in Article 119 TFEU.

Conflict resolution in the setting of economic policy definition is somewhat similar: the Council has ultimate decision-making capacity, and the Commission manages the procedure administratively. The European Parliament participates in an economic dialogue process with the Commission and the Council on the workings of the supervisory procedure.

As for the role of judicial mechanisms, the CJEU can decide on infringement actions proposed by the Commission or another Member State under Articles 258–260 TFEU concerning Member States' compliance with the supervisory procedures if they disclose or do not disclose information. Therefore, while deliberative mechanisms favour inter-governmental solutions, responding to the interests of national governments, judicial mechanisms are available to assess Member States' compliance with EU law. Furthermore, the purpose of CSRs is not to produce legally binding effects on the Member States but to provide orientations only. In summary, the preventive powers of economic policy supervision comply with the principles of federal adjudication.

In terms of corrective supervision powers, the situation is somewhat different. Member States may be subject to sanctions in the EDP and the EIP if they fail to take corrective action. The Council and the Commission make recommendations on the (in)action of Member States, but what is considered satisfactory for compliance purposes is decided by the Council. If a Member State fails to comply with rules and recommendations and yet not be sanctioned, it is also possible that a Member State will act and get sanctioned. The decision-making character is not based on technical criteria but political ones—for the Council is a deliberative, political body, not an executive and technocratic one like the Commission. Moreover, it is unclear if compliance with the rules is evaluated based on verifying the compatibility of the corrective policies adopted or merely checking the achievement of a factual status considered economically sustainable.

Subsidiarity and proportionality could be endangered in the determination of corrective recommendations and in the application of financial sanctions for non-compliance. The EDP's history highlights the complexity of sanction applications, while the EIP, with its more ambiguous compliance criteria, makes implementation more challenging due to the technical discretion of the Commission and the political discretion of the Council in identifying an imbalance. Given the array of elements that could cause a macroeconomic imbalance and determine recommendations that limit or make significant fiscal policy choices, the EIP could be exploited by EU institutions to influence national fiscal policy.

The only federal interests represented in supervision procedures are those of national governments, for two reasons. Firstly, the primary decision-making body in these procedures is the Council. Thus, the deliberative modes of decision are once again executive and inter-governmentally composed. Secondly, the TFEU bars the use of infringement actions (articles 258–260 TFEU) against Member States concerning compliance with excessive deficit rules, as per article 126(10). No limit is in place regarding other judicial mechanisms, like the action of annulment set in article 263(1) TFEU. This means that Member States are safeguarded from the Commission and the CJEU in an action for infringement, while being able to challenge the Council's decisions through an action for annulment in the EDP or EIP.

In sum, concerning federal adjudication, the powers of corrective supervision pose a risk to the principles of subsidiarity and proportionality, such as the Council's political discretion in deciding and defining what constitutes appropriate corrective action. This situation is problematic as it impacts the federal balance within the adjudication logic. Furthermore, the EU has limited judicial powers to ensure compliance with the federal interests at stake.

7.3.3.3 Federal Adjudication and Powers of Economic Policy Assistance

The most problematic setting of powers in terms of federal balance has been, so far, powers of economic policy assistance. The problematic character persists when considering them in light of the principle of federal adjudication.

The EU and its Member States provide economic assistance through either the EFSM or the ESM. Although one is part of EU law and the other is (formally) not, EU institutions produce legally binding acts in both, obligating them to comply with EU law principles and values. Therefore, MoUs (in the EFSM) and MEAPs (in the ESM) must comply with subsidiarity and proportionality as acts undertaken in the exercise of a coordinating competence, according to article 5(3) of the TEU.

There is a significant risk for MoUs and MEAPs to fail the tests of subsidiarity and proportionality. The aim of these acts is to set conditions for national governments to fulfil in exchange for the disbursement of assistance funds. Typically, conditions include achieving specific economic thresholds and targets (deficit and debt reduction, through the reduction of expenses and the increase in income—the usual "recipe") via the enactment of detailed measures pertaining to virtually every domestic policy sector.

However, financial assistance programs have another goal: to aid the State in meeting financial obligations and avoiding bankruptcy and to "reform" the State and its economic policy structure to make it more compatible with the EU's general principles of economic governance. It can be problematic to determine to what extent any measure is strictly necessary to achieve the result and, more concerning, what reform measures are needed to achieve the Treaty's objectives and do not exceed them. Additionally, the involvement of creditors' representatives in the definition of economic policy plans can over-limit government autonomy, making it problematic from the perspective of subsidiarity and proportionality. In sum, EU intrusion in national political policy definition can be abusive and impact the federal balance.

Regarding national interest and federal institutional power, economic assistance is controlled by national governments and by the EU executive. Institutions must inform the EU Parliament, but the latter's powers are limited to informal supervision. The Commission and the ECB, technocratic institutions, oversee compliance with economic conditionality, while the Council decides on the conditions for assistance and subsequent amendments. National autonomy for negotiating conditions is limited in practice, given the financial vulnerability of assisted States.

As for modes for resolving federal conflict, the CJEU has jurisdiction over reviewing institutional actions involved in economic policy assistance procedures, including MoUs in the EFSM and MEAPs within the ESM. The CJEU has already ruled on several cases concerning the relationship between EU law and MoUs based on individual claims about their alignment with the Charter of Fundamental Rights and the principle of the rule of law.[36] However, there has been no CJEU evaluation of financial assistance regarding federal principles like subsidiarity and proportionality. Practically, a claim would likely need to be navigated through national courts and the preliminary ruling procedure before reaching the CJEU, a process that could be time-consuming. An action for annulment would likely have to be initiated by a Member State or an institution. However, given that the Commission and the Council negotiate MoUs, it is hard to imagine circumstances where they would have an interest in annulling them.

Regarding ESM actions, the CJEU has jurisdiction to resolve disputes among its members over the interpretation and application of the TESM. The CJEU declared in the *Pringle* case that a dispute concerning the interpretation and application of the TESM is related to the subject-matter of the treaties, as the criteria for providing financial assistance are partially determined by EU law.[37] Therefore, EU law applies to a certain extent to the interpretation of the TESM itself, besides applying clearly to MEAPs enacted under EU law.

7.4 The Federal Legality of EU Economic Governance: A Constitutional Appraisal

According to the EU's constitutional charter, the *locus* of political authority in the policy area of economic governance remains with the constituent units, meaning that the Member States are the ultimate decision-makers in economic policy. These policy choices, however, are bound by Treaty rules that set limits for budget deficits and public debt, ensuring sound public finances and economic convergence among its members to support the EMU. This situation is akin to other federal systems, such as the US and Germany, where the Member States enjoy significant political autonomy in determining their economic policies and budget choices. The distinction lies in that both the US and Germany facilitate substantial fiscal transfers from the federal budget to the constituent States' budgets, thus compensating for economic asymmetries between the States.

---

[36] See, by this order, by the CJEU: Ledra Advertising Ltd and Others v. Commission and ECB, 2016, Joined Cases C-8/15 P to C-10/15 P; Eugenia Florescu and Others v. Casa Judeţeană de Pensii Sibiu and Others, 2017, Case C-258/14; Associação Sindical dos Juízes Portugueses v. Tribunal de Contas, 2018, Case C-64/16 and BPC Lux 2 Sàrl and others v. Banco de Portugal and others, 2022, Case C-83.

[37] CJEU, Thomas Pringle v. Government of Ireland and Others, 2012, Case C-370/12, para 174 and Lenaerts et al. 2014, p. 698.

The choice made in the EU Treaties concerning the allocation of political authority leads to two conclusions: first, Member States are confined by binding rules set in the Treaties regarding the direction of economic policies that Member States should follow (articulated broadly in article 119 TFEU and more specifically in article 126 TFEU), and second, the EU powers are limited to aiding Member States in coordinating their economies to achieve their collective goals as EU Member States. These coordination powers do not enable the EU institutions to effectively control national public finances. This balance serves as the normative paradigm guiding the structure and exercise of economic governance powers by EU institutions. Federal integrity must be strictly preserved, while federal loyalty is more constrained since there are few obligations (from a normative standpoint) to follow. Moreover, such obligations, typically soft law in legal character, are considered as obligations to achieve a goal rather than to adopt specific means. The federal interest represented is the interest of national governments (that maintain the competence of defining national budget policy together with national parliaments), preserved through the participation of the Council, the most powerful decision-making body in the EU's economic governance framework. Additionally, the EU interest is expressed by the Council as an inter-governmental body and by the EU Commission, while the European Parliament lacks competence in this area.

Furthermore, the preferred federal mode for conflict resolution is political and administrative, as the CJEU is prohibited from evaluating the EDP. The use of soft powers by EU institutions in economic policy definition and supervision procedures does not aid this issue. However, the CJEU has gained more control over assistance procedures over the years, and it can review actions taken in preventive and corrective supervisory procedures outside of the EDP (in the EIP).

Federal balance is maintained concerning powers of economic policy definition, and there are no infringements of integrity or principles of federal adjudication. In terms of loyalty, the perspective should be reversed. Since economic governance is an area where the Member States take the initiative, their loyalty must be evaluated based on their commitment to enacting the BEPGs in the Council and the European Council. The situation can be challenging given that the BEPGs have not been issued since 2016.

The powers of preventive supervision do not pose problems concerning federal legality. The scenario regarding powers of corrective supervision is different due to the presence of sanctions, the dependency of sanctions on a Council decision, and the potential for sanctions to pressure the Member States to take measures that are disproportionate or exceed the Treaty's objective of coordinating fiscal policy. There is also a risk of EU institutions unjustly discriminating against Member States when implementing supervisory procedures and rules. In fact, considering the States' power in the Council, they can evade the application of sanctions or manipulate their application to other States. This situation undermines the principle of loyalty and jeopardizes the principles of integrity and adjudication.

The most significant risk for federal balance appears in the context of economic policy assistance because it is the strongest set of powers that the EU possesses in the field of economic governance. While supervision relies on the effectiveness of formal soft law acts, assistance is based on conditions set in legally binding contractual acts. However, these contracts are made with the Member States, who have very limited negotiating autonomy, and with the Council and the Board of Governors of the EMS. The conditions are comprehensive and encompass various social, health, educational, and fiscal policy areas. In these assistance procedures, the EU can exert its influence and, on occasion, even dictate the implementation of national policy.

While this may be an exception to the rule and a necessary consequence of the EU's fiscal federalism framework, it poses a risk to a constitutional community (a community committed to upholding constitutional values, principles, and rights) where fundamental aspects of national identity and structure are to be respected. Encouraging national ownership of recovery measures may help, but a governmental void must be addressed to ensure fiscal balance and harmony among the Member States.

Considering the inter-governmental structure of economic governance, the interest of the EU federation, which combines the interests of the EU's peoples and governments, is not fully represented, especially in corrective supervision and financial assistance procedures. Involvement of the Parliament could offer an additional layer of legitimacy, and therefore a more robust moral basis for government, to such decisions, ensuring that the federal balance is not compromised and that equilibrium between political authorities is maintained. As it stands, the situation is problematic.

Constitutionally, federal authority in economic governance leans towards the Member States. From a normative standpoint, they should possess the ability to define their fiscal policy according to their preferences, while adhering to the principles and rules established in the Treaties. These principles and rules are obligations of result rather than means, with the most stringent obligation being the prohibition of running excessive deficits. The structure and procedures of economic governance respect this balance to an extent, in the sense that the institutional and power-structure of EU economic governance is intergovernmental and executive. Specifically, the Member States, via the Council, are competent to manage, with the support of the Commission, the system of economic governance and to decide on key aspects, such as the application of sanctions in case of non-compliance. This area demonstrates stronger obligations of federal integrity (generally consisting of duties to respect Member States' rights) applicable to the EU than duties of federal loyalty (generally consisting of duties to respect the obligations that Member States are under in EU law) applicable to the Member States.

The issue with the intergovernmental nature of economic governance lies in its informality, which allows exercises of power by the competent institutions without adequate legal safeguards for contestation. Economic governance is managed and executed by the national governments, leaving a vital policy area for the political (and financial) stability of the EU in the control of only one of the three federal interests at stake, that of the Member States. The interest of the EU (of the federation and its people) is underrepresented. Although the Commission is the second most powerful institution in economic governance procedures, it is "heavily exposed" to pressures from Member States, resulting in its highly politicized actions.[38]

Such informality and flexibility can lead to one of two unfortunate consequences for federal order. The first is the potential for economic governance to be overtaken by national interests, transforming it into a tool of power dynamics between Member States. In essence, this would reduce the EU to an agent of dominant Member States' interests. This scenario inevitably leads to an over-centralization of economic policy definition under the influence of dominant interests at the centre, thereby diminishing the breadth of national autonomy in the budgetary space for other Member States. Such behaviour infringes both the principle of federal integrity, concerning the respect for national political structures and equality of States, and the principle of federal loyalty.

The second undesirable outcome stands in stark contrast to the first: the Member States could simply cease applying EU rules, thereby obstructing the effectiveness of the system. In this situation, economic policy definition becomes over-decentralized, leading to a diminution of the EU's capacity as a provider of order in the field of economic policy. States would consequently run their policies in blatant disregard not only of EU rules but also of EU goals and objectives.

By jeopardizing the principles of federal order in various ways—challenging integrity by overstepping into the national sphere; questioning loyalty by failing to offer adequate commitments to EU goals and principles such as equality of Member States; and disputing adjudication by not representing more than one federal interest in decision-making procedures—the legal framework of economic governance resembles a Bermuda Triangle within the EU's constitutional order. In other words, it becomes an area where legal authority vanishes, and power runs rampant with little control, adversely affecting the balance of powers that a federation must inherently possess.

In conclusion, the EU's supervision of national budgets generates issues of federal legality, which compromises the principles of constitutional order and the integrity of the EU's federal settlement.

References

Balassa B (1961) The Theory of Economic Integration. Allen and Unwin

Broadway R, Shah A (2009) Fiscal Federalism: Principles and Practices of Multiorder Governance. Cambridge University Press

Brunnermeier MK et al (2016) The Euro and the Battle of Ideas. Princeton University Press

Craig P (2016) Economic Governance and the Euro Crisis: Constitutional Architecture and Constitutional Implications. In: Fabbrini F et al (eds) The Constitutionalization of European Budgetary Constraints. Hart Publishing, pp. 19–40

Dermine P (2022) The New Economic Governance of the Eurozone: A Rule of Law Analysis. Cambridge University Press

[38] Dermine 2022, p. 124.

Dyson K (2014) States, Debt, and Power: 'Saints' and 'Sinners' in European History and Integration. Oxford University Press
Fromage D (2017) Executive Accountability to National Parliaments in Post-Crisis EU Affairs: The Persistent Shortcomings in the Council and European Council Oversight. In: Jancic D (ed) National Parliaments after the Lisbon Treaty and the Euro Crisis: Resilience or Resignation? Oxford University Press, pp. 159–175
Fromage D, Markakis M (2022) The European Parliament in the Economic and Monetary Union after COVID: Towards a Slow Empowerment? The Journal of Legislative Studies 28:385–401
Guarascio F (2016) EU gives budget leeway to France 'because it is France'. Reuters. Available at https://www.reuters.com/article/uk-eu-deficit-france-idUKKCN0YM1N0 accessed 15 August 2025
Hodson D (2011) Governing the Euro Area in Good Times and Bad. Oxford University Press
Kilpatrick C (2015) On the Rule of Law and Economic Emergency: The Degradation of Basic Legal Values in Europe's Bailouts. Oxford Journal of Legal Studies 35:325–353
Landesmann M (2015) The New North–South Divide in Europe: Can the European Convergence Model be Resuscitated? In: Fagerberg J et al (eds) The Triple Challenge for Europe: Economic Development, Climate Change, and Governance. Oxford University Press, pp. 60–87
Lenaerts K et al (2014) EU Procedural Law. Oxford University Press
Madison J (2009) Objection That the Number of Members Will Not Be Augmented as the Progress of Population Demands Considered – Federalist No. 39. In: Genovese M (ed) The Federalist Papers. Palgrave Macmillan
Matthijs M, McNamara K (2015) The Euro Crisis' Theory Effect: Northern Saints, Southern Sinners, and the Demise of the Eurobond. Journal of European Integration 37:229–245
Menendéz AJ (2012) La Mutación Constitucional De La Unión Europea. Revista Española de Derecho Constitucional 96:41–98
Meyer C (2004) The hard side of soft policy co-ordination in EMU: the impact of peer pressure on publicized opinion in the cases of Germany and Ireland. Journal of European Public Policy 11:814–831
Musgrave R (1959) The Theory of Public Finances. McGraw-Hill
Oates W (1999) An Essay in Fiscal Federalism. Journal of Economic Literature 37:1120–1149
Peers S (2012) The Stability Treaty: Permanent Austerity or Gesture Politics? European Constitutional Law Review 8:404–441
Pérez S (2019) A Europe of creditor and debtor states: Explaining the north/south divide in the Eurozone. West European Politics 42:989–1014
Rodden J (2004) Hamilton's Paradox: The Promise and Peril of Fiscal Federalism. Cambridge University Press
Rodden J et al (2003) Introduction and Overview. In: Rodden J et al (eds) Fiscal Decentralization and the Challenge of Hard Budget Constraints. MIT Press
Shah A (2007) Introduction: Principles of Fiscal Federalism. In: Shah A (ed) The Practice of Fiscal Federalism: Comparative Perspectives. McGill-Queen's University Press, pp. 9–21
Spahn PB (2007) Equity and Efficiency Aspects of Interagency Transfers in a Multigovernment Framework. In: Broadway R, Shah A (eds) Intergovernmental Fiscal Transfers: Principles and Practice. World Bank, pp. 75–106
Tuori K, Tuori K (2014) The Eurozone Crisis: a Constitutional Analysis. Cambridge University Press
von Hagen J (2007) Achieving Economic Stabilization by Sharing Risk within Countries. In: Broadway R, Shah A (eds) Intergovernmental Fiscal Transfers: Principles and Practice. World Bank, pp. 107–129
Yilmaz S, Zahir F (2020) Issues in Intergovernmental Fiscal Transfers: Public Finance and Political Economy Considerations. In: Yilmaz S, Zahir F (eds) Intergovernmental Transfers in Federations. Edward Elgar, pp. 30–40

Chapter 8
Requiem for EU Economic Governance

Contents

Abstract This chapter concludes the book with an epilogue that connects with the introduction. It examines the paradoxes of EU economic governance through both national and European lenses. It begins with the Portuguese experience under António Costa's government and the role of Mário Centeno, highlighting how Portugal defied austerity expectations while achieving fiscal balance. The narrative then shifts to the EU framework, portraying economic governance as a constitutional theatre dominated by intergovernmental politics, where Member States selectively apply rules and protect national autonomy. The euro crisis exposed structural weaknesses, leading to stricter rules, new supervisory mechanisms, and financial assistance frameworks, yet intergovernmentalism still prevails. The conclusion reflects on reform proposals, acknowledging their ambition but stressing the structural dominance of national interests and the improbability of sweeping federal change. The EU remains trapped in a fragile balance: too integrated to act solely as a collection of sovereign States, yet lacking the constitutional federal order to ensure democratic legitimacy and equal treatment among its members.

Keywords EU economic governance · Fiscal federalism · Intergovernmentalism · Euro crisis · Constitutional legitimacy

8.1 The Devil and Mário Centeno

Lisbon, 20 July 2019. The National Convention of PS is being hosted at Pavilhão Carlos Lopes. Almost four years have passed since the party came to power, and three since Pedro Passos Coelho, then still leader of PSD and member of Parliament, told his fellow party members to enjoy the summer, because afterwards "the devil

M. Lucas Pires, *The Federal Legality of EU Economic Governance*,
https://doi.org/10.1007/978-94-6265-747-2_8

will come".[1] By the devil, Mr. Passos Coelho meant the degrading of economic and financial conditions due to the expected policies of the government of prime-minister António Costa, with its promised policies for reverting austerity. At the time, Mr. Costa's government was still in its infancy: its first budget would be proposed after the summer. Mr. Passos Coelho believed that the measures announced by the socialist party would affect the country's financial credibility that his own government fought for while implementing the financial assistance program during the years of the euro-crisis. There were a lot of expectations in the air.

That summer prophecy came undone. Fast forward three years from Mr. Passos Coelho's warning and to another summer. In the heat of July, in Lisbon, the mood was far from hellish. Parliamentary elections were on the horizon and PS was leading the polls, eventually ending up securing a majority in Parliament (although without sufficient seats to completely discard the support of its former partners, BE and CDU). Expectations were overturned: instead of a deficit rise and degradation of public finances, the country was heading for a budget *superavit*—which would happen, for the first time in Portuguese democratic history, at the end of 2019.[2] The National Convention of PS was held in a celebratory atmosphere. After all the initial suspicion and controversy surrounding its array into power, they were now seen as one of the socialist parties in Europe still in power, having managed to reverse austerity while maintaining sound public finances. Therefore, one of the main figures of the National Convention was, inevitably, the person Mr. António Costa nicknamed the "(Cristiano) Ronaldo of Public Finances", Professor Mário Centeno.

Professor Centeno's stature in national and international circles had risen considerably during the government's mandate, with the arrival of the budget surplus and the election as president of the Eurogroup. It was symbolic of the change of tone in Europe, after the euro crisis, that a President of the Eurogroup coming from the Netherlands, who became famous for his harsh positioning towards the assisted Eurozone Member States (ending up saying that southern countries only care about women and drinking)[3] was replaced, after his mandate ended, by the Minister of Finance of one of the those southern countries assisted during the crisis. Was this a sign that Europe was finally healing, after the crisis?

It was also interesting to note Professor Centeno's choice, as minister, to follow a path of strong fiscal consolidation towards compliance with those same rules, despite his initial remarks on the value of EU fiscal rules (where, it should be remembered, he seemed to dismiss the EU framework of economic governance as a mere "algorithmic procedure"). During the National Convention of PS, Professor Centeno spoke about "balanced finances" being a mark of the government's mandate.[4] While

[1] Rodrigues (2016) available at https://www.publico.pt/2016/07/21/politica/noticia/psd-dramatiza-situacao-economica-vem-ai-o-diabo-1739062 accessed 15 August 2025.

[2] Varzim (2020) available at https://eco.sapo.pt/2020/03/25/portugal-com-excedente-de-02-e-a-primeira-vez-em-democracia/ accessed 15 August 2025.

[3] EURACTIV and AFP (2017) https://www.euractiv.com/section/economic-governance/news/indignation-grows-over-eurogroup-chiefs-sex-and-women-remarks/ accessed 15 August 2025.

[4] Quintas (2019) available at https://ps.pt/contas-certas-do-ps-foram-marca-da-legislatura/ accessed 15 August 2025.

Professor Centeno declared the need to increase public investment, he also mentioned that economic growth had to be sustainable. One of the ways of achieving such sustainability was through balanced budgets and debt reduction, with PS expecting Portuguese public debt to be below 100% GDP by 2023 (it was 130% at the time).[5]

At the end of the speech, Professor Centeno lashed out against the opposition parties from the centre-right, stating that "fiscal policy cannot be left to demagogy". He stated:

> Four years later, it seems that everything is now easy and therefore fiscal policy is up for auction. We cannot allow fiscal policy to be handed over to demagoguery. We also know that right next door there is the auction of public spending, which now seems an unlimited good.[6]

PS's electoral program for the 2019 elections had, right after its first chapter on the topic of "Good Governance", the title "Balanced accounts for convergence". The party would repeat the mantra of fiscal balance in the electoral program for the snap elections of 2022 (with António Costa as prime minister, but without Mário Centeno, who meanwhile became the Governor of the Bank of Portugal).[7] As one of Mr. Costa's former ministers stated, PS was now the only responsible party, the party of "*contas certas*".[8]

8.2 Does Brussels Really Vote in the Portuguese Parliament?

What to make of this constitutional theatre that is the federal legality of economic governance in the EU, and the powers that the EU has regarding Member States' competence in fiscal policy definition?

Historically, the stage was set from the 1970s onwards for EU economic governance to be a supporting competence to the competence of monetary policy definition. While the latter was exclusively regulated by the EU, the latter was only subject to the EU's authority to the extent necessary for achieving the objectives of the Treaties and for protecting the stability of the EMU. Member States remained free to define their respective fiscal policies as they wished, although having to follow and comply, to the best of their efforts, with EU-issued guidelines on economic policy, and with two binding rules concerning budget deficits and public debt levels. The EU had limited mechanisms for reacting to economic shocks in place, since central budget

---

[5] Partido Socialista (2019), p. 9, available at https://ps.pt/wp-content/uploads/2021/02/Programa-Eleitoral-PS-2019.pdf accessed 15 August 2025.

[6] Quintas (2019) available at https://ps.pt/contas-certas-do-ps-foram-marca-da-legislatura/ accessed 15 August 2025.

[7] Partido Socialista (2021) available at https://ps.pt/wp-content/uploads/2021/09/Programa-Eleitoral-PS2022_v5_6Jan_pagsoltas.pdf accessed 15 August 2025.

[8] Ação Socialista (2019) available at https://ps.pt/fica-claro-qual-e-o-partido-da-credibilidade-e-das-contas-certas/ accessed 15 August 2025.

transfers were insufficient and emergency mechanisms for financial assistance to be used strictly. The no-bailout rule, together with the inter-governmental control of the preventive and disciplinary system of economic governance, confirmed the constitutional ascendancy of national autonomy in the procedure. In sum, the structure of the legal framework of economic governance—inter-governmental control, the executive role of the Commission, the use of soft law—meant that national governments were in control, and that success of economic governance depended heavily on their commitment.

The first act of the play, however, showed that Member States were not willing to abide by the rules, either because they did not like them, or because they did not believe in them, or because they found it undesirable to follow them during certain periods, for personal reasons. The consequences of the intergovernmental character of the system of economic governance came to the fore when the two largest Member States voted against the application of sanctions in the EDP to one another, while exercising their influence amongst other Member States that, by supporting them, could expect to claim reciprocal protection in the future if they ever found themselves in the same situation. The Member States then asked and inserted more "flexibility" regarding the rule-application to save face, assuming that maybe the rules were not that good in the first place. But the damage to the credibility of the system was done. More than being fiscally disciplined, it was *necessary to pose as being* fiscally disciplined. It also showed that some Member States are simply bigger than others, and that when intergovernmentalism reigns supreme the protection of federal rights—which are rights regarding the just balance of powers and interests of the federation—are jeopardized, thus generating a constitutional imbalance.

The following act was dramatic, both literally and symbolically, with the emergence of a sovereign debt crisis that revealed the colossal failure of the EU's normative system of economic governance. It was an act defined by urgency, with a substantive state of emergency applied to the resolution of the crisis.[9] Executive federalism, the rule of national governments through intergovernmental institutions (Council, Eurogroup, European Council) took over, with the bailout of the most affected economies by the most robust ones, leading to a political and popular stand-off between different governments and peoples, between *creditor and debtor States*. While some ushed austerity as a cure, others saw it as a form of punishment. The euro became a contested end, with the cost of commitment to monetary integration proving much more demanding, especially for some Member States that saw their sovereign autonomy limited to an extreme for the sake of safeguarding the stability of the eurozone. What was worse, was that such Member States (Portugal, Greece, Ireland) became dominated by the other Member States through intergovernmental mechanisms of a contractual nature,[10] the constitutional substance of which seemed at odds with the rights established in EU Treaties, even if the CJEU formally framed them as valid in *Pringle*.

[9] See, on all this, Larsen 2021, pp. 163–190.

[10] Craig 2014, pp. 28–30.

How do you recover from trauma? The EU and its Member States decided to do two things. First, they decided to renew the social contract of economic governance and the commitment to the fundamental rules of the system: regular coordination and prohibition of excessive deficits and high public debts. This was done by hardening the procedures of economic governance with the setting of the European Semester, with the enactment of regular monitoring and orientation, and with the setting of new supervisory procedures such as the EIP. "Euro plus" pacts and stability Treaties were signed, setting more obligations in EU, international and national law for Member States' governments to follow. The idea was for turning the rules of economic governance—that set a duty to collaborate and follow to their best effort commonly devised guidelines and orientations on the definition of national fiscal policy—into "gold", that is, into fundamental precepts of constitutional significance. In this way, there would be no doubts regarding the true character (both *political and legal, symbolic, and practical*) of EU obligations of economic governance. They were fundamental objectives of EU law establishing strong normative duties.

The second option, followed by the EU and the Member States in response to the crisis, was, to put it simply, to institutionalize trauma itself. Norms, be they principles or rules, can be effective, but there is nothing more effective than fear: fear of the consequences that apply to those who do not follow the rules. What did the EU do then? It was decided to establish a framework for economic assistance and constitutionalize the contractual setting of bailouts, with the creation of the EMS and of a legal framework for sovereign financial intervention. If economic governance failed, and emergency loomed, the only solution would be to go the hard way and implement an assistance program in exchange for the provision of funds. Assisted Member States would see their fiscal autonomy suspended for the purpose of safeguarding the euro, accepting (as debtors) to have their policies discussed by the other Member States (the creditors) for a short period of time until being ready to return to the markets. The experience of financial assistance was hard; to repeat it or to have it (particularly when it is now a viable option to react in the event of crisis) is something that most Member States would not be very willing to try, I suspect. Therefore, the shadow of financial assistance also works as a deterrence for Member States that would avoid complying with the rules.

In summary, the EU and the Member States established a new structure of economic governance, with more rules (and, therefore, more obligations for the Member States) and allowing EU institutions to intervene to a larger extent than before in the Member States' space of fiscal autonomy. Did this revolution, enacted with urgence in a space of emergency, change anything? Can we say that it was successful, in any way? What is the state of play?

It is beyond doubt that the framework of economic governance is a space of authority, in the sense that there are obligations in place and institutions for applying rules and supervising their application. The legal character of some obligations (for example, the "golden rule" of budgetary equilibrium transposed to national laws) is stronger than before, and the European Semester and its operation brought more importance and public attention to the importance of economic governance. Furthermore, the existence of a mechanism of financial assistance and the capacity to use it allows for central intervention in the event of economic crisis and generates a corrective mechanism that is effective and to counterbalance possible limitations of the preventive mechanisms of economic governance.

More rules do not necessarily generate more compliance. The history of the legal framework of EU economic governance is full of doubts, amendments, and contestation. The problem is (as has always been, and as it will continue to be) the management of the system, more specifically *regarding who holds authority over the system*. The EU framework of economic governance continues to be controlled by the Member States. It is up to the Council and the European Council to set the guidelines of economic governance, to analyse Member States' fiscal plans, and to issue CSRs. Crucially, it is up to the Council to issue sanctions when there are significant deviations, excessive imbalances, and excessive deficits. Finally, it is also the Member States who have competence to decide on the granting of financial assistance and the approval of the conditions of MEAPs. Economic governance is, therefore, and without any doubt, an area ruled by intergovernmentalism and its constitutional mechanisms and logics: reciprocity, opportunity, dimension, and compromise. It is an area ruled more by power-considerations than technical considerations or legal logic. And that is the most problematic aspect of the framework, due to the risks that it poses for the constitutional equilibrium of the EU.

This book wishes to answer two questions. The first is: how binding are the EU rules of economic governance? The answer is: they are binding to the extent the Member States wish them to be. The system of authority that is in place is flexible enough to be very effective or not effective at all, depending on the political compromise between the Member States and how they wish to "play" the part. Economic governance, in this sense, is a theatre of authority, which can be piercing and dramatic, or loose and plastic.

The second question this book wishes to answer is: is the framework of EU economic governance constitutional, from the perspective of the organization of federal authority? The answer is no, because the system allows for its own capture by national, sovereign interests, depending on what most Member States' governments believe is the right option to take. By putting the focus on national interests, which are over-protected and over-represented at the federal level in this matter, the interests of the EU (which include respect for national autonomy, national constitutional structures, and equality of States) are put at risk. The federal balance can be affected, and the legitimacy of the framework destroyed. The German and French saga regarding the EDP threw a lasting shadow on the procedures of economic governance that still haunts the scene; the periphery (of States) seems weak in face of the centre (controlled by certain States).

The situation is more problematic in the procedures of financial assistance than in the procedures of definition and supervision due to the stronger legal character of the instruments at stake. While the space of authority in the latter procedures seems limited to best-effort obligations, in the former there are contractual, legally binding obligations that must be implemented; otherwise, the non-compliant party shall be liable—and, consequently, shall risk losing the funds necessary for their solvency. Therefore, procedures of financial assistance risks leading to situations of dominium between Member States that are against the principles of federal balance of the EU legal order—integrity, loyalty, and adjudication, particularly of the deliberative type. James Madison, ever the pragmatist, warned that "[a]mong the numerous advantages promised by a well-constructed Union, none deserves to be more accurately developed than its tendency to break and control the violence of faction".[11] The fear is that the EU system of economic governance does the opposite, that it *allows for the exacerbation of faction*, particularly in such sensible areas such as fiscal autonomy.

It is quite the paradox. The federal authority of economic governance belongs to the Member States; however, thanks to the legal framework of the system, it is possible for some Member States to use the EU to impose their view on the others. Such intergovernmental character allows Member States to subvert EU constitutional rules by claiming to protect national autonomy regarding fiscal policy. The interest of the EU's peoples is not considered, given that there is no Parliamentary participation in the procedures. To survive, Member States enter the theatre and play it to their interests, understanding the inherent political character of the system and how everything depends on compromise and discussion—something that the Portuguese government understood very well from the start since 2015. All is theatre, all is politics.

8.3 Final Considerations

There have been many suggestions for reforming the system of economic governance.[12] The purpose of the suggested reforms is to make the system more compliant with constitutional principles such as the rule of law and democracy (enhancing its legitimacy, in this sense) while also being effective at guaranteeing the financial stability of the eurozone. Most suggestions of reform include institutional change, rule amendment, and the setting of new instruments allowing for the transfer of funds to help enact structural reforms and therefore enhance economic stability, as well as for the issuance of debt instruments by the EU. The setting of the Next Generation EU Funds created after the COVID-19 pandemic to support the economic recovery of the Member States have been described as a possible blueprint for a future system of central, federal grants to be issued by the EU and transferred to the Member States with strict conditions and supervisory mechanisms in place to check their due implementation. There could also be a reform of fiscal supervision, with the setting of a dedicated body (a European Fiscal Authority) responsible for supporting economic governance and managing its three procedures, with the final decisions to be made by a council composed of members from the EU Parliament, the Council and the Commission, and whose decisions could be subject to judicial review by the CJEU.

---

[11] Madison 2009, p. 49.

[12] See the works of Dermine 2022, pp. 353–358; Markakis 2020, pp. 303–331; Adamski 2018, pp. 394–401; Craig and Markakis 2020, pp. 1400–1498; Arnold et al. 2022; Blanchard et al. 2021, pp. 197–236.

All of this involves, necessarily, the transfer of more powers to the EU in the field of economic governance, as well as new budget powers and funds. Some reforms would require the Treaties to be amended.

What to say about these suggestions for reforms, all of them thoughtful and much wished for, and what can this work offer anew? A song by the American band The Mountain Goats comes to mind, in which the character—a person that is dying—states the following:

> There was a chance we'd make it through this
> It's safe to say now that we missed it
> And I will never lose hope, and I haven't lost hope
> I'm just realistic[13]

The suggestions proposed in the literature are based on two (hopeful) objectives: one, that it is necessary to overhaul the system of economic governance and change the fiscal rules to allow for more flexibility while maintaining the target of achieving compliance with the rules; and two, that it is necessary to strengthen EU integration and the relation of powers between the EU and the Member States to turn the EU into a more complete federal framework for the redistribution of wealth.

Regarding the first idea, realistically speaking, the change of fiscal rules will most likely have little to no effect *if the basis of the system remains*, that is: if Member States control, as they do now, the authority of economic governance. National interests will always prevail, unless it becomes necessary to demonstrate to the markets that the system works, and that a small Member State is unlucky enough to be put in that situation. Otherwise, there will be no sanctions for Member States that violate fiscal rules. What can make coordination work for a while is the fear of a financial crisis erupting, leading to Member States requiring financial assistance. If that risk exists, and if markets start to look suspiciously at national accounts, then national governments will, for the time being, avoid imprudent economic behaviours. But politics will be politics, and no one can maintain austerity for long (as we are seeing nowadays with Germany), and so no one knows what will happen when the memory of the financial crisis fades and the need for more expansionary policies arrives. Therefore, a change in the fiscal rules, specifically the one occurred in 2024, in my view only amounts to a mere legal and economic cosmetic operation, subject to failure at the first instance of tension. Meaning: the first moment when acting tough becomes necessary.

Regarding the second idea, there will be no Treaty Amendment soon, and once a process as such opens, there will be many important questions to answer. Most likely, it will entail a refoundation of the EU as we know it, with military cooperation, the establishment of procedures against the backsliding of fundamental values, and the reinforcement of the EU's budgetary and economic capacity. Governance changes will occur, together with institutional developments. But the complexity and the magnitude of the process, together with the difficulty of assessing what Member

[13] The Mountain Goats (2022) available at https://youtu.be/pB9MsCzN7ik accessed 15 August 2025.

States and their peoples want from EU integration makes any speculation, realistically speaking, difficult. Will (all) the Member States agree to overhaul the framework of EU economic governance to the point of setting up a redistributive system for fiscal transfers at the EU level? And will (all) the Member States agree to let go of their authority in managing the application of fiscal rules? Will the Member States agree to make the EU more democratic, and more—whisper it—*constitutionally federal*?

The EU is at an existential crossroads: too politically and legally integrated, too interdependent in important matters such as monetary policy and market rules, but at the same time with important shortcomings concerning the federal legality of some of its governance mechanisms, and the democratic legitimacy of its actions. To make it worse, it is difficult to understand at this stage what EU citizens and national governments want from the EU. The question of Europe has never been more complex than nowadays. On the one hand, it is something to continue improving, since it does not look at all as a *fait accompli*, but on the other hand there is no clear path to where to move forward with this integration.

It seems highly unlikely, based on its history, that the EU will make sweeping changes to its constitutional structure and make them all in one go. The opportunity to improve might have passed by the Member States at this stage. Perhaps the EU will become more democratic, more legitimate, and more federal through small amendments and changes; perhaps new emergencies will lead to new mutations and social agreements. Or perhaps it will remain in its unbearable *status quo* of complex constitutionality for the sake of maintaining some form of political stability that is good and necessary but could have been so much better and more ambitious. An EU where the interests of all and not just of the large Member States are considered, where law and order are based on constitutional values and not on mere force and interest, and where the future, even if unclear, is exciting. The study of the federal legality of the EU's supervision of national budgets shows these paradoxes between *building through* the EU or *playing with* the EU.

References

Adamski D (2018) Redefining European Economic Integration. Cambridge University Press

Arnold N et al (2022) Reforming the EU Fiscal Framework: Strengthening the Fiscal Rules and Institutions. IMF Departmental Paper No 2022/014. Available at https://www.imf.org/en/Publications/Departmental-Papers-Policy-Papers/Issues/2022/08/31/Reforming-the-EU-Fiscal-Framework-Strengthening-the-Fiscal-Rules-and-Institutions-The-EUs-518388 accessed 15 August 2025.

Blanchard O et al (2021) Redesigning EU Fiscal Rules: From Rules To Standards. Economic Policy 36:197–236

Craig P (2014) Economic Governance and the Euro Crisis: Constitutional Architecture and Constitutional Implications. In: Adams M et al (eds) The Constitutionalization of European Budgetary Constraints. Hart Publishing, pp. 19–40

Craig P, Markakis M (2020) EMU Reform. In: Amtenbrink F, Herrmann C (eds) The EU Law of Economic and Monetary Union. Oxford University Press, pp. 1400–1498

Dermine P (2022) The New Economic Governance of the Eurozone: A Rule of Law Analysis. Cambridge University Press

Larsen S (2021) The Constitutional Theory of the Federation and the European Union. Oxford University Press

Madison J (2009) The Same Subject Continued: The Union as a Safeguard against Domestic Faction and Insurrection – Federalist No. 10. In: Genovese M A (ed) The Federalist Papers. Palgrave Macmillan

Markakis M (2020) Accountability in the Economic and Monetary Union: Foundations, Policy and Governance. Oxford University Press

Index

M. Lucas Pires, *The Federal Legality of EU Economic Governance*,
https://doi.org/10.1007/978-94-6265-747-2

MIX
Papier aus verantwortungsvollen Quellen
Paper from responsible sources
FSC® C105338

If you have any concerns about our products,
you can contact us on
ProductSafety@springernature.com

In case Publisher is established outside the EU,
the EU authorized representative is:
Springer Nature Customer Service Center GmbH
Europaplatz 3, 69115 Heidelberg, Germany

Printed by Libri Plureos GmbH
in Hamburg, Germany